THE DNA OF DOCTOR WHO

THE PHILIP HINCHCLIFFE YEARS

ROUNDEL BOOKS
A division of 5064 Enterprises Ltd
46 Venice Court
Samuel Ogden Street
MANCHESTER M1 7AX

The DNA of Doctor Who
The Philip Hinchcliffe Years

First published 2024

ISBN
978-1-80517-387-8 (Hardback)
978-1-80517-386-1 (Softback)

Publisher
Gareth Kavanagh

Project Editor
Gary Russell

Design and Layout
William Brooks

Copy Editor
Paul Simpson

Gothic A1 © Toby Hadoke 2024
Morality and politics © Matthew Sweet 2024
The use of returning monsters © Sophia Morphew 2024
The representation of disabled characters in *Doctor Who* © Alex Kingdom 2024
The hybrid film vs VT technique in 1970s television © Hannah Cooper 2024
The US invasion © Kim Pfeifer-Adams 2024
Borrowing from the classics © Simon Guerrier 2024
Possession as a recurring theme © Hayden Gribble 2024
The non-television stories of Philip Hinchcliffe © Kenny Smith 2024
Real science vs fantasy science © Mick Schubert 2024
On Target! © David J Howe 2024
Sparking the imagination © Robin Ince 2024
Female companionship © Ian Winterton 2024
Using the show's heritage © Matthew Toffolo 2024
Revealing the dangers of orthodoxy © Trey Korte 2024
Building the worlds © Philip Newman 2024
The Representation of ESEA characters in *Doctor Who* © Emma Ko 2024
Whose Philip Hinchcliffe © Matt Dale 2024
Philip chats about … © Gary Russell & Graeme Burk 2024
Foreword © Gary Russell & Graeme Burk 2024
Last Word © Gary Russell & Graeme Burk 2024

Cover photo of Philip Hinchcliffe © Leigh Wood 2024
Photo of Louise Jameson, Page 10 © Mirrorpix

The moral right of the authors and illustrators has been asserted.

All rights reserved. No part of this book may be reproduced, stored in or introduced into a retrieval system, or transmitted, in any form or by means (electronic, mechanical, photocopying, recording or otherwise) without the prior written permission of the publisher. Any person who does an unauthorised act in relation to this publication may be liable to criminal prosecution and civil claim for damages.

A catalogue record for this book is available from the British Library.

This book is sold subject to the condition that it shall not, by way of trade or otherwise, be lent, re-sold, hired out or otherwise circulated without the publisher's prior consent in any form of binding or cover other than that in which it is published and without a similar condition being imposed upon the subsequent publisher.

The editors would like to thank
Samira Ahmed; Colin Brockhurst; Matt Charlton; Gary Gillatt; Tai Gooden; Deirdre Hinchcliffe; Louise Jameson; Justin Johnson; Tony and Jane Kenealy; Allan and Erica Lear; Joseph Lidster; Shaun Lyon; Sean Mason; Steven Moffat, Mark B Oliver; Nicholas Pegg; Andrew Pixley; Paul MC Smith
and, of course, *Philip Hinchcliffe*, without whom …

All the *Philip chats about …* essays herein, plus Louise Jameson's *Foreword* and Steven Moffat's *Last Word*, have been compiled from a series of interviews conducted with Philip, Louise and Steven exclusively for this book by Graeme Burk between 2021 and 2023.

CONTENTS

10 Foreword by Louise Jameson

12
GOTHIC A1
by Toby Hadoke

20 Philip chats about ... starting out

22
the Ark *in* Space
Morality and politics   *by* Matthew Sweet

30 ... Exorcising the past

32
the Sontaran Experiment
The use of returning monsters   *by* Sophia Morphew

40 ... The genesis of villainy

42
Genesis *of the* Daleks
The representation of disabled characters in *Doctor Who*   *by* Alex Kingdom

50 ... Making BBC drama

52
Revenge *of the* Cybermen
The hybrid film vs VT technique in 1970s television   *by* Hannah Cooper

60 ... Tom Baker

62
Terror *of the* Zygons
The US Invasion   *by* Kim Pfeifer-Adams

70 ... Inspirations

72
Planet *of* Evil
Borrowing from the classics   *by* Simon Guerrier

80 ... Incidental music

82
Pyramids *of* Mars
Possession as a recurring theme   *by* Hayden Gribble

90 ... Creatives

92
the Android Invasion
The non-television stories of Philip Hinchcliffe   *by* Kenny Smith

100 ... Writing *Doctor Who*

102
the Brain *of* Morbius
Real science vs fantasy science   *by* Mick Schubert

110 ... Writing Doctor Who outside the BBC

112
the Seeds *of* Doom
On Target!   *by* David J Howe

120 ... Historical trappings

122
the Masque *of* Mandragora
Sparking the imagination   *by* Robin Ince

130 ... Companions

134
the Hand *of* Fear
Female companionship   *by* Ian Winterton

142 ... The NVLA

144
the Deadly Assassin
Using the show's heritage   *by* Matthew Toffolo

152 ... Being a producer in television drama

154
the Face *of* Evil
Revealing the dangers of orthodoxy   *by* Trey Korte

162 ... His early days in television

164
the Robots *of* Death
Building the worlds   *by* Philip Newman

172 ... Actors

174
the Talons *of* Weng-Chiang
The representation of ESEA characters in Doctor Who   *by* Emma Ko

184 ... The show's survival

186
Whose Philip Hinchcliffe
What Philip Hinchcliffe did next   *by* Matt Dale

194 Last word by Steven Moffat

CONTENTS

Digital artwork on pages 12, 22, 32, 42, 52, 62, 72, 82, 92, 102, 112, 134, 144, 154, 164, 174, 186 and 194 by Will Brooks
Photographs on pages 20, 30, 40, 50, 60, 80, 90, 100, 110, 120, 130, 142, 152, 162 and 172 by Richard Lloyd
Digital artwork on pages 27, 36, 47, 56, 68, 75, 86, 95, 107, 116, 127, 137, 149, 160, 167, 179 and 189 by Aaron Lowe
Photographs on pages 9, 70 and 184 by Karen McBride   Photograph on page 193 © Philip Hinchcliffe

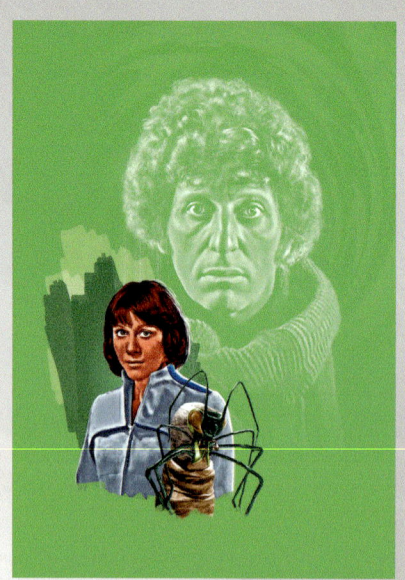

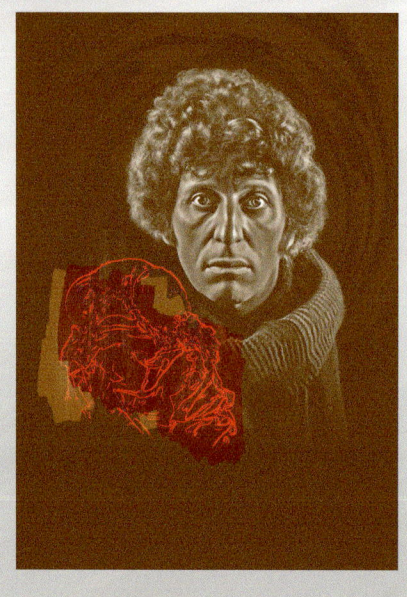

This book is respectfully dedicated to our friend, colleague and favourite jaffa-cake supplier, Matt Dale

1980 – 2023

Doctor Who had been very popular, with Jon Pertwee, during Barry Letts's era. Therefore Robert Holmes and I were lucky because we inherited a very healthy programme.

Philip Hinchcliffe, 2023

This book is dedicated to our Kickstarter Producers

Rowan Bridge	Jeremy Paul
Gary Buckden	Ian Pritchard
Paul Castle	Stephen Southart
Paul Clifford	Richard Starkings
Darren Floyd	Jonathan Symonds
Christopher Glenn	Richard Thomas
Steven Warren Hill	Philip Wenderoth
Christopher Meredith	Stuart Wilson
Marcus Palmer	

Foreword: Louise Jameson

Philip was my first producer on *Doctor Who*, I adore him and I've always thought of him as a bit of a 'grown-up'. You see, it's very difficult to be an incredibly good producer, which he is, and to be really popular with everybody all the time – that's probably almost an impossible thing to achieve, because you have to make some unpopular decisions sometimes as producer. Yet Philip managed it because has an incredible sense of his own self-worth, he has gravitas and he has that air of authority about him that goes with being a good leader. Philip, quite rightly, always sought to make the best possible production he could achieve and as an actor, you really cannot ask to be involved in anything more than that.

I love Leela and was proud of the fact that Philip pushed hard for a very intelligent but uneducated companion because that made for a *perfect* combination; you've got a quick-thinking, brave person who's very instinctive, alongside the biggest brain in the universe.

So thank you, Philip. For everything.

GOTHIC A1

TOBY HADOKE

We've materialised at the correct point in space,
but obviously not in time. A temporal reverse?
Some vast impulse of energy has drawn the TARDIS off course.

IF it ain't broke, don't fix it.

Well, it wasn't, but he did anyway. (Well, *Doctor Who* was always broke, that's why it made monsters out of condoms, but it wasn't *broken*.)

The first episode to have Philip Hinchcliffe's name on the title doesn't, on the surface, look much different from its immediate predecessors. He's inherited a Doctor, and even the new Doctor's opening titles feature similar visuals to those from the previous season. The theme music is unaltered and the incidentals are provided by the stalwart composer of the Jon Pertwee era, Dudley Simpson. As for the script, that is by regular writer (and now script editor) Robert Holmes. Hinchcliffe doesn't have the chance to stamp his style on the show by altering any of its fundamentals.

And yet *The Ark in Space* is *so* different from what has gone before. It announces itself almost immediately when its leading man gives a portentous homily to the virtues of indomitable mankind. Pertwee could deliver a moral lecture with righteousness, sure, but Tom Baker adds an otherworldly mystique to his wanderer in the Fourth Dimension, and it's the confidence with which the producer gives this new Doctor his commanding monologue that shows how ambitious, how serious this era will be.

What choice did Hinchcliffe have? No-one wants to take on a new job and keep everything the same. Producer Barry Letts and script editor Terrance Dicks had guided Pertwee's Doctor through a consistent and much-admired five-year stint: they'd transformed an ailing show and upped its ratings, producing some classic stories as they did so.

Letts's success came after he'd been given a new Doctor and a format that was not of his choosing. Hinchcliffe, too, inherits his leading cast and first few scripts, all by rehired old hands, and he soon sets about remoulding them – which is bad news for both John Lucarotti and Gerry Davis, who quickly learn that they're yesterday's men. Lucarotti's *The Ark in Space*, becomes Holmes's, replete with alien parasites laying their eggs inside a human who are then consumed, body horror, possession, a high death count and a hard edge. Initially, they may have inherited scripts featuring familiar foes – the Sontarans, the Daleks and the Cybermen – but as quickly as possible, Hinchcliffe and Holmes commission stories with no past enemies at all, phasing out old friends the Brigadier, Benton, Harry and finally UNIT itself along the way.

That's not to say the show suddenly becomes hugely original. Its roots are often on display, but it nourishes itself with the best: *Pyramids of Mars* invokes the Mummy films, *The Brain of Morbius* is a Frankenstein riff, *Terror of the Zygons* and *The Android Invasion* have *Invasion of the Body Snatchers* elements, and *The Talons of Weng-Chiang* plays with *The Phantom of the Opera*, Sherlock Holmes and the real-life Jack the Ripper. Hinchcliffe and Holmes are well-read and they know what works, and this level of scholarship gives their stories an intellectual ballast. The confident young buck of a producer and the veteran writer-turned-script-editor are certainly of a like mind. The success of Hinchcliffe as a producer cannot be celebrated without acknowledging Holmes, whose mordant wit, predilection for scares, and gift for world-building – his characters always exist in a wider universe that we do not see – are consistent strengths of this era. The latter is often rendered with deft, economical and evocative vocabulary: Findecker's time-travel experiments taking Earth down a technological cul-de-sac; the march on Reykjavik by the Philippine army; the murder of the commissioner's family by the Peking Homunculus. Noises off that ring loudly in the vividly drawn world of *The Talons of Weng-Chiang*. There are similar examples in most of the other stories. *The Robots of Death* invokes the crew's the Founding Families caste system, robophobia and the world of Kaldor City, and unseen worlds and characters enrich the dialogue of *Planet of Evil*, *The Masque of Mandragora* and *The Deadly Assassin*.

What choice did Hinchcliffe have? No-one wants to take on a new job and keep everything the same.

Hinchcliffe immediately makes the show more muscular in its storytelling – which considering that Letts and Dicks were no shrinking violets is some achievement. It's not just in the atmosphere as a whole, but in the attention to detail. Nothing is purely exposition or padding. *Genesis of the Daleks* suggests that the Doctor has been tortured, depicts Sarah sadistically dangled from a ledge by a Thal (who used to be the blond-haired good guys, remember kids?), and has talk of hanging prisoners in order to preserve bullets. None of these moments is essential to the plot but they are economical sketches of the fact that, despite the *joie de vivre* of our heroes, the universe they inhabit is a dangerous one. This is why Tom Baker's wit and comic energy are important (because despite the harshness described, Hinchcliffe's stories are never dry or humourless) and why his rapport with Elisabeth Sladen (and for a while, Ian Marter) is so vital – a sense of humour and the bond of friendship are important kindnesses in a brutal world. The Doctor and his companions aren't armed with anything other than intellect, moral conviction, loyalty to each other and a sharp wit. And those things are, ultimately, better than all the guns and sadism and violence that are toted in these stories. Hinchcliffe's is an unflinching era, but the core morality and optimism of *Doctor Who* remain.

Look at the scene in *The Seeds of Doom* in which the Doctor coldly observes that in order to save his friend Winlett, zoologist Moberley will have to amputate his arm. It's a moment that never transpires because Moberley is dead moments later. An act that never happens and a supporting character who doesn't live beyond Part One are given a lot of weight in the scene in order to up the drama. Through character and situation the stakes are raised without a drop of blood being spilt; it is all about the impact a postulated outcome might have on an individual. It's gripping, superbly acted, and chilling, but it's also, ultimately, human and optimistic: Moberley is presented, with detached pragmatism by the Doctor, with an horrendous prospect – but he agrees to dig deep and do it and gets the Doctor's admiration ("you're a good man, Moberley") but without the need for any blubbing or speeches. Actions speak louder than words, and so we don't need the script to tell us how we are meant to feel.

This is because Hinchcliffe and Holmes don't underestimate their audience – the stories are awash with subtext and they trust us to pick it up. *Genesis of the Daleks* is brazen with its Nazi iconography, but the metaphor of *The Masque of Mandragora* (science versus superstition) is more subtle, and there are grown-up treatises on scientific irresponsibility (*Planet of Evil*) and the nature of faith (*The Face of Evil*). This smartness is not just thematic, though – it pervades the dynamic between Hinchcliffe's mainstays, the Doctor and Sarah. On the surface the Time Lord can be exceptionally grouchy with her: a withdrawn, scowling alien with no time for slower-minded humans who get too easily distracted by the irrelevant things (like grief and empathy). Except Sladen plays off Baker's darker moods with a humouring patience, and an obvious affection which tells us that she knows that the Doctor doesn't really mean a lot of it or that when he does, deep down his benevolence and goodness still linger. It's a clear, complex relationship played pitch-perfectly by the leads, and one based of genuine affection ("she's my best friend"). There's tension too, in his relationship with Leela, where *her* pragmatism towards death alarms *him*; but despite her being a 'savage', she is never patronised by the Doctor or the script. She is intelligent, funny and adaptive – and again, their relationship is based as much on what is not said as what is.

Hinchcliffe knows that Doctor Who needs to be popular, dramatic, dynamic television.

The contrast between the Doctor and his companions is important – *Doctor Who* has always thrived on successful juxtapositions: two apparently innocuous things creating dissonance (a child with a gas mask, a Yeti on your loo in Tooting Bec, a frog on a chair). It also works best when synthesising two apparently incompatible genres. Hinchcliffe's era isn't all one-note. It's not entirely the musty, spooky Gothic Horror it is famed for being – there are certainly a number of adventures which evoke the cobwebby, haunting atmosphere of Gothic Horror (all period settings and ancient evil) but these earlier Baker years have as just much contemporary and futuristic science-fiction in their canon. What Hinchcliffe does do, however, is use the Gothic genre's techniques to tell his futuristic stories, and they benefit from this approach enormously. Alongside the horror film homages like *Pyramids of Mars* and *The Brain of Morbius*, with the eerie chill of the past about them, we have some all-out science-fiction with *Planet of Evil*, *The Android Invasion*, *The Face of Evil* and *The Robots of Death*. And yet when Hinchcliffe does science-fiction successfully it is hard science-fiction with intellectual heft: *The Robots of Death* has its basis in Asimov, *The Face of Evil* has an intelligent discourse about religion and eugenics at its core, and *Planet of Evil* takes *Forbidden Planet* (which itself invoked Shakespeare's *The Tempest*) and amalgamates it with *Strange Case of Dr Jekyll and Mr Hyde*. Hinchcliffe's *Doctor Who* is good science-fiction which lives a dark double life as a troubling psychological horror movie. It has, really, the best of both worlds: the excitement and invention of science-fiction told with the techniques of unnerving ghost stories. Things that go zap, pow and bang also go bump in the night.

Even so, Hinchcliffe knows that in order to work, *Doctor Who* needs to be popular, dramatic, dynamic television – to thrill the kids but keep the adults on board too. Despite its high-minded influences from one of the masters of science-

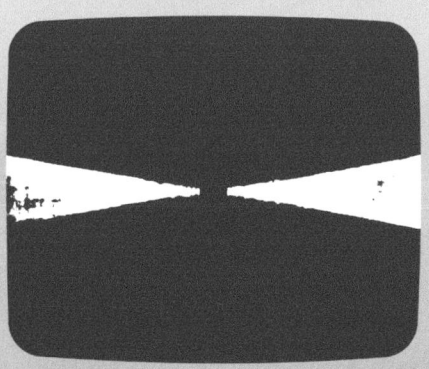

fiction in Asimov, *The Robots of Death* also takes a cue from somewhere much more populist: Agatha Christie. It's a murder mystery, but on a funky space mine instead of in a vicarage. It's a simple premise, but augmented with Robert Holmes-style world-building, deadpan robot killers and a design aesthetic that is original and arresting. Like much of Hinchcliffe's *Doctor Who*, it is a classic because it manages to be *more* than the sum of its parts. Even though it borrows wantonly, it makes something new by sprinkling *Doctor Who*'s smart humour, gift for character and creative verve into the mix. As it happens, this time the world-building was actually Chris Boucher's work and so demonstrates how in synch this young apprentice was with his old hand of a script editor – and what a natural *Doctor Who* writer Boucher was.

So whilst its pilfering must not be seen as a weakness, for the sake of balance one must be honest about Hinchcliffe era imperfections elsewhere (despite, ultimately, forgiving them). Critics of 21st century *Doctor Who* sometimes point to the abruptness of its endings, the *deus ex machina* which wraps everything up all too conveniently. Well, if modern *Doctor Who* *is* culpable of this then its showrunners must share a cell with Hinchcliffe, who commits some denouement atrocities of his own – *The Brain of Morbius* suddenly switches course when the Doctor challenges his opponent to a hitherto unmentioned mind-bending contest that just happens to be lying around. Machina ex Cupboard! All Conquering Classic *Pyramids of Mars* basically re-enacts the last episode of Not All Conquering Classic *Death to the Daleks* (and even has the audacity to quote its source). And the Krynoid in *The Seeds of Doom* isn't defeated by the Doctor at all but by stock footage of the RAF being called in by someone else. But the journey to each destination is so eventful, so carefully mapped and so full of interesting characters that it doesn't really matter. We all know the baddies are going to get blown up anyway, so why make it too complicated? And the productions are so solid (there is very little sloppiness in any art department under Hinchcliffe) that we are diverted from any rare script shortcomings should they occur.

Interviewed at the time – on the *Whose Doctor Who* documentary made by the BBC – Hinchcliffe said, rather bravely, that he would be happy if fifty per cent of the effects the team attempted were successful. It's fair to say his hit rate is higher – for every Skarosian clam there's a Zygon, for every Skarasen there's a sandminer, and for every Sontaran Tea Tray Robot there's a hand of fear. Hinchcliffe marshals his resources to make his productions as achievable as possible. There's a consistent strength in production values throughout the era but that's not to say he's conservative – he tries to erect a jungle indoors (and the film work on *Planet of Evil* is quite magnificent), have a creature the size of St Paul's Cathedral attempting to eat Mick Jagger's house (and the Krynoid, particularly the model, is pretty successful), and has a bash at a giant rat (oh well). And when he takes his team on the road the locations really count (Dartmoor, Portmeirion, Oldbury Nuclear Power Station, the Royal Theatre, Northampton).

He collaborates with the best designers available – costumers James Acheson and John Bloomfield and set genius Roger Murray-Leach all go on to have illustrious careers. The Time Lord costumes and logo of *The Deadly Assassin* endure to this day, the Zygons must surely be one of the show's greatest creature designs, and there are some memorable sets – from the clinically white human dorms of *The Ark in Space* to the gorgeous and terrifying jungle of Zeta Minor in *Planet of Evil*. The Gothic vibe (often characterised by settings like the houses belonging to Marcus Scarman or Harrison Chase) Hinchcliffe aims for tends to make best use of the resources available to him. Historical settings bring with them period costumes, and these have the advantage of being eye-catching and available from the vast BBC costume store. But the era goes beyond that. It even makes one of its potentially most futuristic elements – the TARDIS interior and console – wood-panelled and stained glass-windowed. Visuals from the past always seem more timeless than those of a postulated future, which tend to look dated all too quickly, and even if that TARDIS interior isn't one-hundred per cent successful (the console and column are just a little too incidental) there's intelligence in the idea of swapping the traditional spaceship decor for a library aesthetic. Even in the futuristic *Planet of Evil*, the Doctor's tool bag is an old-fashioned leather case rather than a shiny silver box – it's all ink pens and calligraphy for this era, not BBC Micro and futuristic fonts. Attempts to depict the future are either minimalist (*Planet of Evil*, where the money is spent on Zeta Minor not the spaceship), retro-Earth-sumptuous (*The Robots of Death*'s bold art deco aesthetic), space Nazi (*Genesis of the Daleks*), classical and scholastic (*The Deadly Assassin*) or organic (the Zygon Spaceship) rather than silver boiler suits and flashing control banks, and they look all the better for it. Magnus Greel's time cabinet and murderous mannequin and Sutekh's servo robots are designed to fit into the period in which the stories are set, which create far more pleasing visuals than some shonky android or mass of wires would.

Much of the success of the Hinchcliffe era, though, must be down to his Doctor, Tom Baker. A natural eccentric but an actor of great classical heft, under Hinchcliffe's watchful eye there's little of the waywardness that would sometimes scupper Baker's later performances. A genius needs careful handling and for his first three years Baker is pitch-perfect, and the Doctor a mercurial tough guy. Whilst Pertwee may well have disposed villains with a bit of physical rumpty-tumpty, it was very much at arm's length. Venusian Aikido was a perfect invention for Pertwee – you could administer it without breaking a sweat, ruffling a bouffant or snagging a shirt-frill. Barry Letts, mindful of the kids, wanted something they could not imitate. Baker on the other hand, is a thumper. He fist-fights and bleeds red blood in *The Deadly Assassin*, smacks Salamar in the face in *Planet of Evil* and pummels a chauffeur in *The Seeds of Doom*. In the latter he also flourishes a gun (even though it explicitly states he'd never use it) and gives Scorby an audibly disquieting neck twist. If you told Baker's Doctor to be kind, he'd give you a dismissive side-eye and impatient scowl – he's cold at the death of Marcus Scarman, pragmatic and detached when lecturing Sorenson on scientific responsibility, and incandescent with rage when facing off against Scorby (before ordering him to make a Molotov cocktail!). He's the funniest Doctor to date but he's a spiky bohemian with an air of alien menace and an undercurrent of danger lurking beneath those wide, curious eyes and that playful grin.

But this is where his companion comes in. With Louise Jameson's Leela Hinchcliffe bravely upsets the traditional dynamic by giving Baker a character and a co-star who is more than a match for him – making for a relationship that is prickly and dynamic but nevertheless underlined with mutual respect (art imitating life). It's a bold move but Elisabeth Sladen is a tough act to follow – Sarah Jane humanises Baker, not by teaching him to be better with a trite homily, but by snarking with him and treating his moods as understandable byproducts of an alien life long-lived in the shadow of danger. She forgives him his foibles and so do we – because he's funny, because he's clever, and because sometimes brilliant people are difficult and that's alright because by God it's better than being mediocre. And not much about the Hinchcliffe era is mediocre.

Just as Letts and Dicks had done, Hinchcliffe avoids huge names when filling the guest parts, instead employing an array of recognisable, respected troupers doing convincing, committed work and taking everything with the requisite level of seriousness. There's barely a bad performance in the Hinchcliffe era, and some remarkable turns: with the producer's most noticeable edict being his preference for having a good actor (often possessed) being the mouthpiece of the alien threat, rather than having some doughty thesp having to give a Shakespearean-style performance from behind a rubber mask (and he's right, the Vogans and Kraals are far less memorable than any of the humanoid villains, and even the best monsters, the Zygons, spend a lot of their time disguised as people). Michael Wisher's Davros is the exception, of course, but there's a remarkable alchemy about that memorable creation and it's no wonder the character has endured.

There are so many little moments, so many individual scenes, great performances, and deft touches in the Hinchcliffe era that this overview hasn't had a chance to invoke. The *Doctor Who* that Hinchcliffe inherited was fabulous – witty, exciting adventures told with and gusto and charm. He didn't rewrite the rule book, he just altered the typeface (opting for something Gothic, perhaps, sometimes Grotesque). He darkened the tone, adding edge and bite to the humour and something slightly more foreboding and frightening to the threat of the week. Unlike his predecessors, who resurrected a flagging brand, he took on a show that was riding high, and he achieved the remarkable feat of making it even more successful. He was only twenty-nine when he joined the show – he'd barely learned to walk! And like all *Doctor Who* producers, he had to contend with the programme being a puny and defenceless teatime frippery, having to survive floods of production nightmares and a famine of financial support. Yet he enabled it to begin a new life and created stories that (still consistently holding their own at the top end of fan polls) out-sit eternity. The Hinchcliffe era is inventive and invincible.

It's indomitable.

Philip chats about starting out

PHILIP CHATS ABOUT STARTING OUT

"I officially joined the BBC sometime in April 1974 although there was a lengthy period prior to that when I wasn't actually on the BBC staff. Bill Slater, the BBC's Head of Serials, said the first thing he wanted me to do was take over a show he'd set up.

The Girls of Slender Means is a lesser-known novel by Muriel Spark, about young middle-class girls during the Second World War, and their lives in London. The original producer couldn't get the director that he wanted and he got a bit huffy and basically said he wasn't doing it and waltzed off. This was a problem for Bill Slater as this show was scheduled with crew attached and everything. Moira Armstrong, who was an excellent drama director, was brought in by Bill at the same time as he gave me the producer job. Bill felt it would be a good way for me to get my feet under the desk at the BBC and learn all about it. It was a lovely script, a beautiful adaptation in three parts. I learnt a lot from Moira very quickly because we planned the show together. She'd already worked out most of her casting. I remember Mary Tamm was given a role. And Patricia Hodge, Miriam Margolyes and Judith Paris. Then the BBC went on strike, which was very unusual at that time, but that put the kibosh on that show being made by me at that time – and in fact it was made a year or so later by Martin Lisemore along with Moira. But things turned out well though, because it gave me a longer lead time to work out what I wanted to do with *Doctor Who*.

* * * *

For me, *Doctor Who* began really when Bill Slater introduced me to Barry Letts and I think Terrance Dicks too, in Barry's office. I've got very strong memories of being with Barry, following him all over the place, because he was just such a welcoming and decent man, and nothing was too much trouble for him to explain. He had a quiet strength but he wasn't in-your-face – simply an incredibly gentlemanly, well-mannered man and very straightforward, very honest in his dealings with people. That stayed with me, and I wanted to be the same. Here was a man who'd been doing *Doctor Who* so successfully with Terrance for years. I had enormous admiration and respect for them from the moment we met, because I could see Barry was a man who was on top of everything and still treating everybody like human beings while really delivering the goods. I remember being invited to sit with him in the gallery, because he was the director as well as producer – while they were doing the last episodes of the Jon Pertwee spider story and then seeing odd bits of *Robot* being made straight afterwards. I watched lots of kerfuffle as they played around with CSO and I remember thinking, wow, this was going to be a very complicated and technical show – none of which I knew anything about. It was daunting but exciting at the same time.

I loved the gift of being given the opportunity of producing *Doctor Who* at that time in my life.

* * * *

I think I'm very balanced about the work, knowing what we did and didn't achieve. A lot of the time I spent with Bob Holmes, my script editor throughout my years doing the job – throwing ideas around, or talking to Tom or Lis or Louise enthusing about the programme, which kept the creative part of me very engaged. But the other side of the job was having to be a leader of men, taking the troops into battle if you like. I think it was Carl Sagan who once said creative people always need to keep in touch with their inner child, and I believe that. But also you have to balance the Dionysian and Apollonian aspects of yourself. With the format of *Doctor Who*, it's been said you can do anything. It can go anywhere and that's what's so marvellous about the programme. But if you are not careful, that can get taken too far, and you end up just accepting any old thing because you believe that phrase, without any balance. It can become pantomime, or it can become comedy, or become childish rather than childlike. I think, I *hope*, I had that instinct, and was able to avoid that. I quickly learned how to tell a story using a limited number of sets, where you don't have a lot of location filming and observing the dramatic limits of not having many characters. This means every character, every set, every storyline has to earn their keep. That's one of the great talents that Bob Holmes had and I think some of that transferred to me simply by working alongside him.

The first story that Bob worked on with me, rather than stuff he started with Barry Letts and Terrance Dicks before I joined, was *The Ark in Space*, which was a big job to begin with as we had to rewrite it from scratch. Well, Bob did. I had to get special permission for him to do that from Bill Slater. Bob's story starting point was that he saw it as essential that the Ark leader was going to get infected. That was the first major change and I think I had the *Quatermass* stories as a reference point, where people were taken over by the Martians. I can never give Bob enough credit because so many stories were really written by him or, heavily edited by him and he saw and understood my need to do stories differently."

the ARK *in* SPACE

MORALITY AND POLITICS
MATTHEW SWEET

Long ago humans came to the old lands.
For a thousand years the Wirrn fought them, but you humans
destroyed the breeding colonies; the Wirrn were driven from Andromeda.

AN ark in space. A population in suspended animation. Humanity, amongst the stars, waiting to begin a new life. Sarah Jane Smith, drugged and disoriented, waking up in a new uniform to an unfamiliar voice saying, "welcome, sister".

Invasion of the Dinosaurs was a textbook Barry Letts story. Monsters from Earth. Men from the Ministry. Boots on the ground. An inciting issue torn from the pages of *New Statesman and Society*. (Easy to imagine its review of Sir Charles Grover's *Last Chance for Man*.) And, most importantly, villains who think that they were doing the right thing; villains with whom it might be possible to go to arbitration.

> As Doctor Who demilitarised, the series left Earthly things behind.

Seasons Seven to Eleven of *Doctor Who* are often characterised with reference to Nigel Kneale and Ian Fleming. Jon Pertwee's Earthbound Doctor was a maverick government employee, driving his souped-up classic vehicle to the next alien landfall. (*Invasion of the Dinosaurs* gave him the magic car moment for which James Bond had to wait until *The Man with the Golden Gun*.) But an equally strong thread of the Pertwee era was one we might associate with another authoritative bouffant-haired icon of the Seventies. Under producer Barry Letts and script editor Terrance Dicks, the Doctor was frequently trying to broker a negotiated settlement; to put something in place of strife. As tensions escalated between Earth and Draconia, Sir Reginald Styles was menaced by Boaz and Shura of the 22nd Century Popular Front and miners glowed green beneath Wales or downed tools below Mount Megeshra, the Third Doctor seemed to be asking himself – *what would Barbara Castle do?* This is not a question that would trouble his successor.

What changed when Philip Hinchcliffe, his script editor Robert Holmes and his new star Tom Baker inherited *Doctor Who*? Why were the space arks of Seasons Eleven and Twelve so very different? It can't be explained by an infusion of new writers. Bob Baker and Dave Martin were Pertwee people. Terry Nation, Louis Marks, Gerry Davis and John Lucarotti went back to Hartnell's time. (Two of them seemed stuck there.) Chris Boucher was the only genuine discovery of Hinchcliffe's tenure. Half his new writers were Robert Holmes under a pseudonym. Yet the change of direction is profound.

It went deeper than loosening ties with UNIT or rejecting the convention of monsters invading the Home Counties in groups of six. As *Doctor Who* demilitarised, the series left Earthly things behind. Out went gasometers, chain-link fences, folders marked top secret, barbed wire, MOD signs and army jeeps – the accoutrements of *Quatermass*. (Though *Doctor Who* was not done with Kneale: our peep into the hive-mind of the Wirrn was the show's most outrageous theft from him since the opening moments of *Spearhead from Space* back in 1970.) As these were phased out, something more fundamental was rejected – the moral and ideological framework that Letts and Dicks began establishing as the series switched to colour.

Hinchcliffe and Holmes are to the political right of their immediate predecessors. The

problems of collectives did not much interest them, just as they did not interest all those people who switched off Letts and Dicks's BBC's mid-Seventies science-fiction series *Moonbase 3*. Hinchcliffe and Holmes were also unfascinated by diplomatic process. Their stories did not hinge upon peace talks, summits, decolonisation efforts. Their monsters had lairs, not modernist embassies in Hampstead.

Orwellian dystopias held no excitement for them. Despite the distant dark age sketched with few lines in *The Talons of Weng-Chiang*, Hinchcliffe and Holmes seemed more optimistic about the human future. The big speech in *The Ark in Space* set out their vision. Our species is indomitable – not, as *Doctor Who* had recently insisted, the agent of imperial and industrial forces that turn everything on Earth to ash and clinker, and the moon into a prison for left-wing academics. That grim joke in *Frontier in Space* about the family allowance in New Glasgow rising to two children had no place in the landscape of Hinchcliffe's futures, which looked like *Forbidden Planet* or Gaudi or art nouveau and never the South Bank Centre on a damp Wednesday morning. Families and children barely figure. Were there any men on Karn? Were there any women on Voga? Did anybody but Professor Watson have kids to kiss goodnight? In the UNIT years, companions dated, poachers and plastics manufacturers had spouses, and the Brigadier wore a watch from Doris. In the Hinchcliffe universe, was anyone actually having sex?

Not everything is different. The subject of empire stayed on the agenda – how could it not, when Robert Holmes was with the Black Watch and the Queen's Own Highlanders in India and Burma during and after the Second World War? – but we were no longer being offered parables on the Raj. We made visits to the imperial past – where Marcus Scarman dismissed his assistant Ahmed as a superstitious savage and Sergeant Kyle was sure that a Tong member will "jaw-jaw plenty by and by" – or travelled to more distant imperial futures, ones that gestured to the worlds of Isaac Asimov and Frank Herbert, or books with Chris Foss covers that Philip Hinchcliffe might have read on his way to the office. (*The Robots of Death* borrows both Asimov's laws and Herbert's dunes: if only the sandminer had been painted with candy pink stripes.)

Something Copernican had happened. Morestrans could identify Earthlings but betrayed little curiosity about them. Did the Founding Families of Kaldor come from Earth? What about the wearers of Skyfall Seven spacesuits? Nobody asked. Perhaps nobody cared. It all seemed too long ago, too far away. When, with a fussy note of pride, Harry Sullivan told Nyder that he is a human, the Kaled Security Commander informed him, glassily, that their greatest scientist has decreed such people impossible. Three years later, Harry was long gone and Leela was the Doctor's brawn – a woman to whom Earth was a slightly annoying place where she had to wear peculiar underwear and go easy with the blowpipe.

Even the Time Lords had forgotten us. Back in Season Ten's *The Mutants*, the High Council considered Earth's imperial policy sufficiently important to require some subtle celestial intervention. In *The Deadly Assassin*, the obscurity of Sol Three in the Mutters Spiral was a running gag. When Gallifreyans say it, it sounds like they're dropping the name of an obscure prog rock band. "Rather an interesting little planet, I understand," twitters Engin, before Castellan Spandrell dips his enthusiasm in cold water. (And later, of course, starts using terrestrial slang picked up from the Doctor.)

Exchanges like this were part of the reason why fans formed by *The War Games* and *The Three Doctors* took such exception to *The Deadly Assassin* and wrote, more in anger than in sorrow, to the *Doctor Who* production office. Some of the replies they received were not wholly polite. As fan discourse began gathering its skirts in the mid-Seventies, both Hinchcliffe and Holmes found themselves called upon to defend their decision to demote the Time Lords from demi-god status. Holmes, troubling himself to write for the fanzine, *Gallifrey*, in late 1977, declared that "a weakness of the serious *Who* fan is that he will take everything said in the programme as holy writ." If the Time Lords are such elevated beings, he asked, why do they produce a "disproportionately high number of villainous megalomaniacs"? The Shobogans and Patrexes and Runcible the Fatuous Dimblebying away on the Panopticon floor are Holmes's answer. "This new hypothesis," he wrote, "seemed to fit better than the old belief that Time Lords were lofty-minded cosmic Buddhists." Here theology enters the chat, to offer another way of reading the tonal shift between Letts and Hinchcliffe. Hinchcliffe's stories contained one allusion to Buddhism. It occurred during the decompression unit scenes in *Terror of the Zygons*, where "a trick … picked up from a Tibetan monk" gets the Doctor and Sarah out of an airless trap. It's a narrative convenience straight out of Edwardian pulp fiction. Barry Letts was not above the use of such devices – the jump-cut "transmigration of objects" in *The Ambassadors of Death* springs to mind – but for him, Buddhism was the moral and philosophical ground of the series.

Letts was a Catholic convert who turned to Zen Buddhism as a way out of the Problem of Evil, which, as the years went by, had reduced him to silence as everyone else at Mass said the Creed. In a 1981 interview for *Doctor Who Monthly*, he made his first explicit statement on the subject. "I am a Buddhist (though I dislike such labels), and although not many people realised it at the time, the *Spiders* story was a parable about Buddhist meditation." He may have underestimated the audience – in Pertwee's final story, *Planet of the Spiders*, the Doctor's old teacher from Gallifrey, living as a Buddhist monk in the Home Counties, sent his pupil to a CSO mountain to free himself from the burdens of pride and despair. For anyone who missed the message, Letts's later writings left no room for doubt. "Zen Buddhism," he wrote in his memoir, *Who and Me* "was central to the persona of the Third Doctor."

In Buddhism, evil is neither an external force nor a fundamental human component. It is a contingent phenomenon – the product of our anger, greed or thirst. The Letts era was ill at ease with the idea of elemental evil. 1971's *The Mind of Evil* – in which it seems to be a particular form of mental energy that can be siphoned from convicts and held in the bottle of the Keller Machine – is an outlier. More typical is that same season's *The Dæmons*, for which Letts brought the Devil himself to the screen. Only he wasn't the Devil. He was a confused alien, who, having moulded humanity like a Nigel Kneale Martian or the beings in an Erich von Däniken paperback, seems unable to understand the results of his work. After failing to compute Jo Grant's love for the Doctor – or her compassion for a chicken destined for the black sabbath pot – Azal of Dæmos suffers a fatal ethical headache and stumbles away to oblivion.

In the novelisation, published in the gap between *Planet of the Spiders* and *Robot*, Letts added lines in which the Doctor offers his own advice on how to tackle a problem like Azal – a paraphrase of the Zen concept of Kenshō. "Oh yes," laughs the Time Lord, as Jo frets over the daemonic Armageddon brewing in a church crypt up the road. "But that's not now. That would be tomorrow – or this evening – or in five minutes time. And right now, the sky is blue. Just look at it!"

In an interview with J. Jeremy Bentham in the 1983 *Doctor Who Magazine Winter Special*, Philip Hinchliffe looked back on his time on *Doctor Who* and described his dissatisfaction with what he perceived as the moral simplicity of the Letts formula. "What I think we wanted to lose was the Cowboys and Indians approach – of men in red hats shooting at men in blue hats." With Pertwee's departure, Hinchcliffe argued, the time was right to move away from the idea of the Doctor as "a moral stereotype ... who fights evil on a galactic scale. Baker's Doctor is certainly more morally ambiguous than his predecessor. His complaints in *Terror of the Zygons* about human reliance on mineral slime may sound like Pertwee on his high horse, but it's impossible to imagine the Third Doctor in *The Seeds of Doom*, recusing himself from the amputation of Charles Winlett's infected arm. And as for "evil on a galactic scale" – Letts abolished it from the universe of his *Doctor Who*, where even Satan is open to negotiation.

The great triumph of the Hinchcliffe and Holmes version of the programme was the result of their decision to end those negotiations and restore evil to its throne. For them, the Problem is Evil was no problem at all. It made stories happen and motivated the Doctor's enemies – few of whom, from 1974 onwards, seemed willing to go to mediation. As Tom Baker once said of his first producer and script editor, "the two of them opened a door to a dark winter's night and let some evil into *Doctor Who*."

It returned slowly. The Wirrn were not evil. They were, like the Krynoids, just doing their thing – which happened to be infiltrating human bodies and dissolving them from inside. ("Hungry," as Peter Capaldi's Doctor says in 2017's *The Pilot*, "looks very like evil from the wrong end of the cutlery.") The defining feature of the Wirrn is that they are beyond reason. It is the human residuum of Noah that the Doctor persuades to lead the swarm to incineration. No insects are involved in the conversation.

In the Hinchliffe years, we were never told to suspend our judgement.

In *Genesis of the Daleks*, evil seemed to be something you can see under a microscope. Ronson tells us that Davros "took living cells, treated them with chemicals and produced the ultimate creature ... immoral ... evil." The Doctor shares Ronson's moral language. The Daleks, he says, are "totally evil." Their creator, however, rejects that view. Like some chamois-leather Oppenheimer, Davros sees the Daleks as a means to end all wars. It's an argument that the Doctor is forced, in part, to accept – and it seems significant that when he asks his celebrated question outside the incubator room (borrowed from a thought experiment by Dostoevsky), Sarah replies by appealing to the authority of the Time Lords. The Doctor, she argues, can put his moral responsibility to one side. If he blows up those writhing things on the other side of the door, he will only be obeying orders.

In the new world of *Doctor Who*, such decisions ought to have been easier. We've been told since 1965 not to judge by appearances. *Galaxy Four* warned that a walrus that smells

like the cat litter tray on a hot day may be more virtuous than a mini-skirted lady with a beehive hairdo. (Perhaps the urinal tang of the Rills haunts the Third Doctor's nostrils as he salutes the chickens in the hold of the SS *Bernice*.) The Axons – shiny people in yellow body stockings who offer to pay our heating bills and make our frogs bigger than ever before – taught this lesson in the Letts years. But they couldn't quite stay on message. Once their moral ugliness was revealed, they became as repellent as Krynoids.

In the Hinchliffe years, we were never told to suspend our judgement. The Zygons were sucker-studded babies that drank milk from a sea serpent. Field Major Styre had none of the easy wit of Commander Linx's Connecticut Sontaran in Irongron's court: he was a squat Mengele crushing rib cages on Dartmoor and recording the results on his Dictaphone. The Cybermen shot sparks from their heads and wanted to blow up Voga.

The safe bets of Season Twelve, however, clearly reduced Hinchliffe's enthusiasm for what he termed "race[s] of monsters of the 'rubber suit' variety" – and neither he nor Holmes had much love for alien threats that operated, like trade union delegations, as collectives with a single spokesperson. For Barry Letts's successors, villains with individual motives were much more attractive than platoons of Autons, Mutants and Gelguards. (Little wonder they never revived the Sea Devils, whose Chief seems to be the only member of his species with a functioning jaw.)

It all had to change. It always does. After the alien invasions, the Chinns and Brownroses, the UNIT family, the moments of charm, *Doctor Who* turned to evil. Gone were the radicalised idealists, the noble lizards of Draconia and Wenley Moor.

Evil things look like evil things. No use spitballing planet-sharing ideas with Sutekh the Destroyer. His moral world is the reverse of ours. ("Woe unto them that call evil good, and good evil," says the Book of Isaiah, "that put darkness for light, and light for darkness.") There was no chance of a fencing match and some Jack and Algy repartee over sandwiches with the Master of *The Deadly Assassin*. Like so many evil figures in the Hinchliffe universe, his moral decay was also a state of physical decay. Hinchliffe villains drooled and suppurated. They waded through sewers and sucked the life essence out of prostitutes. They lived in basements, sometimes in tanks of bubbling water in basements. If the Letts mantra was *never judge by appearances*, the Hinchliffe one is *never trust a man with dirty fingernails*.

The first time Sarah Jane Smith awoke on an ark in space, it was a zone of human folly; an idiot trap for wealthy celebrities sufficiently foolish to believe they could travel to a new world in three months, and sufficiently immoral to think themselves fit to lead the people they would find there. She had them sussed in moments. She knew who they were. Their names, their histories, their vanities. She probably had her first paragraph for *Metropolitan* magazine sketched out.

When it happens a second time, Sarah awakened into a very different world. She was millennia from home. She was on a real spaceship in real space. Soon, she would meet a sadist who wears a Nazi iron cross. She would be blinded. She would feel the wrath of a deranged Egyptian deity. She would see a man chained to a bed, his body transforming into a hideous green mass, who yelled and bellowed that she was just as bad as the psychopath who made him that way. She would live in Philip Hinchliffe's new world of gods and monsters.

Philip chats about exorcising the past

PHILIP CHATS ABOUT EXORCISING THE PAST

"It was odd at the start because I didn't do Tom Baker's first story, *Robot*, although I was aware of what was going on – it was actually made in the same block as Jon Pertwee's last story, so it fell to Barry Letts to produce before I really arrived.

Robert Holmes and Terrance Dicks and Barry had already planned out the basics for most of my first season as producer, so I inherited a lot of ideas and scenarios and stories. Somebody must have come up with the idea of building this spaceship with the ring. I don't know if it was Bob but clearly someone said we can use that twice and save money. So that was *The Ark in Space* and *Revenge of the Cybermen* sorted. For *The Sontaran Experiment*, they allocated it all the outside filming days. This story fitted the style of Bob Baker and Dave Martin, who were very filmic writers. I believe Barry had found it very difficult to contain them in the studio. When they told a story, they always wanted big, sweeping locations and the budgets to go with that. But all this pre-planning worked in a way for me, I could pick up and run with what had been loosely plotted out for us. Bob wanted to bring back the Sontarans, he'd created them I believe during Jon Pertwee's era and probably thought we could get a nice short story out of them. Then I had the Daleks returning and the Cybermen – Bob probably thought that's what we needed, all the favourite monsters. He was really hedging his bets big time. Also he got a royalty if we used the Sontarans! Seriously, that wouldn't have been his overriding reason, but it probably crossed his mind. That's how all these old enemies came together during that initial series.

Now, I have to say, I was frustrated at the time by this. If the younger members of the audience loved the Cybermen then they were okay because it's not a bad story and so it worked for that section of the audience. But I found it annoying, this endless parade of past glories – it wasn't the vision I had for the series at all.

Another problem with *Revenge of the Cybermen* were the scripts. Gerry Davis was a big name on *Doctor Who*, so I had to be respectful, but actually he was mailing the script in from somewhere and it really showed. I think Terrance Dicks had originally suggested Malcolm Hulke to do that story, but he passed on it, so Gerry came in. Of course, it was improved by Bob's rewrites but although he did what he could in the time left, he really couldn't put his stamp on it as he had rewriting *The Ark in Space*.

I was very lucky that I had such a very talented script editor. Everything starts with the script – if you don't get the script right then it doesn't matter what you do, it'll fail. I was a hard taskmaster but I was very, very lucky that I had Bob because another script editor wouldn't have been able to rewrite as well or as fast as him. There were so many times he had to do a page one rewrite because someone just hadn't quite got the show, or had burned out. Bob would have to step in and do all this additional work but that was because both of us believed you had to have high standards and want to fulfil them. Otherwise, if you're prepared to just let stuff go through, the show is bad. People used to say that's the nature of making television drama – but it's particularly demoralising when you realise that nothing really is salvageable and you're on that production treadmill. As a young producer wanting to make my mark on the world, I'd read the script with these hackneyed old monsters like Cybermen and saw disaster staring me in the face. It had to become a complete rewrite, retaining the good bits of the idea and hopefully we made it work. Ultimately after that first season, well from the Zygon story onwards, I believe we achieved what I wanted to do. And we did it by banishing the Daleks and the other old monsters."

the SONTARAN EXPERIMENT

THE USE OF RETURNING MONSTERS
SOPHIA MORPHEW

I'm a sort of travelling time expert. As you can see, Earth's been habitable for several thousand years, but they didn't wake up. Why? Clock stopped. Overslept. So here I am.

IN the 2006 story *The Girl in the Fireplace*, Madame de Pompadour makes the following remark about the nature of the Doctor: "The monsters and the Doctor. It seems you cannot have one without the other." The observation is equally valid about the show as the man. Just imagine *Doctor Who* without its familiar pantheon of monsters … No Cybermen or Zygons. Imagine bringing up *Doctor Who* in polite company and not hearing a variation on the joke about Daleks not being able to get up stairs. Returning monsters provide a sense of continuity and familiarity in a show whose DNA is rooted in flux (sorry. Not sorry). Companions and showrunners come and go, our protagonist alters their face, gender, and persona at will, but here's a Silurian so we're in the correct part of the universe after all, be it Sunday teatime or a weeknight. Those Daleks, whether at the bottom of the stairs or the top, are just as iconic as the blue box and the madman inside it.

Distinctive in everything, the three seasons of the Hinchcliffe era – amongst the highest rated, most popular and tonally unified in the show's history – are singularly un-reliant on returning monsters, save for Season Twelve, an anomaly within an anomaly where three serials out of five feature a returning monster. This can certainly be viewed as an attempt by the outgoing commissioning team of Barry Letts and Terrance Dicks to provide the viewer continuity mentioned above, but how do these stories, in particular the first of them, *The Sontaran Experiment*, fit within the wider Hinchliffe run? Let's go take a look …

Once upon a time – the viewer's distant future, Season Twelve's remote backstory – Earth was ravaged by solar flares. Humanity fled – some in ships to the distant stars, others to a space station, Nerva, to wait in cryogenic hibernation. By the end of *The Ark in Space* the Doctor has offered to return the Nerva survivors to Earth. It's this task that propels us into *The Sontaran Experiment* as the Doctor, Sarah and Harry materialise in a fairy ring of transmat circles, parked out on a hillside like the galaxy's most improbable sculpture park (as we're talking about returning things, it's gratifying – from both a viewer and production standpoint – to see them pop up again in *Revenge of the Cybermen*).

I found *The Sontaran Experiment* a disorienting watch the first time I saw it. Unsurprising, with hindsight, as I'd never seen *The Ark in Space*, of which it's as much a continuation as it is a standalone story. But *The Sontaran Experiment* isn't just an interlude between bigger and better things, a kind of editorial corridor. It's a great place to get an overview of a show in a state of transition. The first of the breakneck almost direct pickups between serials that characterise this season might land us slap bang in the middle of Piccadilly Circus, but we're already a million miles from home in terms of how the show feels and where it sits tonally. Gone is the largely cozy and contemporary Earth of the Pertwee era, with outside threats being detected and defeated by the Doctor and UNIT. *This* Earth is an altogether less comforting proposition – rather like the brashly bohemian man who now calls himself the Doctor, packing Harry and Sarah off into the wilderness with instructions to "Enjoy yourself!".

I'm yet to get to the monsters, but then neither has the serial. It's not until what is both the episodic hook and serial midpoint that Sarah is captured by our titular Sontaran. Why a Sontaran? Wouldn't this middle serial be a good place to bring out the show's big guns? The answer comes when

Sarah sees the face of her captor. Afraid, but also confused, she has one word to say …

"Linx!"

The Sontarans are here because Sarah, our one remaining link with the Jon Pertwee Doctor, is here; both made their debut in the previous season's *The Time Warrior*. It's a neat piece of story-lining, reuniting friend and first foe, at once legitimising and reassuring. However, Sarah's captor *isn't* Linx, but Field Major Styre. Exact same face, very different person. Styre chides Sarah for the mistake – "Identical, yes. The same, no" – before adding (in what is possibly the greatest retort to catcallers imaginable) "Your opinion of my looks is of no interest to my program."

The Sontarans are a smart pick for an outing here. They provide some level of continuity with what's gone before, but they're not – at this point in time – iconic enough to carry much baggage with them. Even the episode title was unlikely to be a spoiler-ish as it sounds to modern ears. After all, there was no of rewatching or checking what species the creature from *The Time Warrior* was. This leaves the Sontarans ripe to be made this era's own, so we find out some juicy new details about them. Sarah's Styre/Linx mix-up is because Sontarans are a clone race (it *is* amusing to note, for a race of clones, how different they look from serial to serial …) and they're not merely fighting a war as we're told in *The Time Warrior*, but at *perpetual* war with something called the Rutan Cluster (a titbit so successful it resurfaces in Season Fifteen when the Rutans get to star in their own story).

Styre has lured a human ship to Earth to have living subjects for experiments to establish the capacities of humans as military foes. He adds Sarah to his store of subjects, testing her mental resilience with a series of unpleasant hallucinations, and we start to uncover a collection of story elements and preoccupations characteristic right across the Hinchliffe era. Styre's science projects gone bad mark the first of several incidences of 'unnatural experiments,' as well as a preoccupation with mind control, both owing far more to horror than the action adventure of the Letts era. The violence starts to feel more real too; both the Doctor's fight with Styre and the tortures Styre metes out display a harder edge, which was to increase across Hinchcliffe's tenure. The Sontarans themselves, recognisably people albeit, as Sarah points out, ugly ones, and the hierarchical military society they live in makes them an astute choice to give us a preview of a series of grotesques, dictators and dysfunctional regimes that will populate later episodes.

The serial following *The Sontaran Experiment* is among the most surprising and terrifying stories of Hinchcliffe's era, a surprise that starts with it being a Dalek story by Terry Nation. From the destabilising opening sequence of an apparent First World War battlefield to the Time Lord in *Seventh Seal* cosplay charging the Doctor with the extraordinary mission of preventing the creation of the Daleks, it's a wild ride before you're even halfway into the first episode. Welcome to *Genesis of the Daleks*.

In a supremely confident editorial move, this six-episode serial contains barely any Daleks.

Audience expectations are raised, but what is delivered is a claustrophobic exploration of the dangers of authoritarianism, heavy with parallels to the Nazis and seething with anxiety but with about half an hour tops screentime for the iconic pepper pots themselves. All done so deftly that there's no dissatisfaction as the script teases the presence of Daleks like a burlesque fan dance – promising much, revealing little, making us feel that we've seen it all. Leftfield and irreverent, *Genesis of The Daleks* succeeds in breathing new life into the previously overexposed Daleks.

Upstaged in their own origin story, the Daleks allow a new figure to take the stage: their creator, Davros. His conflict with the Doctor, an intellectual equal but moral antithesis, sets the serial alight – would he be the antagonist that defines this Doctor, as the gentlemen's club rivalry with Roger Delgado's Master had helped to define the Third Doctor? With hindsight, no, although it would have been fun to speculate. Careless of its riches, the Hinchcliffe editorial team was never to revive

Davros or the Daleks. As with the Sontarans, however, a new returning villain had been established, and this alternate Enmity of Ages (and Davros's equally fractious relationship with his own creations) drives many subsequent stories. If *The Sontaran Experiment* uses its returning monster as a dry run for what is to come, *Genesis of the Daleks* presents a show that has fully taken up the reins of its power, choosing exactly what pleases it best from the show's history and leaving the rest.

Displaying a surprisingly relaxed attitude to time keeping, the Time Lords return the Doctor to Nerva millennia before he left it. Waiting for the TARDIS to find its way to him, the Doctor encounters the final returning monster of the season, Cybermen. The decision to revisit Nerva at an earlier point in time, rather than heading somewhere else, reveals more than a canny approach to budgeting for sets. Like Earth in *The Sontaran Experiment* and Skaro in *Genesis of the Daleks*, Nerva gives us a setting we think we understand, presented to us in a way that we perhaps don't. This reveals an emerging preoccupation with recurrence and return, found both in the geographical anchoring of Season Twelve around Nerva and in the structure of *Revenge of the Cybermen* itself. The Doctor returns to Nerva *before* he left it, and the mythical planet of gold re-emerges from hiding, just as the seemingly vanquished Cybermen are also crawling out of the dark folds of history.

Structure is probably the most interesting thing to examine in *Revenge of the Cybermen*. Where the previous two serials take charge of their returning monsters, revealing new facets to them and infusing them with the characteristic flavours of Hinchcliffe's tenure, *Revenge* feels disinclined to dish out the same secret sauce to the Cybermen. The only thing really leant into is the hard-edged violence of the era, and the scenes of the Vogan soldiers hurling themselves, lemming like, into the Cybermen's superior fire power are the closest the serial comes to raising an emotional response for me. It's a shame, as the Cybermen are particularly suited to the cocktail of body horror, corrupted power and science gone bad that features in so many other of the era's serials, especially as they already owe such a debt to *Frankenstein*, gleefully used as a touchstone in later seasons. The contrast with how *Genesis of the Daleks* strips the Daleks back to their true horror – not machine but something once all too much like us – is marked. The failure of *Revenge of the Cybermen* to sup from this particular grail of nightmare fuel does both the Cybermen and the viewer a disservice.

Although not intended to finish Season Twelve, it feels somehow fitting that *Revenge of the Cybermen* does so, with its final outing for a classic monster under Hinchliffe's tenure. But the recursions and return baked into the structure of the serial invites us to look at the following two seasons a little differently. To do so I'd like to briefly resurrect a monster from my own past…

I am ten, more or less, and I've just been to the library. I'm now sitting in the airing cupboard with my treasure like some tiny low-rent Whovian Mitford. I've got The Book, the Target Novelisation checked out on heaviest rotation. I'm both appalled and compelled by it – the story, but also the picture

on the cover, unusual for a book illustration in being so much worse than anything you had imagined on your own. That face, huge eyes so alive compared to ... Well, to anything else about it. Before going to bed it's imperative to make sure The Book is facing downwards. Teeth. Wash hands. Hide That Face. Mary Whitehouse would, I am sure, have had a field day.

'The Book' was, of course, *The Deadly Assassin* and can you think of a more accurate description of what a *Doctor Who* monster is supposed to do, how one is supposed to make you feel, than that? This incarnation of the Master – an almost corpse kept going only by grit and spite – scared the life out of 10-year-old me, and he did so in a way that Roger Delgado's Master never could have done. The original Master was power-hungry, manipulative, and dastardly, but also rational, sometimes reasonable, acutely aware of where his own self-interest lay, and very occasionally even capable of something approaching fondness for his 'best enemy.' In *The Deadly Assassin* this is all gone and the Master's actions are profoundly irrational – from bringing the Doctor to Gallifrey in the first place to persisting in tampering with the Eye of Harmony. He's prepared to destroy not only Gallifrey but himself with it rather than either lose or stop and think. The man who would destroy only what he could not win by stealth is well on the way to becoming the woman who would cheerfully burn cities just to see the patterns that the smoke made. The monstrosity comes not just from his *Dawn of the Dead* looks but from a character now acting from a place of unreason, who is past being reasoned with, that is both more and less than the Bad Man we used to know. The Hinchcliffe era has returned the Master to us as a monster.

We've met someone very much like this version of the Master before, if you'll allow me to loop back to Season Thirteen … A figure from the Time Lord hall of infamy, now existing in very much reduced circumstances with only a loyal acolyte and the strength of his mind to help him climb back up to the top of the tree. Morbius. There are similarities with other Hinchliffe era villains too – think, for example, of Magnus Greel, reduced to feasting on waifs beneath a Victorian music hall. Or Sutekh. Or Eldrad. Although the era of the returning classic monster is over, there is a certain type of villain, a recurring idea of what is monstrous, that runs across all three seasons. The checklist for these recurring villains was already being put in place back in *The Sontaran Experiment*: the grotesque, the deposed authoritarian, the disruptor of reality, the mad scientist (this last played for particular joy in *The Brain of Morbius* – Morbius was accused of committing 'unnatural experiments' by the Time Lords and then himself winds up being one as Solon builds him a body out of the odds and sods of travellers lured to Karn). This group of villains seem to *themselves* recur in the sense that they are all reawakened menaces previously believed vanquished and destroyed, but which cling on and resurface from the past. The idea of the returning monster now itself functions as a returning monster.

The Brain of Morbius owes an obvious debt to *Frankenstein*, already wistfully namechecked when discussing *Revenge of the Cybermen*. This referencing and reworking of works from Hammer Horror to Asimov is yet another way for serials of the Hinchcliffe era to create a sense of familiarity and continuity for the viewer without relying on returning classic monsters. The success of the Hinchcliffe era in avoiding the recurring monsters so traditional to the show in part rests on its ability to create its own internal sense of recurrence and familiarity, borrowing both from outside sources and from itself.

The ultimate drawing together of all these ideas comes in Season Fourteen's *The Face of Evil*. Possibly taking inspiration from *Strange Case of Dr Jekyll and Mr Hyde*, again we have a powerful figure from the past returning to cause havoc, and again that figure is a renegade Time Lord. Except this time the unwitting cause of all the trouble is the Doctor himself – or rather, part of his personality, unwittingly trapped in the distorted circuits of a supercomputer. Hang about the universe long enough, it seems, and everybody gets to be somebody's monster.

As with many things, when looking for returning monsters in the Hinchcliffe tenure, you just have to know where to look. In fact, this is an era underpinned by the idea of recurrence and return, from the expansion and refashioning of the Sontarans and Daleks in Season Twelve, where the familiar is used to orient us in a radically new direction, through to the invoking of classic texts of horror and the recurrence of a particular kind of villain – often themselves making a return from the past (or future). The germs of all this are in *The Sontaran Experiment* – not just an editorial corridor or a short adventure curio but a hatchling pond for what is to come. Even the idea that came to fruition much later in *The Face of Evil* that, given world enough and timey-wimey (Again, sorry. Not sorry), something will crawl out of your past or future to bite you, and that you might just have to take your turn as the monster, can be found there.

In *The Ark in Space*, the Doctor asks the Wirrn why they are using the humans of Nerva to complete their breeding cycle and is told the following tale: "You destroyed us … Long ago, humans came into the old lands. For a thousand years the Wirrn fought them, but you humans destroyed the breeding colonies. The Wirrn were driven from Andromeda. Since then, we have drifted through space searching … Now we shall use the humans in the cryogenic chamber."

At the mention of Andromeda, Vira, the de facto leader of Nerva, exclaims that the Wirrn story confirms that the 'star pioneers' – human colonists from what is by now her very distant past – survived. Even this early we come across the idea that actions from ages past might well resurface to bite (quite literally in this case) the unsuspecting inhabitants of the future. It gets better – arriving on Earth in *The Sontaran Experiment*, we get to meet the descendants of those 'star pioneers' in the crew of the ship Styre has lured there, the GalSec. Their ancestors are exactly the sort of people who would have colonised the breeding grounds of the Wirrn, thus setting up the threat from the past that the Doctor has just helped Vira battle. But, for the GalSec, Nerva and Vira's people are only figures of deepest myth. Meanwhile they themselves are being preyed upon by a superior alien race. It's a pleasing, if slightly dizzy-making, spiral path in which we humans are capable both of setting up our own returning monsters and of being someone else's monster too. How strange to find that sometimes the face of the ugly idol in the glass is in fact your own.

Philip chats about the genesis of villainy

"*Genesis of the Daleks* was a great story, but I confess, its commissioning was nothing to do with me. As I understand it, Terry Nation importuned Terrance Dicks and Barry Letts to do a Dalek story every year, but he delivered a story that Barry and Bob Holmes were just not happy to accept, it was too similar to a couple of his more recent ones. My memory of the situation is that Barry Letts asked why Terry didn't look at the origins of the Daleks, and do a story about that?

* * * *

I was I think eighteen or nineteen when I saw my first *Doctor Who* story. I may also have seen bits of the Dalek story in the first series, or I might have seen another one later on. But I always knew what a Dalek was because they became an iconic figure in children's television. I didn't really watch much television when I was a teenager, although I remember seeing *The Forsyte Saga*. But the television was often on in people's homes where I was visiting, so I saw snippets of Daleks. In my mind they went hand in hand with *Doctor Who* – that all *Doctor Who* episodes featured Daleks, that was the take I had on it. But I had enough sense to realise that something couldn't have become so iconic if there wasn't something special about it. Little children absolutely loved Daleks and were terrified at the same time. And I'd have been a fool not to acknowledge that when I was starting as producer of the series. They just weren't to my taste for the sort of storytelling I wanted to do.

Therefore we did that one big story, *Genesis of the Daleks*, which I thought was very successful, and Davros was a fascinating character. Terry created him on paper – a stroke of genius I think – but the look, the design was not really there, so early on I brought in David Maloney and his designers. I think it was me and David who really sorted out his paraphernalia, the chair and all the rest of it. As a boy, I remembered reading the comic *Eagle* with the *Dan Dare* strip which had the Mekon as the villain. Not many people had seen someone on television who looked like the Mekon, so that was my contribution – I told John Friedlander, who was building the mask, to look at the Mekon. Terry Nation's script said he only had one eye, and we were all pitching in other ideas. The voice came from Michael Wisher, the actor who played Davros; David and his team created the look and all the design around him, and so it all came together and everybody had a bit of the pie and could claim success for that. A proper group effort, not just one person, created this brilliant, now iconic, television villain. Davros was great because he's what the Daleks needed. Beforehand it'd been like having the Nazis without Hitler. With Davros, suddenly you had a Hitler and it all made sense.

* * * *

The only other returning villain we used was the Master. Bob Holmes was very keen on the Master and again, I only had the vaguest of notions who he was. I hadn't seen recordings of previous episodes he'd been in, but I understood that the Master was a sort of Moriarty to the Doctor's Holmes and in a long running series, that's a good thing. However, I got the impression from Bob that back in Pertwee's run, the Master was appearing too frequently as the villain. By the time I took over, Roger Delgado, who played the Master so well and popularly, had died, and I wasn't keen to recast this ready-made villain so soon – I preferred doing new stories in new places with new villains. Bob, I think, was still pushing to bring him back, but he waited till our third series, by which time I was more relaxed and ready to go for it. I agreed with him that it would be good to see that adversary again, just once for *The Deadly Assassin*. And the more you can personalise the adversary the better the adventure. We worked out that you need the Master to outwit, ambush and stay ahead of the Doctor. And by putting him in the state we did, damaged and enfeebled, it meant we weren't just trying to replace Roger Delgado but again, move the character on, make the return worth having. It was a new step forward, not just redoing what had happened every week during the Barry Letts/Jon Pertwee stories."

GENESIS *of* the DALEKS

THE REPRESENTATION OF DISABLED CHARACTERS IN DOCTOR WHO
ALEX KINGDOM

You will tell me the reason for every Dalek defeat. With that knowledge, I will programme them. With that knowledge, they will know their errors and how to avoid them. With that knowledge, there shall be no defeats!

IN April 1975 *Doctor Who* fans were introduced to the creator of the Daleks in the Fourth Doctor story *Genesis of the Daleks* – it was revealed that the person who made these villainous creatures was a scientist, called Davros. We see him first at the end of the first part of the story, demonstrating the movement of his new Mark 3 Travel Machine which he would later develop properly into becoming a Dalek. Davros's appearance is striking, with his disfigured face and misshapen hand, but one of the most striking features is the chair that he uses to move around in. The design of the chair is similar to that of the base of a Dalek, which immediately tells the viewer to not trust him. This is one of the first times in the show that a major character has had a disability, and it could also be argued that it's the first time that a disabled person is written to be taken seriously in the show. Because although Davros has his physical disadvantages (which the Doctor and other characters would take advantage of during this story and those beyond) he is still one of the story's strongest characters. Within two hours we see just how twisted this man is; the moment when he reveals his plan to erase emotions from the Daleks is chilling, and when he first demonstrates extermination, this is equally effective in telling the viewer this is a person to take seriously. Ultimately, Davros goes too far with his Daleks's programming, and they end up turning on their creator and, it seems, ending his life. Of course it turns out this was not be the case and he would sporadically appear in the series going forward.

When looking back at *Doctor Who*'s history it needs to be made clear that the quality of disability representation is a product of the time that it was made. Also, it should not be suggested that the show was the only television programme not giving adequate representation. With that having been said … whilst disability representation in the media is something that has slowly got better over time, looking back at the early years of the show, there isn't a whole lot of disability representation and what little there is, not all of it is positive. However, there are still some moments of brightness that have been remembered fondly.

After Davros's appearance in the show, disability representation became sparse and whenever someone with a disability *would* appear, they would normally be a background character or have very little impact on the story. This is indicative that any representation of marginalised groups was rare and frequently lacked much depth. Now this doesn't mean that there wasn't any representation and in fact some disabled actors would land some significant roles in the classic run of the show. Deep Roy would first appear in the Season Fourteen story *The Talons of Weng-Chiang* as Mr Sin and he would then land another role in the show during the twenty-third season in *The Trial of a Time Lord*. There he would play an alien, a Posicarian, although this would be a less important role compared to his first. Interestingly, the same episodes of *The Trial of a Time Lord* would see the return of the villain Sil, portrayed by the actor Nabil Shaban who was diagnosed with a brittle bone disease called *osteogenesis imperfecta*. *The Trial of a Time Lord* wasn't Sil's first appearance in the show – he first showed up in the Sixth Doctor story *Vengeance on Varos,* in the previous season. There, Sil was the lead antagonist and was certainly one of the more memorable characters from that period of the show. Sil's design is also unique as he doesn't have the most powerful appearance or use

any mechanical aids; it is Shaban's performance that makes Sil such a formidable foe for the Doctor. With his cackling laugh, fierce intelligence and total unpredictability, he really is a villain that holds the viewers attention.

In the most recent Children in Need mini-episode, *Destination Skaro,* we saw Davros for the first time in nearly a decade. However, in this short he was able-bodied, and moving as if he hadn't suffered any physical injuries. My assumption for this change at first was because it was a prequel to *Genesis of the Daleks* but upon watching behind-the-scenes show *Doctor Who: Unleashed* we found out this physical change may be permanent going forward. Returning showrunner Russell T Davies discussed the negative correlation between 'disability' and 'evil' in the media. When speaking about Davros specifically he said: "This is how we see Davros now." Firstly, I want to say I have nothing against making this decision – in fact I think it is absolutely necessary to change the way disability is represented within media and I respect Russell for taking such a massive risk with one of the show's most iconic characters. I have known young people who have been in wheelchairs all their lives who have been called Davros and slurs like that, and we need to set an example that likening people in chairs to evil villains just isn't right. On top of which, this doesn't change Davros's personality at all; he will still be one of the most evil-spirited characters in the show I'm sure.

There are a lot of stereotypes used in the media when featuring disabled people and many of them are not pleasant. One stereotype for instance that is particularly bad is when a disabled character is miraculously healed of their disability during the events of a story. A good example of this is Elizabeth Rowlinson from the Seventh Doctor story *Battlefield*. Elizabeth is a psychic who is blind. During the events of this serial, she is given her sight back, which is treated as a triumphant moment – and this is where the conversation becomes complex. There is a question a lot of disabled people get asked, which goes something along the lines of "If you could fix your disability, would you?" Now, this is a difficult question to answer and of course the answer would differ between people. My issue with the question is with the word 'fix', or indeed any similar words, which to me automatically has a lot of negative implications. If I'm honest I don't see my own disability as an outright negative (I have cerebral palsy) so when characters in fiction suddenly get their disability removed, I find it conflicting to watch. It's a complex topic as although someone being healed is a good thing on paper, what about the viewers who live with those disabilities and enjoy seeing characters like them on the screen, only for that relatability to be taken away? *Doctor Who* certainly isn't the only television programme or film to do this, and it was certainly more of a common trope back in the Sixties and Seventies and thankfully, something we don't see too often anymore. In the case of *Battlefield*, it sticks out more as even at this point in the show's history, disability representation still wasn't something that the show did very often.

One topic of debate that often occurs is the cliché of the character with a disability having to be the villain and whether that balance can be struck between a good character who happens to be disabled (villain or otherwise) and the use of the visible disability as a form of lazy shorthand to tell the audience that 'this the bad guy'. Characters like Davros and John Lumic from the modern series are, thankfully, both interesting characters who work as effective antagonists. The issue comes when the percentage of disabled characters in the show that are villainous compared to the good guys is reasonably high. Just because the show leans into this stereotype doesn't automatically make the character outright bad or offensive until you weigh it against the lack of positive disabled ones – and that makes the 'disabled villain' representation more frustrating, especially when the villain doesn't demonstrate much depth.

Take for example Max Capricorn from 2007's *Voyage of the Dammed*. Now he is not the nastiest villain in the history of *Doctor Who* – far from it – but what is unfortunate is the way this story builds up to his reveal, only for him to be a goofy head on a chair with a gold tooth that shines after he says his name – it just takes away all of the fear factor from the character, leaving him as a comedy villain whose disability is his only trait. This is a bad use of representation, as it seems that the only reason he is in the chair in the first place is to pull the rug out from under the viewer and to get a striking visual. The best villains have multiple layers that allow you to understand why they feel that what they are doing is right. Which is why villains like Davros and Lumic work so well – although they're horrible people who have no empathy for the people around them, you still get their point of view. Both of them see their roles as trying to improve life around them, despite the wishes of the people they're trying to 'save.' Their villainy therefore comes from their determination to do what they believe to be right, regardless of cost. Lumic is established as being the creator of the Cybermen and becomes slowly more despotic as time passes – so much so, that when he eventually turns into a Cyberman, it's because there could be no redemption for him. What makes him such an interesting person is how desperate he is – unlike Davros, who is creating the Daleks to win a war and later conquer the universe, Lumic just wants to improve humanity to its highest capacity although he too is eventually blinded by power, in a similar way to Davros. Where they really differ, however, is in the visuals. Davros has an incredible design which makes the viewer uneasy from the first time they see him, whereas Lumic, with zero prosthetics, relies on his presence and eccentricity which immediately commands your attention. At the end of the story Cyber-converted and sat on a massive throne, Lumic is a great piece of imagery and although presented as the stereotypical disabled villain it doesn't necessarily mean that the character is badly written. A question that does need asking is, other than drawing an immediate visual parallel with Davros as creators of *Doctor Who*'s two biggest threats, did John Lumic need to really be in a wheelchair at all?

If you were to ask a fan to name ten *Doctor Who* villains, there is a high chance that Davros would be on that list. This demonstrates how large a legacy that character has developed after almost fifty years

since his first appearance, and that development continues right into the 21st century. In the Twelfth Doctor story *The Witch's Familiar* we saw an additional side to the character – he appears to be near death and has a heart to heart with the Doctor, before slyly tricking the Time Lord into giving him some regeneration energy. However, this then leads to a controversial scene in which we see the Doctor having a laugh, riding around in Davros's chair, which implies that the Doctor somehow physically removed Davros, a disabled man who relies on the chair to sustain life, from it. A number of viewers suggested they saw this as an unnecessarily antagonistic action and people struggled to imagine the Doctor doing this, however evil Davros may have been.

One thing that may be overlooked when discussing *Doctor Who*'s representation of disability is how the non-disabled characters behave around the ones with disabilities. This is important because as disabled people we want to be treated like everyone else and so when we see our favourite characters interact with people like us in a respectful manner it means a lot. *The Witch's Familiar* aside, the Doctor generally talks to and about people with disabilities positively. The Eleventh Doctor is one of the best at this – in *Cold Blood* he meets Elliot, a kid who is struggling with dyslexia. The Doctor makes Elliot feel just as valued as the rest of the group without resorting to saying "just because you have dyslexia doesn't mean you aren't valued". This still means a lot to young viewers with disabilities as it shows that one of the most intelligent beings in the universe sees value in anyone, despite their problems.

Since *Doctor Who*'s return in 2005, disability representation has become more frequent, and finally not just via villains. We are slowly starting

to see more characters with disabilities actually impacting stories in big ways. *The Crimson Horror* introduces us to the character of Ada, who lost her sight due to being cruelly experimented on by her mother. There's a dramatic moment towards the end of the story where she has the opportunity to kill her mother in an act of revenge, but she doesn't go through with it (she does, however, kill Mr Sweet, the alien parasite for whom the experiments were in aid of). Blindness takes centre stage again in the Thirteenth Doctor story *It Takes You Away*. This is potentially the most mature story in the show centred around a disabled character so far, Hanne, who has to live independently whilst being blind, since her dad has gone missing and her mother has passed away, although his desertion of her is almost forgotten about in order to tell the main plot of the episode – luckily this makes Hanne a more impressive and resilient person. What was additionally nice is that this is another instance of the character being played by an actor who has the disability in real life.

One of the Thirteenth Doctor's companions was Ryan Sinclair, who has dyspraxia. This was a great decision by the production team as this would be the first companion to have a disability. In the early episodes of his time on the show, there would be moments in which the character would struggle with certain situations like riding a bike and climbing ladders. Sadly it would quickly become an afterthought and be barely mentioned. There would be some moments of development such as him being able to throw a circular ball after struggling to play basketball earlier in the series and again learning to ride a bike at the end of the character's time in the TARDIS but it was only really utilised when the writers needed it to be. Whilst Tosin Cole, who played Ryan, did a solid job for the most part, perhaps this element of the character would've been better explored if an actor who actually had dyspraxia had been cast as perhaps this might have allowed the condition to be a much bigger part of the character's arc.

The first episode of the 60th anniversary specials, *The Star Beast,* introduced UNIT's newest scientific adviser, Shirley Anne Bingham. Shirley was a wheelchair user and, as performed by Ruth Madeley, was smart, funny, and strong – she really was one of the best characters to come out of those anniversary specials. From her very first scene where she met the Doctor, her personality shone. She was far more excited about the potential bonus she would get as a result of meeting the Time Lord than other characters who worked for UNIT within the modern era in the show, as many of them were simply shown to be massive fans of the Doctor. The fact she told him "I've got this" and sent him away so she could get on with her job spoke volumes about how confident she was within UNIT. The moment later in the story where she rescued the Doctor and the Noble family, using darts hidden within her wheelchair, was incredible; I have to say it's one of the rare times that I audibly cheered while watching the show. Then, when the Doctor questioned her about having weapons hidden in her wheelchair she simply replied "We all have" – and then went on to blow up a wall saying "It doesn't just fire darts, mate." This is fantastic because we always talk about the importance of the younger *Doctor Who* fans and for the longest time, young wheelchair users would always have to act like a Dalek or cosplay a Dalek but now, they don't have to. Now they can be Shirley or their own member of UNIT with different tools within their own wheelchair and I think that is just brilliant. *Doctor Who* now has a character in a wheelchair that people can look up to – Shirley was such a great addition to the show.

Unfortunately, the social media reaction to Shirley was mixed, with some people asking as to how disabled actor Ruth Madeley, who was born with spina bifida, could move her legs or stand and still need a wheelchair? Or made suggestions that UNIT should have had the resources to 'fix' her. These comments were horrendous, but I think Ruth handled them wonderfully, being very tongue-in-cheek and making fun of these remarks. But it's posts like these that prove disability representation like this so important, as it demonstrates that a large number of people are so ill-educated when it comes to respecting people who are disabled, and reminds them that not everyone wants to be 'fixed'!

In *The Giggle,* the last of the three anniversary specials, one element of the storyline was that people were starting to believe that whatever they think was automatically correct. UNIT personnel all wore an object called the Zeedex which allowed the user to be unaffected by this, and keep them level-headed. However when UNT boss Kate Stewart deactivated her Zeedex, she began a rant, during which she shouted at Shirley, saying "I've seen you walk!" Now I think this moment is important as it demonstrates that saying things like this is unacceptable. I do understand though that some disabled viewers did find this went too far and was triggering so I can only speak for myself by stating that I believe you do need to show the struggles people with disabilities go through – both physical challenges and also dealing with people's prejudices.

At the end of *The Giggle* we discovered that the TARDIS is now wheelchair accessible – at last people with limited mobility can imagine themselves as companions. I really like the line "You finally caught up with the 21st Century" as it's the production team acknowledging this is something that should have been done a long time ago. Perhaps we will see wheelchair users inside the TARDIS in the not-too-distant future.

Inclusion in the media is something that has gotten better with time and *Doctor Who* is no exception. Though there are some frustrating and incorrect depictions of multiple disabilities throughout the show's past, that is for the most part a product of the time it was made. Television, when *Doctor Who* began, was part of a very different landscape to the one we are all experiencing today. Slowly but surely the industry has started to become more inclusive across the board, but there is still work to do. Just because there is more representation doesn't automatically mean that it's good. When trying to represent a certain group, accuracy is most important and that single aspect seems to be what a lot of creatives have struggled with. *Doctor Who* has shown positive signs of representation over the years which has slowly been improving. Davros's first appearance back in 1975 was groundbreaking in the show, presenting a villain with a disability who, despite that, was still a force to be reckoned with and would go down in history as one of the show's greatest characters. The show means so much to so many people and a good percentage of fans will hopefully have more characters to relate to than I had growing up watching the show.

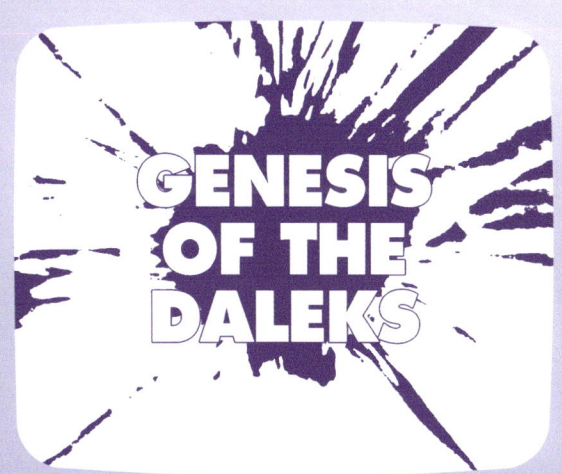

Philip chats about making BBC drama

"The *Doctor Who* production office was in Union House in Shepherd's Bush. It was an odd building, very plain, very 1950s, where one side was called Union House, the other side Threshold House – the same building with a central staircase that acted as the divider. The BBC put all the drama Series and Serials teams down there rather than at TV Centre up the road in White City.

Bob Holmes and I were based in Union House with our secretaries and as new directors came in to work on a story they got a temporary office with their assistant directors and so on. That was the same for every drama series. Oddly, BBC plays like *Play for Today* were up at TV Centre, alongside Comedy, Light Entertainment, Childrens etc. Only Series and Serials were banished to Union and Threshold Houses. This was a pain in the backside really as we still had to go up to TV Centre for recordings and meetings. Up at TV Centre were all the main production servicing departments: scenery, wardrobe, design, graphic design for titles, engineering. Plus of course all electronic post-production, dubbing and editing, because all the tape machines were in the bowels of the White City. They were the hardest commodity to book, the highest of premium access. You had to gain access to the tape machines, firstly to record your programme in live time while you were doing it in the studio, and then you needed to get access again to the same machines later on to edit your programme together and assemble it.

This meant we spent a fair bit of time walking from Union House up Wood Lane or sometimes through Frithville Gardens alongside the park, to go via the back entrance, which was a slightly shorter walk. This was the era when there were no useful domestic tape machines, no VHS tapes we could sit in our offices and watch comfortably in our own time.

TV Centre was revolutionary at the time, a purpose-built home for massive studios just to make television. It was built on a circular design so that they could throw open the studio doors and access them by a perimeter road, meaning all the scenery and stuff could come in easily. In those days the TARDIS sat beside this road when it wasn't in use and I would always check it and find bumps and scratches and bits knocked off.

* * * *

We didn't do filming at TV Centre, just videotaped stuff. Filming was either done on location or up at the old Ealing Studios in West London, where all those famous Ealing films were made. They had a couple of soundstages there but no production offices. It was a very odd way to make television drama, with the split between film and video – but it grew organically out of the BBC originally being a radio service. Hollywood movie studios were purpose built, loads of soundstages and the production offices dotted around on the backlots, which is a much more sensible way of doing it. But television is one industry and Hollywood movies is another.

One thing that was coming in around this time – I think Barry Letts had instigated it on *Doctor Who* – was dramas using new lightweight Outside Broadcast cameras for location filming, so the picture blended better than the mix of film and VT, which was always very noticeable, especially where effects were being used. It helped Barry on *Robot* where they could do the giant robot CSO stuff on location video rather than film, so it mixed better.

* * * *

One of the very first things I discovered when I arrived on the show was that someone, probably George Gallaccio our Production Unit Manager, had booked the OB cameras months in advance for *The Sontaran Experiment*, because the decision had been made to do it entirely on location on videotape, not film. It was a new gimmick for Series and Serials, and the benefit of using it for *Doctor Who* was twofold. One, you could actually make more convincing pictures because you haven't got the wobble that comes with shooting 16 millimetre film and secondly it enabled you to shoot at least twice as much, if not more, pages of dialogue between actors. Although you're on a location, you're not doing every shot as a new set up, as you would with film; you had a multi-camera set-up so could knock off a lot more minutes using these lightweight OB cameras.

We did that again for *The Seeds of Doom*, thinking of Barry and his giant CSO robot, because we wanted to make the Krynoid get bigger at the house we were shooting at. We specifically planned that script knowing what we would be able to achieve with the lightweight OB cameras.

* * * *

As producer, I wasn't there every minute of every day when they were filming at Ealing or on location although I'd tend to try and visit when I could. Once that was done, the TV Centre-based stuff was rehearsed up at the purpose-built rehearsal rooms at North Acton – we'd have a read-through there and I might go once to the actual rehearsals, just to kind of take the temperature. Plus, I would go for the Producer's Run, which was the day before everything transferred back down to TV Centre at White City to be recorded in the studios. When I wasn't doing that, I'd be meeting writers, planning new scripts, talking to the script editor, or casting with the next director. It was a busy, full-time job being a producer."

REVENGE *of* *the* CYBERMEN

THE HYBRID FILM vs VT TECHNIQUE
IN 1970s TELEVISION

HANNAH COOPER

You've no home planet, no influence, nothing.
You're just a pathetic bunch of tin soldiers
skulking about the galaxy in an ancient spaceship.

THERE were changes both behind and in front of the cameras for the twelfth season of *Doctor Who*, but there were also some for the cameras themselves. For the first time, the series used Outside Broadcast (OB) cameras to record location scenes on videotape. It had previously always been standard practice to record to videotape within an electronic multicamera studio and anything on location with, by the 1970s, 16mm film. Despite being the fourth story starring Tom Baker to enter production, this meant *Revenge of the Cybermen* became the first story of Season Twelve to employ film for its location work. Yet OB wouldn't become so dominant again on *Doctor Who* for another decade, and this videotape and film combination was far more representative of the wider world of British television drama throughout the 1970s.

These hybrid videotape-film practices came about because film had always been expensive. As a result, television drama departments limited its use where possible. The videotape cameras used in studios were heavy and impractical to take outside, so film was used instead – sparingly. When OB cameras arrived as a way to use videotape outside the studio, they were mainly used to broadcast live events like sport. There were numerous experiments with using OB for drama in the 1960s, and the increasing cost of colour film prompted renewed interest in OB drama during the 1970s. But it would take a long time for the balance to shift.

Different directors and production staff developed their own preferences for film or OB. Most television personnel were aware of a picture difference when jumping between videotape and film, which was eliminated by the use of OB. It also offered speed through multicamera recording and live editing by a vision mixer, which meant more shots were completed each day, making it far more cost effective. For some, this trumped everything.

In 1973 the BBC had installed two new lightweight OB cameras in an old technical vehicle and named the experimental unit as a Lightweight Mobile Control Room (LMCR). Further and more advanced OB scanner vans would be commissioned by both the BBC and the various ITV television companies during the rest of the decade. However, the size and noise of them meant they still needed to be set up some way from any performance. This was a problem encountered on *The Sontaran Experiment*, recorded entirely on OB, with director Rodney Bennett having to choose whether to be in the scanner van or at the actual recording location. The distance between the two meant it would take too long for him to keep moving from one to the other, so he elected to mostly remain in the scanner van with the vision mixer. In this sense, directors chose to surrender some control for OB recordings, compared to the closer oversight they had with film. *The Sontaran Experiment* was *Doctor Who*'s first story to be recorded entirely on location with no interior studio scenes. As with other drama productions that committed to stories solely on OB, this meant there was no opportunity to remount scenes in the studio if the crew encountered technical issues, which was always a risk.

The OB cameras had to be connected by cables to backpacks that contained their circuitry, then the backpacks would be connected to the LMCR's control units. These connections and other electronics sometimes proved unreliable, forcing the production team to either delay action while a camera was repaired or improvise their planned multicamera recording with a single camera. This all took up precious time, which the OB cameras were actually supposed to be saving. In addition, they could produce various electronic picture problems, rendering the shots unusable. It was standard practice that OB units would be rested at repair rooms whenever they had a few spare days between programmes to enable inevitable electrical and mechanical repairs.

With only two cameras in the lightweight units used for taping drama, they could be viewed as more limited than a more numerous multicamera studio, without offering the freedom of film. While some liked multicamera OB for swifter recording and editing, others saw film as the more flexible medium. Editing choices could be delayed as spontaneous filming opportunities were found and there was also always the risk that sound could be compromised on location, with film providing better potential for redubbing.

These hybrid formats were not used by all television drama. Among the notable exceptions were the series made by ITC, a finance and distribution subsidiary of ATV (the commercial television franchise for the Midlands). Best known for their 1960s' action-adventure series such as *Danger Man*, *The Saint* and *Randall and Hopkirk (Deceased)*, they repeatedly gambled on making programmes with global appeal entirely on film, hoping it would result in sales to the lucrative US market. To maintain cost-effectiveness, ITC operated a streamlined model and their productions were predominantly studio-bound, with limited location filming. However, after several years of success (including helping ATV win the Queen's Award to Industry for Export) by the mid-1970s ITC's television ascendancy had started to wane. Due to rising costs, some ITC series had been made on 16mm film (*Jason King*, *The Adventurer* and *The Protectors*), rather than the higher quality and thus more expensive 35mm that had been used on their earlier televisual fantasies. *Space: 1999* was an extraordinarily expensive 35mm production and much anticipated by both science-fiction viewers and the television industry; however, its viewing figures quickly floundered and the ITV companies soon shunted it into less competitive and less appetising timeslots. ITC had already begun a move towards feature films and would shift its focus away from television as the decade progressed.

Away from ITC, 16mm stock was more common, but film was still primarily only bestowed upon what were regarded as 'prestigious' productions, which generally meant classic literary adaptions (such as M.R. James's *Lost Hearts* and Charles Dickens's *The Signalman*) and some original one-off plays. The latter were often transmitted as part of anthology strands like *Armchair Cinema* and, on the BBC, *Play for Today*. The number of *Play for Today*s shot on film would increase throughout the 1970s. Yet series drama would come to eclipse the single play, partly as cost-conscious departments looked for ways to overcome the effects of the decade's double-figure inflation; unlike plays, most series could reuse sets and costumes week to week. Euston Films – a subsidiary of Thames Television, the weekday commercial broadcaster in London – were to make a notable impact with *The Sweeney*. The scriptwriters of this police series were encouraged to make some use of the standing studio sets and limit the number of locations per episode, while prioritising them for action. However, overall filmed drama series continued to be in a minority. The cost of film and the additional time it required to complete a production remained a barrier, so the videotape-film hybrid remained the norm.

The format could be used in different ways, but some productions simply had to make do with what they were given, even when it wasn't ideal. During the mid-Seventies, the first series of the BBC space opera *Blake's 7* was given the 'strike filming' that had been efficient on their other programmes, such as police procedural *Softly, Softly: Task Force*. Effectively, this meant that each episode was allocated a few days filming, regardless of its content. This set-up could work on ensemble shows where the regular cast rotated: as they weren't needed in every episode, there could be overlap, with some filming on location while others were recording in the studio. But this was not the case for *Blake's 7* and left the show in a 'use it or lose it' situation; if nothing was pre-filmed, more minutes of episode footage had to be taped on the videotape studio days. With several episodes requiring little to no location work, studio segments were sometimes shot on film at the BBC's Television Film Studios at Ealing to make the most of the filming days. However, this production set-up did not suit the programme's overall needs and ultimately timings fell behind, so it would be abandoned for future series of the show.

Other programmes were more fortunate. The concept of some productions led them to use videotape and film in ways that suited them. In *Doctor Who*, this was reflected in the way each season could be planned, with some stories crafted to be entirely studio-bound, thus allowing others the time and money to venture further afield for location filming. For instance, *The Robots of Death* used the standard murder mystery trope of having its suspects all trapped in one place, so it was ideal as a multicamera studio production, with minimal film work. *The Deadly Assassin,* however, was a story that refined the approach within a single serial by concentrating its film work to a single episode, balancing it with the studio work for the others. Being a series made up of serials clearly gave *Doctor Who* greater flexibility compared to many productions.

There were programmes conceived that could comfortably be almost entirely studio-bound on videotape. A huge Sunday night success for the BBC, and indeed overseas, *The Brothers* followed the fortunes and feuds of Hammond Transport, a South-East London haulage company. The series was built around the squabbles, subterfuge and tense wrangling among the members of the family-owned business. The element that truly kept its large audiences gripped was these boardroom machinations between the eponymous warring brothers, as well as others connected with Hammond Transport. Significant amounts of location filming at working haulage yards with trucks manoeuvring

around would have been impractical, so instead odd scenes are peppered, ensuring the series still has a grounding in the world it's set in. *The Brothers* was a truly character-driven series and the studio recording meant there was a tad more allowance for retakes of scenes with complex, business-heavy dialogue than during expensive film location shooting.

Terry Nation's BBC drama *Survivors* was another television ensemble piece where the characters's interactions drove the series, but it took a different approach to the videotape and film balance. The story begins with the swift rise of a new virus that wipes out the majority of the planet's population, with the series concentrating on the remaining minority's attempts to survive. The biggest threats to the last remnants of humanity are often other people. These sorts of series relied on strong acting choices to succeed. *Survivors* was an interesting example of a programme splitting a series between studio videotape, film and OB recording. In the earlier episodes, the characters were often on the move outdoors, eventually becoming less nomadic meaning fewer locations per episode. Despite the 'lightweight' description of the mid-Seventies OB cameras, moving the equipment between different places on a tight location shoot was still more time consuming than with film. Therefore the series was shot on a mixture of film and studio videotape for its first few stories before settling down and being shot entirely on OB for later episodes.

In contrast, film was more essential for other series to create the strong sense of place and focussed action that their stories required. *Gangsters* had started life as a *Play for Today* shot entirely on film. When an on-going series was commissioned, the budget was just a quarter of that of the original two-hour play, so it needed to be balanced with some studio recording. But for stories drawing on the culture of gangs and violence in Birmingham, as well as its great ethnic diversity, only the real place would do. The distinctive Bullring shopping centre, Aston Expressway and Rotunda building were all prominently on display in location footage, as were local shops, restaurants, clubs and parks that all depicted the post-war make-up of Birmingham's people. The city's ongoing clearance/regeneration during the late Seventies was clearly visible, with scenes set at the abandoned Snow Hill station and some actually filmed within a house whilst it was being knocked down, as part of clearances. There's also a clear sense that the crimes we were witnessing were part of the real wider world, with sweeping panoramic shots over Birmingham's skyline before panning down and zooming in on the main characters.

When *Gangsters* does have to move indoors onto videotape, it is cleverly written to reflect the medium. It can seem similar to the likes of *The Brothers* in this way, using the opportunity for limited action to engage its various criminals in roundtable discussions. Back on *Doctor Who*, this approach is evident in *Revenge of the Cybermen* too, as dialogue-heavy scenes with exposition take place in the studio parts of Voga and Nerva Beavon.

Outdoors, lightweight film cameras depicted *Gangsters'* enclave in an almost documentary style, with handheld shots in underpasses and darkened corners which enabled us to feel close to the action across a large variety of locations. Sometimes it even felt as though we were forced further into their world with crash zooms. Unusually, this handheld style was replicated using the videotape cameras in the studio, helping to provide a continuity with the location footage, which means the viewer's outside and inside realities didn't jar quite so much. It's important to note that there were different crew for studio, film and OB work, i.e. separate camera operators and different people responsible for editing and lighting on each medium, so this blend wasn't necessarily straightforward. Other productions in this period also aimed to provide visual continuity between their film location footage and studio videotape. In *Revenge of the Cybermen*, this could be seen through the set design and lighting choices, respectively the responsibilities of Roger Murray-Leach and

Derek Lee, with the Vogan chambers in the studio designed to replicate the aesthetics of the Wookey Hole filming location.

As the amount of location work for television increased during the late 1960s and early 1970s, production departments gained more experience with many having learned how to make the videotape-film format work best for them. This mix could help sculpt a programme's style, as individual productions worked to take advantage of both formats. While attempts were sought to make the join as seamless as possible, the hybrid format could also enable productions to achieve different looks and styles for different parts of a show – whether within an individual episode, or across a series as a whole.

Wookey Hole's underground caves provided a sense of scale for *Revenge of the Cybermen* that would have been impossible solely in the studio. OB cameras certainly wouldn't have been practical there. A dark and moody look was achieved, with atmospheric shadows, and the actors's voices echoing around the caves. The multicamera studio scenes on Nerva Beacon worked for very different reasons. The studio lighting achieved a more controlled and consistent look for the manmade space station, and the brightness contributed to the feeling of a clinical environment, which the crew have maintained since the apparent plague outbreak.

Another contrast was used to effect in *1990*. This series depicted a dystopian future where Britain, run by a totalitarian communist government, was facing an exodus of skilled professionals. A great many of its qualified doctors and engineers were attempting to leave behind a nation evidently in decline, and stuck in the past. *1990*'s concept means that, despite being set over a decade in the future from when it was first made in 1977, the then-present day of mid-Seventies Britain was ideal to represent a future version of the country that wasn't progressing.

Grainy winter location filming helped to convey a particular level of grimness: covertly clustered meetings with potential escapees took place with their breath visible under the grey skies, on lorry parks where the only real signs of change were the vehicle registration plates. Episodes followed both the escapees and the people smugglers into a cramped hold on a cargo ship at the harbour. It all seemed so tangible.

The show's lead was Jim Kyle, a journalist on the only remaining independent newspaper – although it's been mandated that eighty per cent of their advertising revenue must come from the state. He spent much time watching appeal proceedings at the courts, where prospective emigrants were routinely denied exit visas, being cooly told that the state insisted they could still obtain the medical care and education they sought within Britain. The court corridors seemed drab and stark, with the harshly bright studio lighting helping to emphasise the clinical detachedness of the entire atmosphere within the building. In the country's pubs, citizens were allocated alcohol rations based on their perceived contribution to society. The drinking establishments depicted in *1990* were cold and bland, empty of any joy and the usual atmosphere of a pub. The characters huddled together, eking out their rationed alcohol, with government signs looming over them:

CITIZENS ARE WARNED THAT BEVERAGE CARDS ARE VALID ONLY FOR THE WORK STATUS MARKED.

There is a certain irony for a series set in a world where citizens expect to be constantly watched and listened to, that it was most likely to occur when they were indoors, being taped from several angles in a multicamera studio. In contrast, their efforts to avoid government eyes and ears for clandestine activities tended to happen in front of a single film camera.

While film was mostly needed for outdoor filming, there were also certain advantages to utilising it for specific elements of studio work. The BBC's Film Department was based at Ealing Studios, which the Corporation had acquired in 1955, and the premises included both studios and editing facilities. Drama productions could construct sets that would be impractical in the smaller studios at Television Centre, or for scenes too risky because they used fire or water.

As television's audiences became increasingly experienced viewers, many could tell the difference between the grain of film and the smoothness of videotape and became used – either consciously or unconsciously – to the visual association of video inside/film outside. As a result, shooting on film offered an advantage of verisimilitude if a production needed to create an outdoor location within a studio.

One of *Doctor Who*'s constant challenges was in creating convincing fictional worlds in which each story took place. Filming for *Planet of Evil*'s jungle set, superbly designed by Roger Murray-Leach, enabled the production to bring the outside in on a far grander scale. Ealing offered greater lighting control over both a real location and a studio that used videotape, with film more forgiving of lower light levels. Shooting with a single camera also meant that very specific shots could be achieved to create the effect desired. Film helped gain more perspectives and combined with the atmosphere created by the design and lighting, an appropriate sense of mystery. This was an alien outdoors suitably created indoors on Earth. It was successful enough that a similar venture would be repeated the following season for *The Face of Evil*'s jungle planet.

For the BBC's early Seventies wartime drama *Colditz*, Europe's Iron Curtain made it impossible to film at the eponymous castle that had held Allied prisoners during the Second World War. Unable to shoot in East Germany, various locations within Britain often stood in, with Stirling Castle among those doubling for the 'escape-proof' POW camp. However, Colditz Castle's large courtyard would feature regularly in the series, so the production actually opted to build a vast set inside Ealing Studios where scenes could be shot on film, thus matching other 'exterior' sequences.

The combination of videotape and film was a key characteristic of the majority of television drama during the 1970s, including *Doctor Who*. Yet production departments didn't take a single approach with it. From Skaro's grim and misty surface in *Genesis of the Daleks* and the eerie atmosphere of *The Face of Evil*'s jungle on film, to *The Android Invasion* and *The Deadly Assassin* making audiences question realities while moving between studio and location, the programme succeeded in a number of ways. Increasingly creative and experienced production teams could make the most of videotape and film's advantages over the era's alternatives and ensure each format was used in the best way for their individual programme.

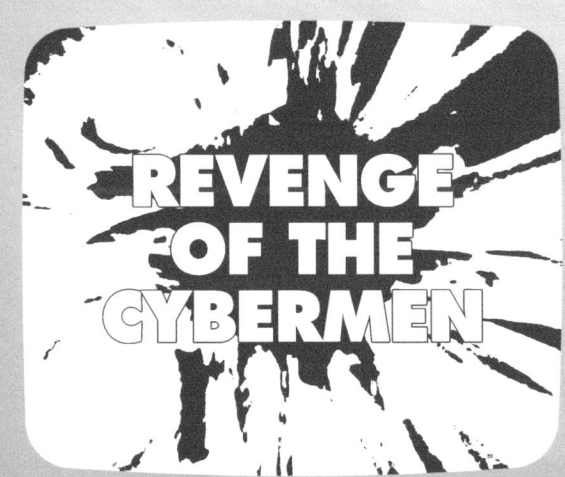

Philip chats about Tom Baker

"I didn't cast Tom Baker, that was Barry Letts, and I am so grateful that he brought Tom onboard. There was talk, I later learned from Bob Holmes, about casting someone much older, or more comedic. As a result, Bob said to me, he had to invent Harry Sullivan as an athletic, younger male companion because there were so many rumours going round about these decrepit actors in the frame for taking over from Jon Pertwee, and if that was the case, Harry would have to take on the action in the stories. Which is a terrible idea, to be honest, I mean why would you cast a lead actor who can't actually *be* the lead character?

Looking back, it seemed to me that they must have been struggling really to find someone to carry on after Pertwee, who was really quite a presence to replace. Maybe there was nobody who was an obvious casting for the Doctor. Or maybe they tried people and got turned down. I don't know. I do know it was Bill Slater who should get the credit for Tom initially, because he remembered this rather zany actor, Tom Baker, whom he'd directed in Shaw's *The Millionairess*. I believe the story is that Barry Letts and Terrance Dicks, on Bill's suggestion, rushed off that afternoon to see the Sinbad film which Tom was in, and then obviously came back and said to Bill what a great idea Tom was. They got him in for a meeting and I imagine Tom utterly charmed them. I think if I had been given that responsibility, when I had so little experience of producing, I would have been really at a loss and I might have made a terrible mistake because I just didn't have the depth of knowledge of actors back then.

Therefore I was totally okay with Barry's decision – I wouldn't have been if Tom had turned out to be not very good or wrong, of course, that would have been a terrible situation to be in, to have inherited the show with the wrong leading man. Truth is, I never really thought about that because Tom was a fait accompli and by having Tom, I think Bob Holmes and I were lucky. We already had a really clear strategy in our minds about how the new Doctor would be. Brilliantly, Tom immediately bought into the character that we were hoping he would be become, he kind of intuitively moved towards it. We didn't have to say to him "You're not doing it right, Tom, could you do it like this?" He just found his feet so quickly. I think that by *Genesis of the Daleks*, you felt this was a commanding performance and he was already confident, so by the time we reached *Terror of the Zygons* and *Pyramids of Mars*, we had the Doctor that we all wanted, including Tom. He made the viewers feel that there's always something more going on inside his head, he's not just a hero who can run around and zap people with a sonic screwdriver; he doesn't know everything in the world. Sometimes he meets people who are more powerful, like Sutekh in *Pyramids of Mars*, and you realise they're more powerful and he can't solve it in five minutes. That brings real depth to a story and to the Doctor.

Tom of course was younger than his predecessors. Not young, but *younger*. Not like Peter Davison and David Tennant, but he seemed younger because the earlier Doctors had grey hair, seemed paternal. Tom had a kind of bohemian thing going on, looking like the sort of somebody who tramps around the universe, very anti-rules, which was what I wanted. I didn't want an out-and-out rebel, more of a radical which was the zeitgeist in the Sixties and early Seventies – a bit Woodstock, a bit student riots and anti-Vietnam and all that. He's obviously the maverick Time Lord, not the one who just toes the line. I think that was my feeling about the character purely from the point of view of how he should be written and how we should approach him. Tom naturally had a lot of that and there was his humour as well. I don't mean cracking jokes so much as witty, intelligent, the humour of a sophisticated mind. Tom could do that, could deliver that.

I think that the costume department took these discussions literally. They went to images of Bohemia and bohemians, one of the most famous of whom was Aristide Bruant, as painted by Toulouse-Lautrec, which was the French impressionist era version of what a bohemian looked like. And while I think that the costume people went a bit too far with it, on the other hand, that iconic image does serve the Doctor in a very nice way – the hat, the scarf. It gives Tom's Doctor a style, an image. really. Yes, it was a bit of a cliché in one way, but it also has a power and elegance. They also gave him a shortish shooting jacket, a Norfolk jacket. But it seemed to me that it'd be better for him to have a long coat, so I made that change. Perhaps I was thinking back to cowboy movies, where they gave them long coats to give actors power and potency.

Tom once claimed that I gave him the note to play the Doctor with a sense of 'Olympian detachment'. It was one of those phrases I made up on the spur of the moment, and to be honest, as an acting note, it's probably the most feeble and useless one to give to an actor. Yet it obviously struck a chord with him. It wasn't a throwaway idea though, because that was my view of the Doctor: if you look at the history of the Doctor, he's not human yet he looks totally and utterly human. So I was trying to encourage Tom to somehow portray that that he wasn't human. He was *helping* the human race, but he had to have a certain distance otherwise he just becomes like any other hero. So, there was a bit of seriousness behind the remark and I'm glad Tom went with it."

TERROR of the ZYGONS

THE US INVASION
KIM PFEIFER-ADAMS

It's about time the people who run this planet of yours realised that to be dependent upon a mineral slime just doesn't make sense. Now, the energising of hydrogen...

"IT'S 10:00 o'clock – do you know where your children are?"

The year is 1979 and all across the United States television announcers issue this ominous query just before the nightly news. In New York City, the admonition was voiced by presenter Lou Steele. From 1969 to 1973, Steele (under the pseudonym 'The Creep') also hosted the local late-night horror show *Creature Feature*. Not unique to New York, these monster-movie-of-the-week shows, hosted by various local personalities, often in the guise of a vampire or ghoul, are a popular staple for many local stations across the country. Hearing the voice of 'The Creep' warning you to check on your children is more than just a public service announcement, it is a reminder that the world is a dangerous place – not just from kidnappers and ne'er-do-wells, but from things that go bump in the night. It would seem that the only thing Americans love more than being scared is scaring their children.

The American appetite for horror began in the 1930s, coming of age in with the Universal classic Monsters and later, the Hammer Films from the UK. But by the 1970s a new era of horror had taken the USA by storm. Unlike the scary movies of the 1950s (in which good always prevailed) the 1970s saw a darker movie mythos emerge. The good guys didn't always win, the body count was high, the deaths were graphic and gruesome, the enemy was *us*, and the call was coming from inside the house. In contrast to the post-war atomic age where we externalised our fears into larger-than-life monsters that we could defeat, the 1970s saw us internalise those fears. Nothing was as it seemed and maybe there was no silver lining. It's no wonder that we took comfort in the classics of the Fifties and Sixties. A late-night Monster Mash or Saturday afternoon double feature ignited nostalgia and, perhaps, a collective yearning for simpler times.

Like so many American fans, Tom Baker was my Doctor

Although many of these shows aired after the watershed, for eight-year-old me, in Buffalo New York, *Sci-fi Theater* aired on Saturday afternoons featuring classic monster flicks from the 1950s as well as Japanese kaiju films of the 1960s. To be honest it wasn't unusual for me to watch the late-night shows either. These movies were a staple of my childhood. But prime viewing for me was during the hours after school, from 3:30pm to 6:00pm, which consisted of a collection of shows on Canadian channels and the American PBS (Public Broadcasting Station). After standard kid fare like *Sesame Street, The New Zoo Revue*, and syndicated shows like *Bewitched, The Munsters* and *Lost in Space*, came the unmistakably eerie, synthesised sounds of Ron Grainer and a different kind of show altogether. At 6:00pm weeknights, on PBS Channel 17, there was *Doctor Who*.

Like so many other American fans, Tom Baker was *my* Doctor. I know now, owing to the detailed research of websites like BroaDWcast.org this is largely because these stories were the first to air in the US, at a regularly scheduled time and in proper order. Airings of *Doctor Who* in North America began a few years prior, with a batch of Pertwee stories, but the unpredictability of their schedule and the very real possibility of being left on a cliffhanger meant the show couldn't really establish an audience. Of course, I didn't know any of this at the time, nor did I know that Philip Hinchcliffe was the man behind the curtain, guiding this era of *Doctor Who*. What I did know is that these episodes were scary. So scary that I wouldn't really watch an episode all the way through until their second (or perhaps third) run on PBS. By this time *Doctor Who* was a PBS staple and the Tom Baker stories aired on a loop. Once WNED NY reached the third airing of the Baker stories, it was no longer necessarily solitary viewing. A consistent schedule and complete stories in order meant there were others watching the same show I was watching, at the same time. I remember a couple of friends at school were also watching *Doctor Who* (albeit boys) and we could talk about the Doctor and his infamous scarf. I wouldn't have called it a cult following then, but it very much was, and we felt special. Just like his companions, we had an exclusive invitation to travel with *Doctor Who*. As PBS channels are publicly funded stations, the viewers spoke with their pledge dollars each year during fundraising drives, and already Americans were saying yes to *Doctor Who.* Hurdles in broadcasting logistics aside, however, *why* were we saying yes? And, specifically, why was *I* saying yes, despite being afraid to watch? Thinking back, what I remember most about *Doctor Who* from childhood is in bits and pieces; flashes of imagery – a monster here, a set piece there, a vague notion of a particular time, place or planet. So, when I sat down to ponder what made this era in *Who* special, I thought I'd better take a look back at a story that would have been airing when I was watching and eventually resulting in me saying "yes".

I nestle into my time machine (a red tartan throw blanket, my living-room sofa and a subscription to Britbox) and set the dial for North America, 1979. The episode is *Terror of the Zygons*, and the opening title sequence makes me feel like a kid again. The TARDIS lands in the Scottish Highlands with the Doctor in a tartan scarf and tam o'shanter. The Brigadier is sporting a kilt, when we meet him, lest we forget where we are. In fact, it almost seems made with the American viewer in mind, every Scottish trope (haggis and bagpipes anyone?) thrown in for good measure. Within the first few minutes of the episode, we know that something is destroying oil rigs in the North Sea and that UNIT has dispatched a call for help to the Doctor. The locals are acting strangely, but nobody (other than the Brigadier) seems terribly concerned about any of it, least of all the Doctor, who thinks being called in to save our ability to further exploit Earth's fossil fuels is a waste of time. Enter the Zygons. They are scary. Even by modern standards the make-up and costume design of the Zygons holds up remarkably well. We can forgive the limitations of the visual effects budget in appreciation for the set design of the Zygon ship and console alone. It all feels organic, and very slimy. Their ominous, hissing voices making them even more menacing, the Zygons are easily one of the more disturbingly impressive television monsters of the time.

The plot seems simple enough: the locals are superstitious, the oil company and military are baffled, but of course it's aliens all along. What I'm most aware of at this point is that there are lots of accents – English accents, Scottish accents,

more English accents. Is that an American accent? Now a different Scottish accent. Wait, maybe that was supposed to be a Canadian accent. Before my ear can even become attuned to the dialects, the action is ramping up. The operator on the rig that was attacked in the opening scenes is still alive, he stumbles out of the sea and collapses. Harry is there. (*Why* is Harry there?) He comes to the man's rescue, but there's another creepy local there too, off in the distance. I know he is a local because of the red bushy beard and kilt. He's carrying a rifle and he shoots the dying man before he can say what attacked the rig. He shoots Harry too, who collapses to the ground. Harry's in sick bay now, not dead, and he'll likely recover. But just when you think he's out of the woods and starting to speak, the nurse (a Zygon in human form) attacks him. Sarah, who has left Harry's side to call the Doctor, is attacked too and there we have our first cliffhanger for this story. Were it really 1979, I'd have to wait until the following day to find out what happens next, but thanks to my time machine, today I can watch all four parts at once. I do.

As I'm watching, I am struck by the pacing; I was expecting it to feel slow, like many older serials seem to upon contemporary viewing. It does not. There's a lot of dialogue, and I'm not sure I'm catching it all, but I'm along for the ride, and thinking, "This is just as I remember it. This is silly and thrilling and brilliant." Over the course of the four episodes, I learn that the Zygons crash landed on Earth over a century ago and have been hiding out under Loch Ness preparing to take over the planet with their cybernetic loch/sea monster.

They can shape-shift into human form, but only if they capture the human first and keep them in some sort of stasis on their ship. They don't like oil rigs and they can kill with just a touch of their moist, tentacle-like hands. No, wait, I don't think they actually do that. Now that I think about it, I'm not sure what their plan for world domination really was, or why it was taking so long. What was with the sea monster and why was it attacking oil rigs? Why were they spying on the townspeople at the inn through a moose head? What did I just watch? Perhaps I need to watch it again. I do.

It's precisely because it was scary that Doctor Who finally got a foothold with American viewers

Tom Baker's Doctor is irreverent and charming. The chemistry between the companions and he is irresistible. It is too bad that this is Harry's last full story. But I find I'm not entirely fond of Sarah Jane in this episode. On the one hand she's not helplessly getting herself caught by aliens, but she just seems dismissive and aloof; character traits I forgive in the Doctor (he's a Time Lord after all) but Sarah, as a human companion, should hold space for our fears and compassion as well as our bravery and sense of adventure. The former two are missing in these episodes. She laughs in all the wrong places.

The Zygons are undoubtedly grotesque, but they are not the super-villains I imagined them to be. They are not supernatural in their strength or

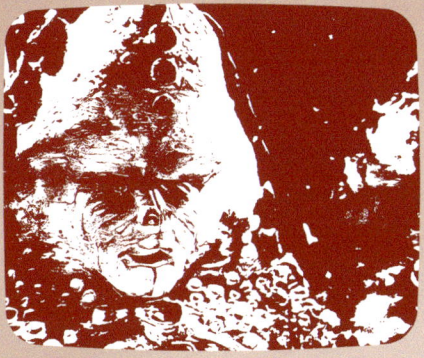

powers. They attack their victims in mostly mundane ways – strangulation, gunshot, bludgeoning (aside from the end of Part Four when they do seem to kill by touch alone.) They aren't particularly bright either. They have a hard time knowing when humans (or Time Lords) are *actually* dead and are surprised when they are not. They behave as if it was completely unpredictable that the entrance to their secret underground spaceship is discovered after leaving Sarah Jane alone exploring the bookshelf where the control to open it is hidden. In the end they are thwarted by the Doctor essentially setting off the ship's fire alarm, prompting them to evacuate the bridge like accountants in a workplace fire-drill. They are conceited and over-confident. What they are good at, however, is exposition. They are only too happy to answer any and all questions about their back story, their capabilities, their plans and their weaknesses. Speaking of plans, they are convoluted, and nonsensical. They are still really unsettling, though and I'm glad this at least holds up on repeat viewing.

The Skarasen (aka the Loch Ness Monster) is less impressive but just as entertaining as any Saturday morning Kaiju. I'm still not sure how it figures into the plot, other than an opportunity to have a couple of big monster moments worthy of a *Godzilla* film. Maybe this isn't the television masterpiece I want to remember it as, but it's still got thrills, chills and exciting cliffhangers. For the little girl in me, it was still scary.

I think, in part, it's precisely because it was scary that *Doctor Who* finally got a foothold with American viewers. These episodes were a particular type of scary that we were ready to embrace; a type of scary that was missing from American television. *Star Trek* showed us an idyllic future where humankind would be united in their exploration of space. Capitalising on the theatrical success of *Star Wars*, 1979 saw the revival of Buck Rogers with the movie *Buck Rogers in the 25th Century* followed by the television series of the same name. But sitting in front of my television set from 1979 to 1981, I decided what to watch by twisting the dial, adjusting the antenna and looking for something that grabbed my attention. These first few seasons of Tom Baker's era grabbed more than just my attention, and looking back now, I think they would have ticked a lot of boxes for the American viewer. They were exciting. They were scary. They were undeniably British. They had a charismatic hero. Moreover, they filled a content gap in American programming that made us want to tune in. *Terror of the Zygons* is an example of how the show could tap into the vein of societal fears and show them through the filter of the monster-of-the-week movie. As the oil crises in the 1970s gave us energy insecurity, we grappled with industry upsetting the natural environment and the change it brought to rural life. A line like "He's been a different man since the oil companies came" foreshadows the Zygons' shape-shifting ability while simultaneously making a commentary on the tension between big industry and small communities. Unlike the real world, however, the evil behind our woes in *Doctor Who* came from another planet. Other science-fiction shows gave us future problems for a future version of humanity to solve. We had plenty of opportunities to look forward to a fantastic

future, but what we didn't have was a way to look at the past and present with that same depth of imagination. *Doctor Who* provided that. Through *Doctor Who*, we could confront monsters, villains, and impossible situations knowing we could prevail – prevail not only in a distant future, but anywhere and anywhen. We could prevail without a battery of weapons, or a fleet of spaceships. On the contrary, we could prevail just by being a little bit brave, a little bit silly, and very clever.

And that hope should help us all sleep a little easier at night.

But while I, and my grade school fan club of four (myself, Todd K., Blonde John, and Little Mike) were trading *Doctor Who* reactions over tray lunches and carton milk in the cafeteria, an entire North American *Doctor Who* movement was underway. In 1980 my world extended to the five or six blocks around my home. Britain was a galaxy away and Los Angeles may as well have been on Mars. But in the December of 1979 on the planet Los Angeles, California, the first North American *Doctor Who* fan convention had already exceeded the expectations of not only the organiser, Lucy Chase Williams, but those of the actors and guests in attendance as well. Pulling in a crowd of over 800 fans, the convention outperformed UK-based fan conventions by half. So many in fact, that autograph sessions with Tom Baker (a last-minute guest owing to the halting of production during a BBC strike) had to extend an additional day and relocated to Venice Beach. These were not the eight- and nine-year-old fans of whom I was a part. These American fans tended to be older even than the fanbase in the UK. They were the adults who opened their wallets and checkbooks to fund *Doctor Who* during PBS pledge drives. They called their local stations to keep the show on the air and pushed for more episodes and in proper airing order. They were anglophiles, and like all the best anglophiles they likely shared an idealised notion of British life and culture; the image of which is reflected in the film, television and music exports that had infiltrated and captivated American audiences for decades. They reflected the demographic of the American PBS viewer at large, who were typically middle class, affluent, and female. That's right, here in America, women made up a comparatively significant proportion of *Doctor Who* fandom. Statistically it makes sense; in the early Seventies PBS had recently made the shift from strictly educational programming (prior to 1970 PBS was NET, National Educational Television) and its viewership included children, academics, and adults interested in learning new things while broadening their cultural horizons. This trend in viewership continued into the following decade.

Women were watching when the show finally found a foothold in North American distribution, so it stands to reason that Tom Baker's youth and charisma played a part in the show's popularity with them. He wasn't particularly handsome, not by Hollywood standards anyway, but he had sex appeal, wit, a posh accent and a devilish smile. I was much too young to care about those things at the time, but I recognise them now, as I suspect many women of *Doctor Who* fandom did then. Perhaps he was the thinking woman's heartthrob.

In addition to Baker's charm, the chemistry between his Doctor and Elisabeth Sladen's Sarah Jane Smith was a winning combination. If the Doctor was a mysterious stranger whom we could fantasise whisking us away on spectacular adventures, Sarah Jane represented the modern woman with girl-next-door charm. More than just a maiden in distress (although she spent plenty of time being just that) she was intelligent and independent, with an adventurous spirit. She was a journalist with a fearless curiosity. The Doctor's companions have always been our human conduit for experiencing the show and Sarah Jane was certainly not the first (or the last) female companion to show these qualities and hold her own alongside a near immortal time-travelling alien, but she was *our* Sarah Jane, the burgeoning feminist career woman. Flawed, though the character was, and perhaps, more of a trope on the page, it was Sladen's portrayal that gave Sarah Jane Smith her spark. Perhaps it was a bit of that spark that Ms Chase Williams channelled when she organised that first North American convention in 1979. Or, perhaps, it was the other way around – maybe the show itself drew in the type of woman that had that same spark to begin with. Was it a show which reflected back to the viewer the qualities they saw in themselves? Did it show us a version of ourselves, whether in the cleverness of the Doctor, or the courage of his companions that we aspired to? I like to think so.

Whatever the catalyst, these years marked the beginning of a tenacious fandom that would continue to grow, weather the lean years, and expand exponentially with the show's revival in 2005. The perfect storm of the right American audience, watching the right cast, telling the right kinds of stories, at just the right time is as much kismet as design. Like a TARDIS, spinning off into the dimensional continuum, landing in just the right point in space and time, *Doctor Who* landed in America. It gave us an invitation:

Would you like to come travelling? It might be a bit scary, but you'll only need to be a little bit brave, a little bit silly, and very clever.

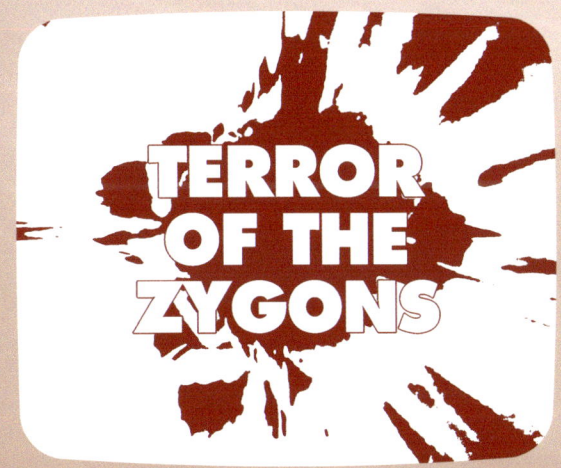

Philip chats about his inspirations

"I have always loved books. When I was young, about ten, I remember looking for something to read on my father's revolving bookcase. There was a French grammar book and I tried to read that and I made progress and discovered I had a gift for languages. There was another book there, *Brave New World*. I remember reading it but not getting the entire gist of it all. There was a phrase in it, something like "she was a pneumatic blonde" and I couldn't work out what this word pneumatic meant. I knew I pumped up my bicycle tyres, so I knew pneumatic in relation to tyres but not what pneumatic meant in this context – in fact there were quite a lot of words in this book that I didn't understand, but it really made an impact on me!

Then I discovered the King Arthur stories, the Roger Lancelyn Green version. That was love at first sight. Eventually I moved onto *Treasure Island, Kidnapped, Coral Island* and comic strips adaptations of *Oliver Twist* and *The Last of the Mohicans*. I also discovered the radio serial *Dick Barton*. Each episode was about fifteen minutes long, went out at seven at night, and he was a special agent, he had a sidekick called Snowy and they were always in a fix or jeopardy. Plus there was dramatic music. I don't remember anything about the actual plots, just that it was exciting and I couldn't wait till the next night to hear what would happen next. It sucked you in, pure adventure, a thriller that gave me a little fix every night. There was *Journey into Space* as well, and I can remember hearing a version of *The War of the Worlds*.

Lots of these became films later on, but I hadn't seen them although Robert Holmes certainly had. *The Hand of Orlac* was something he loved which inspired *The Hand of Fear* but I'd not even heard of it – I'd never even seen *Frankenstein*, or a mummy film.

* * * *

Bob Holmes and I had endless conversations, merging our sources we were bringing to our *Doctor Who* stories. He was film-inspired, I was literary-inspired. Authors like Asimov, Brian Aldiss, Philip K Dick, Frank Herbert, HG Wells and Jules Verne and, of course, right back at the beginning of my journey, Huxley's *Brave New World* – this was the kind of stuff I was familiar with. We never really did that, but I think *Childhood's End* by Arthur C Clarke left a big impression on me, and again from my childhood, John Wyndham's stuff like *The Kraken Wakes* and *The Midwich Cuckoos* – all impacted on my decision-making on *Doctor Who*. Look at *The Seeds of Doom*, that's us doing Wyndham's *Day of the Triffids*. Of course Terry Nation uses a bit of *The Midwich Cuckoos* in *The Android Invasion* – that creepy English village. What I borrowed from *Dune* was the idea of the sandminers (and I wish we could have afforded giant worms) and planetary industrialisation, but the BBC budget meant we could only take these inspirations and then lower everything to a level we could afford to make good *Doctor Who* on. It was helpful to have those big ideas in the background, find a way to somehow bring in these notions and concepts in some way, and accept that once whittled down, you'll end up with one cheap little model shot of a sandminer. The audience had to indulge you a bit and thankfully they did. I'm not taking anything away from, say, Chris Boucher, *The Robots of Death* was absolutely *his* story, but the origins, the basic notion would have been mine, based on these books I had read. Poor Chris, the same is true of *The Face of Evil*. Bob probably knew about big sentient computers from *2001: A Space Odyssey* but there was one very specific element I wanted in there. I don't know where it came from ... I kept coming back to a story where the Doctor has done something and had an effect somewhere and then he goes back there, and he has to deal with it. That story premise was one I kept reaching for in other stories but it never really clicked until *The Face of Evil*. I recalled an image of the faces on a Mount Rushmore and thought what a fantastic moment it would be for the Doctor to come somewhere and to see that he's been deified. So those two elements were what inspired the story from me, but it got married to half an idea, or more, that Chris Boucher had anyway."

PLANET *of* EVIL

BORROWING FROM THE CLASSICS

SIMON GUERRIER

You and I are scientists, Professor. We buy our privilege to
experiment at the cost of total responsibility.

'I remembered as a child seeing [1956 movie] *Forbidden Planet*,' said Philip Hinchcliffe in 2007. He was speaking on *A Darker Side*, a documentary included on the DVD release of *Planet of Evil*. 'I cringe a bit when I look at this [story] because it's a bit too much of a rip-off of that [film].'

Fiddlesticks.

Oh, *Forbidden Planet* is certainly an influence on *Planet of Evil*, at least in the first episode. But Hinchcliffe and his script editor Robert Holmes didn't rip off the film. It wasn't even the starting point of this *Doctor Who* story. Something more complex and interesting was involved in the way they drew from classic science-fiction and a wealth of other sources to create their classic *Doctor Who*. By understanding that process, we can cast light on why, perhaps, *Planet of Evil* doesn't quite work.

The colourful jungle may owe something to the flora and fauna of the alien garden in Forbidden Planet.

Let's start with the similarities between the film and the *Doctor Who* story. Both involve a spacecraft arriving at an alien world to find out what happened to a group of humans with whom contact has been lost. The crew of the spacecraft discover just one survivor of the group and a lot of graves. This sole survivor is oddly reticent about the unusual manner in which his comrades died. The crew are then surprised to find two unexpected people on the planet – a sardonic robot and young woman in the film, a Time Lord and young woman in *Doctor Who*. Crew members are attacked by an invisible creature and initially suspect the robot/Time Lord. Later, the attacker manifests as a glowing red outline of a large, nonhuman creature. The crew use parts of the ship to build a forcefield to hold this creature back, with limited success. Ultimately, the attacks prove to be the result of the survivor's own human frailty. When this issue is resolved, the surviving members of the crew leave in their spaceship.

That's mostly plot. Some of the design of *Planet of Evil* also suggests an influence. As well as the red-outline creature, the spaceship control room in both film and *Doctor Who* story features a mezzanine level, while the crew wear blue-grey uniforms. The colourful jungle in the *Doctor Who* story may owe something to the colourful flora and fauna of the alien garden in *Forbidden Planet*. But the enclosed, claustrophobic dark jungle is in direct contrast to the film's wide-open spaces, where even an underground system of caves is breathtakingly vast and spacious.

Another aspect of the story is the opposite of what happens in the film. In *Forbidden Planet*, survivor Dr Morbius has dabbled with the ancient technology of long-dead alien beings and unleashed a dangerous aspect of his own mind – in effect, he is the creature. The disturbing implication is that inside all of us are such 'monsters of the Id'. By contrast, in *Planet of Evil*, survivor Sorenson's single-mindedness antagonises a living alien entity which enacts revenge, transforming Sorenson into a monster. The monstrousness is imposed on him rather than already there. This element of the television story has nothing to do with *Forbidden Planet* and came from a completely different source: the 1886 gothic novella *Strange Case of Dr Jekyll and Mr Hyde*.

There's a third key source for the television story. In the film, we're invited to guess the shape of the ancient, long-dead creatures from the shapes of the doorways and corridors in the underground complex, and glimpses of the red-outline creatures. But the latter turn out to be conjured from Dr Morbius's dreams – we never actually see the real aliens. In the *Doctor Who* story, the red outlines *are* the alien beings, which emerge from an apparently bottomless, dark hole in the ground. We're told these are beings of antimatter. This idea was apparently the first ingredient of the story devised by writer Louis Marks, based not on some fictional source but on real science. Hinchcliffe said in the DVD documentary that he, Marks and Robert Holmes 'had quite a few lunches' to develop the plot of the story between them. They took this 'scientific' idea about antimatter, grafted on the Victorian horror of *Strange Case of Dr Jekyll and Mr Hyde* but set it all in a far-future inspired by *Forbidden Planet*. The latter wasn't ripped off so much as used to add some colour.

This is simply how science-fiction – and any genre – works. A spaceship-arrives-at-strange-world story is just as much of a generic convention as an *And Then There Were None*-kind of murder mystery. At the start of such a story, we recognise the generic convention from previous examples and so understand the kind of story to follow and the 'rules' by which it ought to abide. The pleasure then comes from some new element to surprise us. In a murder mystery, we're invited to play along and guess the identity of the murderer; in science-fiction the delight is in some sense of wonder – a bold new idea to astonish us. To achieve this, genre is an ongoing conversation that writer/producers and readers/viewers participate in together. *Planet of Evil* draws from *Forbidden Planet* to establish generic credentials – the kind of story it will be – then quickly subverts them.

I think *Forbidden Planet* does this itself with the character Robby the robot. Robby's core programming won't allow him to harm humans. This and Robby's name are surely a reference to the 'three laws of robotics' devised by Isaac Asimov, one of the best-known science-fiction writers. The first such law, that a robot may not injure a human, featured in Asimov's classic 1940 short story *Robbie* – a story that was originally published, against Asimov's will, as *Strange Playfellow*. The direct reference to the first law of robotics, as featured in many other of Asimov's later robot stories, was added to a revision in 1950, which would have been the version most people would have known when *Forbidden Planet* was released. In the film, the robot's name and inability to harm people surely implies – to anyone familiar with the generic conventions – that the plot will follow Asimov's lead in exploring loopholes in logic to explain a robot's strange, sometimes unpleasant, behaviour. We're more likely to suspect Robby of the attacks on the crew if we know the conventions. The twist is that the robot is innocent.

Forbidden Planet was a big success and became a landmark in the genre, as we can see from all the subsequent science-fiction that drew from it. Michael Kmet's 2013 essay *Gene Roddenberry's Cinematic Influences* makes a convincing case for the impact of the film on the look and feel of *The Cage*, the pilot episode of *Star Trek* made in 1965. Roddenberry specifically asked his team to study the film's spaceship interior and speak to those who built it, but – importantly – not simply to copy what they saw. We can see something similar in the look and feel of *Lost in Space* (1965–68), most notably in its friendly but sardonic robot. Robby from *Forbidden Planet* even made guest appearance in two episodes of *Lost in Space* to battle its television counterpart. Robby's boast in *Forbidden Planet* of speaking "187 other languages, dialects and sub-tongues as well as English" is surely an influence on C3P0 being "fluent in over 6 million forms of communication" in *Star Wars*, twenty years later. The ambience of the Death Star in *Star Wars* owes something to the Krell underground complex; in 2012, sound designer Ben Burtt told Geeta Dayal from *Wired* that he was, "in many ways … keying off *Forbidden Planet*".

Forbidden Planet was a big success and became a landmark in the genre

We can see a similar influence of the film in the very earliest days of *Doctor Who*. The interior of the TARDIS was conceived by designer Peter Brachacki as a single room with living quarters, computer banks and equipment arranged around a central table-top of controls with a large, transparent structure in the centre. In the first two serials, there's a single room with rest area, food machine and computer banks all within sight of the central column. The third serial, *Inside the Spaceship*, introduces the idea of separate spaces including bedrooms and a wardrobe. Compare that original, single room to the interior of the C-57D in *Forbidden Planet*, where the central tabletop of controls is mounted with a large, transparent sphere, in which elements move in line with the progress of the spaceship. In fact, such a mechanism is exactly what Brachacki originally had in mind for the TARDIS. Instead of the column rising and falling to indicate flight, "I planned that when the TARDIS was operated the central column would rise and then, when reaching maximum height, would slowly turn around with lights flashing inside," Brachacki told the fanzine *TARDIS* in 1976. "The column was supposed to be a type of 3D navigational instrument. The Doctor could look at it and be able to see exactly where the TARDIS was in time and space." The very first Dalek story also surely owes something to *Forbidden Planet*, with its underground city complex with doors and corridors shaped to match the proportions of the nonhumanoid Daleks, and the eerie, science-fiction atmosphere conveyed through electronic sounds.

Another early *Doctor Who* adventure owes a much greater debt to the film. In the Season Two story *The Rescue*, an older man, Bennett, and young woman, Vicki, are the sole survivors of a group of humans on a planet that was once home to an advanced civilisation. A rescue mission is expected but the TARDIS arrives first, and the Doctor and his friends are then menaced by an apparently native creature who is revealed to be the older man in disguise. In the film, the young woman Altaira is a 'friend' to various animals including a tiger, which one of the crew shoots believing it to be dangerous. In *The Rescue*, the Doctor's companion Barbara shoots a sand beast she thinks is dangerous but is Vicki's pet. At the end of the film, Altaira leaves in the spaceship; Vicki leaves in the TARDIS. *The Rescue* takes the basic outline of *Forbidden Planet*, swaps in the TARDIS for the spaceship and simplifies things for a largely as-live television production made in relatively small studio space. That's not a criticism; it's just a much more straightforward way of doing things. But comparing that approach to *Planet of Evil* shows how differently Hinchcliffe and Holmes used source material.

In fact, *Forbidden Planet* may have been suggested to them by someone else. Holmes's predecessor, Terrance Dicks, worked a reference to *Forbidden Planet* into Tom Baker's first story, *Robot*, which was the last story made before Hinchcliffe took over as producer. In the film, Dr Morbius tells Robby to shoot someone but this causes Robby distress as it conflicts with prior instructions never to harm people; it's a demonstration by Dr Morbius that Robby *can't* kill someone. Something similar happens in *Robot*, though the person who instructs the robot to destroy Sarah Jane Smith isn't sure what the outcome will be. Again, it takes the same premise but then does something different.

Soon after completing *Robot*, Dicks proposed another *Doctor Who* story that would draw more directly from *Forbidden Planet*. The original idea featured a criminal called Morbius – the name surely swiped from the film – and his intelligent robot, whose spaceship crashed on an alien world. With Morbius horribly wounded, the robot scavenged bits of different dead alien creatures

to produce a new, patchwork body. *The Brain of Morbius* was really a science-fiction version of the well-known gothic horror *Frankenstein, or the Modern Prometheus*, but the initial idea drew from *Forbidden Planet* to establish the science-fictional trappings of the story. That's the same strategy as *Planet of Evil* drawing from *Forbidden Planet* to establish the setting of what's really a sci-fi *Strange Case of Dr Jekyll and Mr Hyde*.

This is the recipe for a lot of *Doctor Who* under Hinchcliffe and Holmes. *Terror of the Zygons*, the story broadcast immediately before *Planet of Evil*, is about the legendary Loch Ness Monster, which we discover is an armoured cyborg. *Pyramids of Mars*, the story immediately after *Planet of Evil*, reworks 1959 horror film *The Mummy* and similar Egyptological stories, but reveals that the mummies are robots. The next story, *The Android Invasion*, does a riff on the Cold War fear of enemies within seen in films such as *Invasion of the Body Snatchers*, again with robots. 'Mr Sin' in *The Talons of Weng-Chiang*, Hinchcliffe's final story as producer, is surely drawn from 'Tonga' in the classic Sherlock Holmes novel *The Sign of the Four*, this time revealed to be a machine with the cerebral cortex of a pig. "This vein of fiction we were raiding, in a way, as our source material," said Hinchcliffe on the DVD of *Planet of Evil*, "[largely] emerged in the romantic era." There's certainly an element of 19th century literature in the romantic and gothic tradition – but it's just one of myriad sources.

What's especially striking is that *Planet and Evil* and *The Brain of Morbius* were outlined, written and produced within months of one another. Surely, if Hinchcliffe and Holmes had thought at the time that they were in any way 'ripping off' *Forbidden Planet* in either story, or at least drawing from it extensively, they wouldn't have used it twice in such quick succession. In fact, they used *Forbidden Planet* again a third time some months later. In season fourteen's *The Face of Evil*, just as Dr Morbius's subconscious creates deadly, invisible creatures, something similar happens when the Doctor hooks up his mind to a computer. But that's just one aspect of the story, which also drew from Aldous Huxley's celebrated science-fiction novel *Brave New World* and other material.

Chris Boucher, the writer of *The Face of Evil*, was well versed in science-fiction. His next *Doctor Who* story, *The Robots of Death* – also for Hinchcliffe and Holmes – drew from Agatha Christie's classic murder mystery *And Then There None* but is peppered with references to classic works of science-fiction. The setting, on a giant sandminer, "was a steal from *Dune*," Boucher told the fanzine *In Vision* in 1989. "I did at least have the decency to change it sufficiently so that it was actually mining storms rather than harvesting sand." He also 'borrows' from Clifford D Simak's 1950 short story *Bathe Your Bearings in Blood!* (later republished as *Skirmish*) and the robot stories of Isaac Asimov, while naming characters after science-fiction writers Karel Čapek (who first coined the term 'robot') and Poul Anderson. These were mixed into the murder-mystery plot, and then director Michael E. Briant and designer Kenneth Sharp gave the whole thing a distinctive art deco

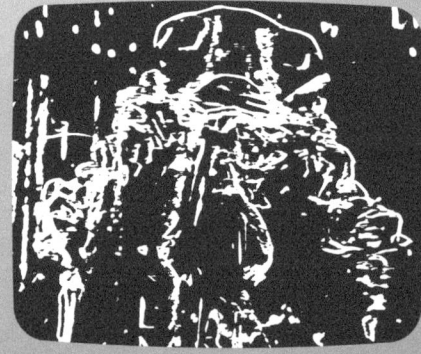

look. The result of drawing together these disparate elements is a richness in both setting and story.

In an interview with Samira Ahmed released by Big Finish in 2023, Hinchcliffe explained how he and Holmes contributed different elements to this mix. Holmes often drew from "old movies … because he was older than me … and had seen [them]. He brought his filmography and I brought my literary, cultural [interest in] the romantic era." That literary interest included science-fiction. As a child he read *Brave New World* and books by HG Wells. But on becoming producer of *Doctor Who*, "I gave myself a crash course in sci-fi I hadn't read. Most of it was basic stuff: Asimov, Brian Aldiss and other people. And I thought 'Wow, this is a really interesting story area'."

Planet of Evil was the direct beneficiary of this: on the DVD, Hinchcliffe says the 'oculoid tracker' – what we'd now recognise as a surveillance drone – was his idea, drawn from one of the science-fiction stories he'd read. There are, for example: automated flying 'eyes' in *This Moment of the Storm* by Roger Zelazny; golden, basketball-like 'copseyes' in *Cloak of Anarchy* by Larry Niven; and 'flying eye' probes in *The Repairman* by Harry Harrison. It's also worth noting that the year in which the story is set, 37,166, recalls the 'galactic era' setting of several of Isaac Asimov's novels, when the "Galactic empire is at its height [and] Earth [is] completely forgotten as [the] origin of humanity.' Between them, Hinchcliffe and Homes were well read in classic literature, acclaimed works of science-fiction and the icons of cinema. All of that fed into their rich, literate *Doctor Who*. The Doctor is likewise richly literate, quoting both *Romeo and Juliet* and *Hamlet* during *Planet of Evil*. His reading, travel and experience make him articulate. And the stories are at their best when the Doctor meets his match in an articulate foe.

That's where I think understanding the way Hinchcliffe and Holmes used the classics of science-fiction (and other sources) shows up why maybe *Planet of Evil* doesn't quite work. The antagonist is an alien creature lacking the articulacy of other villains of this period. It speaks – but not in our hearing. The Doctor confronts it, makes a deal with it and resolves the central problem. But we don't witness the negotiation and we get no direct sense of the threat. It is all reported afterwards by the Doctor. As we've seen, in *Forbidden Planet*, the disturbing idea of a monster inside an otherwise good and civilised person, suggests a monster inside us all. We can see how that idea is used to good effect in *The Face of Evil*.

But *Planet of Evil* just doesn't draw enough from *Forbidden Planet*. This begs the question, would it be a more effective story if it *were* more of a rip-off?

Philip chats about incidental music

"Music was an important ingredient in *Doctor Who*'s success, not just that theme, but the music and atmospherics created for each episode. I think Dudley Simpson was very versatile, and he knew it needed it to be moody, to underscore the atmosphere, to mark the moments of danger and suspense, then the excitement and thicken up the drama and conflict. *Doctor Who* demands a lot from a composer and Dudley could do all that because he loved the show and could respond to the drama and be very precise. He was never trying to do too much with his music, he understood its role in the overall storytelling. He was incredibly professional and knew *Doctor Who* so well. Some directors wanted to put their own stamp on their stories and thought Dudley Simpson wasn't right for them. They wanted to do something different with somebody else. Douglas Camfield persuaded me to have a go with Geoffrey Burgon, who wasn't very well known back then, on *Terror of the Zygons*. He was a very good composer, but I don't think that Geoffrey, week in/week out, could have done the job that Dudley did.

Michael Briant, a bit like Douggie, wanted to try something new too. He'd worked with Carey Blyton before, and Carey was obviously a composer of note, but completely unsuited for *Doctor Who*. What he came up with was just not appropriate enough for the show. These composers came in full of ideas and enthusiasm but hadn't realised how quickly they'd need to work and I believe it showed in their scores, whereas Dudley could work incredibly quickly, because he was used to the weekly production process. These others were struggling to work at the speed that Dudley could work, from seeing the final cut of an episode to getting his music written and then agree with the director where the cues were going to come, what kind of cues they were etc. Then he had to go and record them, put them to the picture and attend the final dub. It all had to happen very fast.

★ ★ ★ ★

Ironically after I left the show and produced a new crime series called *Target*, I thought I'd give Dudley a chance to join me. He was keen to do something else. However, when he put the music on the first episode it was like ... well, *Doctor Who* music. In the end, I wanted a new feel for this gritty cop show but the music was a bit facile and not doing it for me, not matching the content. I took every cue off, every single music cue was gone. I then had to sit poor Dudley down and explain to him it just wasn't working. In the end I think we did the show without any music. Maybe my assumption that *Target* even *needed* music was the wrong one anyway, but it was horses for courses and Dudley's best horse was *Doctor Who*.

People always talk about the fifth Beatle: Pete Best, George Martin, Stu Sutcliffe, whoever. Dudley was kind of the fifth Beatle of the *Doctor Who* success story. It would not have been the show it was without Dudley. He gave *Doctor Who* a particular spin and was a very major part of the show."

PYRAMIDS *of* MARS

POSSESSION AS A RECURRING THEME
HAYDEN GRIBBLE

Deactivating a generator loop without the correct key is like repairing a watch with a hammer and chisel. One false move and you'll never know the time again.

I always like to think that the Doctor is a rock, a certainty in the show. Sure, he may regenerate every few years, but good will always emerge victorious and he is always on the side of the angels, so there's a reliance on him to win the day. For the younger viewers, that faith is total until the cynicism of watching *Doctor Who* creeps in as a teenager and adult. What you need is a central character who is strong, reliable, dependable, much like a father figure.

However, as brilliant as I think the Fourth Doctor (and Tom Baker's performance as the bohemian wanderer) is, he really unnerves me on occasion.

The Doctor at times can act attached, aloof, flippant and almost as though his mind is off in another galaxy entirely. Remember how odd he is in *Robot*? The great Terrance Dicks only wrote him like that so that the writers who followed after him would calm him down but they never did. He's so odd and yet likeable in that first season and by Season Thirteen, his true alien qualities are really explicit in *Terror of the Zygons*. That million light year stare he burrows out across the cosmos in the first part made me wonder on first viewing if he was indeed possessed himself!

I always found it scary when people I looked up to as a child would act out of character. As a nipper, there is nothing more terrifying than a grown-up shouting when normally they wouldn't, or acting in a way in which you are unfamiliar for them to behave. So, for the Doctor, his otherworldliness could at times cause me to not fully trust him. I know all would be safe and well in the end, but anything could happen when the Fourth Doctor was in town. I once saw an interview with the aforementioned Terrance in which he remarked that he always thought that the Fourth Doctor was the incarnation who would more likely be seduced by evil and he's bang on the money. Baker's otherworldliness, whilst in the main being a fun and trustworthy person, does give his Doctor a rather sinister edge.

Therefore when he is possessed by Sutekh the Destroyer in my all-time favourite story, *Pyramids of Mars*, you can bet that little Hayden was dropping his baked beans and chips in his lap and leaping behind the nearest thing to hide behind. A companion being consumed by evil (as poor Melanie Bush was, when Sutekh made his unexpected return to the series in 2024's *Empire of Death*) seems mild in comparison to the Doctor himself becoming Sutekh's plaything! I can't describe how much I was unnerved the moment he crosses his arms in the murky – yet sometimes very green – cell. It was the moment that the Doctor was

gone. His strange unblinking eyes staring upwards in complete surrender.

Submission of free will is something that had been explored before in *Doctor Who* many times before. Characters had been hypnotised, threatened and copied the name of evil but I think the true horror in *Pyramids of Mars* is possession of those we come to love and trust in the form of the main man himself.

As I watched him transported slowly through that groovy disco time tunnel that took him back to the ominous Victorian mansion, I thought instantly how terrible this was about to get for his travelling companion, Sarah Jane Smith. She's all on her own in this nightmare. The second she sees her best friend and, let's face it, protector, return from Sutekh's prison, her face falls into one of deep despair because she knows that the game is up. All hope is extinguished. We might as well pack up shop and leave at this point as it's about to get particularly nasty. To be honest, it all looked so bleak for little Hayden watching this I was surprised at the sheer nerve the programme makers had in taking the narrative down this dark, scary tunnel. Indeed, why continue the show if the Doctor is gone? It's so rare in the show's history up to this point to see him totally consumed. We're not talking a little bit of crude hypnotism that has floored our hero. He's been possessed by a god!

And what made it worse when the Doctor lost control is that he *is* the show. It's fine for his friends to need rescuing because he's always the gallant hero of the piece, ready to step in and do just that but who can really save the Doctor in this instance? When the Doctor is taken over, the proverbial fan falls over it gets hit so hard! If he's not around the save the day, all bets are off. Earlier in the story the Doctor has already shown us what would happen to Earth if Sutekh wins. It'd be a barren nothingness, a desolate fallen world, among millions around the cosmos who would befall similar fates. Now that's the fate of the universe. All hope is lost. This is why the Doctor's possession is so terrifying.

Incredibly, the Doctor's possession is short-lived and he finds a way to trap Sutekh for all eternity. I breathed a sigh of relief of such velocity I nearly blew the telly into next door's kitchen at the end of my first white-knuckle viewing of this classic.

For all the evil that had overpowered him, the Doctor seemed to be back to cuddly mad old Uncle Tom Baker again at the end. I could trust him again, implicitly. And yet, why was that? I'm pretty certain I was very untrusting of Harry after that Zygon imposter had taken his form and tried to spear Sarah with a rusty pitchfork. It's why I could never really look at Turlough after *Enlightenment* without thinking, "any moment now, he's going to wrench one of the roundels off the TARDIS wall and Frisbee it at the Doctor's neck". Once a companion, or Doctor for that matter, has tried to harm anybody in the TARDIS team, I can't look at them on-screen without glaring at them with an element of distrust but with the Fourth Doctor this seemed okay in my book… It was because the Doctor had taken on a god and won. I knew he could deal with anything after this.

Whatever story I watched after this, nothing would ever amount to him coming so close to a final end again. It restored my temporary wavering faith immediately. He'd chased away the poison in his mind and what's more it hadn't affected him in the aftermath one iota. And all it took was a quick throttle from a Mummy …

The Doctor got off lightly when you look back it. What about poor Marcus Scarman? How horrifying was his total and absolute submission to the evil machinations of Sutekh? There's something more sinister to his part in the story than his master he is serving. Not only do you see him smoke the shoulders of the mysterious Egyptian Namin but he brutally murders his old friend Dr Warlock, whom he doesn't even seem to recognise, he's that far gone! No memories of playing as chums at school can snap him out of this all-consuming trance and Warlock soon pays the price for appealing to Marcus's humanity, which seems to be dead in the water. Despite the Doctor being as firm as he can to reiterate to Scarman's younger brother, Lawrence, that there is nothing left of his sibling, it doesn't stop him from giving it a go in that chilling scene in the lodge. What else would he do? It'd only be natural to think he's the only one who can deliver Marcus from evil. For a moment or two it looks like Lawrence may have managed to find that shred of the real Marcus Scarman that lies somewhere within the pale-faced demon that the latter has become, but soon that hope is extinguished in a really disturbing way. Although the murder of Lawrence takes places off screen, his final plea of, "Marcus …please …" is so childlike, it's almost like the older brother is bullying him remorselessly and they are both the little boys again.

But the terror in his tones echoes on in the episode as the full horror of it dawns on Sarah when she and the Doctor discover Lawrence's lifeless body later on. Marcus Scarman is so far gone, so totally subsumed by the will of Sutekh that he would commit the gruesome murders of his own brother and a childhood friend? He actually gets his hands dirtier than Sutekh himself. The

possessed seemed worse, to me, than the possessor because Scarman was supposed to be human and it was worse to see a man commit such terrible crimes, worse ones than those of a baddie I couldn't identify, making Marcus Scarman's possession equally as scary as the Doctor's. The body count is all on him, and yes I know he's being controlled, but as a little boy watching this on VHS for the first time on a dark December evening, it was Scarman whose red, possessed eyes bore into my nightmares that night, not the green ones of Sutekh the Destroyer.

Ah yes, it's time for my confession. You see, I didn't grow up in the Seventies. I didn't even make my grand appearance until the final six month of the Eighties; to me the Seventies was a far and distant country. The only memories of that decade I have, barring *Doctor Who*, is of annoying compilation shows on BBC2 in the early Noughties and movies that had stood the test of time, such as *Star Wars* and *Jaws*, alongside films like *Carry On Girls*, which hadn't. So you'll forgive me, whilst I bask in my relative youth, if I didn't catch the glorious Hinchcliffe era on its original run, but you'll have to blame my parents. And whilst I can assure you that the grey hairs are well and truly bedding in, I was deprived of that sweet sensation of watching early Tom Baker stories as they were originally broadcast. To make matters worse, it took years to catch up. Decades even! Now who's laughing? But I gained an appreciation for the story telling, the entertainment and of course, the ability to scare – plus the recurring theme of possession in this era of *Doctor Who* – and that is what has endeared it to me.

The concept of an entity taking over an individual was one that wasn't just spared for one companion in this time. Let's not forget that Sarah herself succumbed to alien occupancy too. In her final story, *The Hand of Fear*, we bear witness to the Doctor's best friend becoming consumed by the essence of Eldrad. She even shoots a guard or two with blue energy from her hand, like Emperor Palpatine in *Return of the Jedi*. On top of that there's the influence a moment like that has on the viewer. Whilst it may seem fun when your sister runs around the garden with a sandwich box pretending she's wearing an Andy Pandy costume chanting, "Eldrad *MUST* live" at you, it does rather change your opinion on whether there is anyone who can be trusted not to fall to the alien powers of the big baddies in stories. In the real world even family members could, potentially, not be all that you thought they were! My sister's acting must have been convincing!

Possession does seem to be a running theme throughout the Hinchcliffe years, almost as synonymous as the gothic horror tag the era is given by so many. Yet, I tend to think that the two themes go hand-in-hand. After all, the true horror in this concept is the loss of self and the era is littered with reference to this in multiple stories. Indeed, in only the second adventure of his fourth incarnation, *The Ark in Space,* the Doctor runs into a colony of humans who are threatened during hibernation by alien larvae that has infiltrated their space ark.

Sure, the scene with the infected Noah and his green bubble-wrapped hand may seem laughable to audiences nowadays but the fundamental image of a man losing control and becoming taken over by an alien infiltrator is really chilling. Isn't that also what makes *Doctor Who* so brilliant and enduring? It isn't the sometimes unspecial effects that come to mind with us fans; we can forgive little things like that. It's the ideas that stick and indeed the imagery, which in Noah's case is as he transforms into a Wirrn, that become ingrained deep into our memories and nightmares. His body is corrupted and yet his mind is still in there somewhere – enough in fact to lead the swarm into the transport ship, which leaves the Doctor to surmise that it could have been Noah's plan all along: leading the Wirrn off the Ark and saving his friends. A selfless act and a horrifying note lingered in my mind watching *The Ark in Space* that Noah, no matter how much his body had been taken over, was still in there somewhere, a shard of humanity was clinging on for dear life. Isn't that a rarity in *Doctor Who*? To see victory over the possessor by the possessee. Doesn't that give hope that whatever might be poisoning a person's mind, it can be overcome? If an intruder is living in your mind, you too can kick it out ultimately, or briefly, for the greater good of others. There's a tinge of melancholy when I realised that incredible power of will that Noah has in this moment still isn't enough to save himself. True it's because he explodes into a million pieces along with his fellow Wirrn brethren, but that's by-the-by. He's still in there, but there isn't enough to overcome the infection that has spread across his body. Physically, he's more insect than man but that tiny spark of humanity bought him enough time to make a noble self-sacrifice and see to it that the Doctor and his friends lived to see another day. Sometimes I wish the show would remember such moments or heroism more often. Good old Noah. He dies a hero.

The same cannot be said, however, for Arnold Keeler in *The Seeds of Doom*. Blimey, that's a chilling fate! The poor botanist is the epitome of a character being in the wrong place at the wrong time. Surrounded by madness and thuggery, the moment he accidentally comes into contact with the Krynoid you just know he's brown bread. I remember a queasy feeling in my stomach when I watched it for the first time. No matter how much he pleads with Harrison Chase, he won't get any help as he begins to mutate. It's harrowing to watch him begging for help from his sick bed as the Krynoid is eating away at his individuality while Chase's sick experiment continues. Chase wants Keeler to be absorbed. He's even ordered his butler to feed him plant food! How horrific is that? No help, no sympathy, no hope.

In the Hinchcliffe stories that deal with possession I feel unease with regard to this loss of control and awareness of it happening, just like Keeler. I can imagine this might be how it would feel to develop Alzheimer's. Sure, there are fleeting moments where the old persona comes back to the fore but the rest of the time it remains trapped in a brain which is no longer functioning correctly. That to me terrifies me more than other life changing diseases. Who would I be if I wasn't me?

  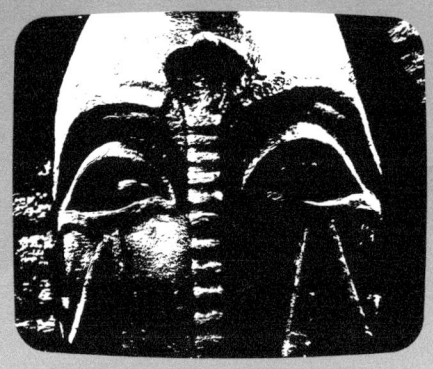

It's a similar situation that befalls another guest character, in the form of Professor Sorenson in *Planet of Evil* – only just for once, like the Doctor's friends, the possession doesn't result in death. Instead, the anti-matter creature that inhibits the scientist only takes over his form temporarily, unlike the split personality character of Dr Jekyll and Mr Hyde, whose story appears to have been the inspiration for the character. It was Phillip Hinchcliffe himself who intervened and suggested that Sorenson survive, a plot point that feels truly unique in the theme of possession during his tenure. It gives hope to viewers that with the Doctor's help, whatever evil encapsulates the poor unsuspecting victims can be drawn out one way or another.

On the flip side of the coin, what if an enemy actually welcomes possession? In *The Masque of Mandragora*, the apothecary, Hieronymous, and his worshippers of the Cult of Demnos welcome the Mandragora Helix with open arms. The members of the cult are all too happy to give their souls up to an unimaginable power. To me, if you are open to cultism, then you most likely won't put up a fight in the face of possession because, much like Hieronymous and his followers, you believe in a greater good that's dangerous and all-consuming. They believe in a higher power, and they will give all that is left of them to see it victorious. That's where a different kind of terror lurks in Mandragora – the horror that some people will believe anything.

Philip Hinchcliffe and Robert Holmes had all the tools at their disposal to make possession one of the cornerstones themes of their era. They had the actors, the inspiration from stories across many forms of media and the knack to make it a constant that is always lurking there, behind the gothic horror trope, in the darkness waiting to show itself when called upon. Whether it be friend or foe, it's always an effective and powerful subject matter that as I get older makes me feel less and less at ease in the real world. I mean, when I reply to a tweet, maybe it is a Zygon after all, pretending to be a follower or when I make plans over WhatsApp, a Krynoid could be posing as a friend and threatening to corrupt me!

In the end, although possession was explored as a theme in other eras of *Doctor Who*, never had it been more prevalent, more unnerving and inventively explored than during the Phillip Hinchcliffe era. Whether it was loss of mind, body or even soul, there was nothing to stop anyone – not even the Doctor – from occasionally not feeling like themselves during this run and for that I thank those storytellers, in an odd way, for scaring the bejesus out of me!

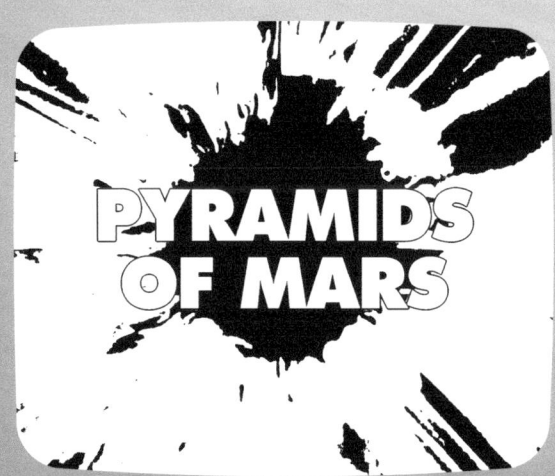

Philip chats about creatives

"I always considered directors to be the most vital part of the *Doctor Who* production process and I had some good ones. There were BBC directors – which means they were on the staff and allocated to you, rather than you hiring them as freelancers. That was Paddy Russell and Chris Barry and Michael Briant (Michael was a whizz with CSO and anything technical and complicated – he could shoot a wristwatch and put somebody's face in it and make it look magnificent all in the studio). Then from outside the BBC I hired people like Douglas Camfield and David Maloney. I think Barry Letts had used all of these directors at least once when he'd been producer, but to me they were just people whose work I had seen on various television dramas and thought were really good. Some of them had also worked on the show much earlier in their careers as production assistants, so they weren't untried, they knew the show and its unique pitfalls. Which was lucky, as something in me started to ring big alarm bells as I quickly discovered this was a very special, esoteric, and difficult show to direct, let alone produce. I was an untried producer so I opted for the safety of people who knew the show; apart from Rodney Bennett who was the suggestion of Robert Holmes, funnily enough. I think he directed a *Dead of Night* episode of Bob's and as always I was able to rely upon Bob's wiser, more experienced recommendations.

The staff directors were assigned to us even before the scripts were probably written, and the outsiders I could assign myself to specific stories. I approached them at the right time, and I was lucky enough that they were free and prepared to join us. Perhaps my ideas made them think *Doctor Who* might be worth doing again. We all forged a very good working relationship and created excitement about the show. They could all handle the animal that was *Doctor Who*.

There was a staff director who had done some very good work at ATV when I was working there. He was quite a modest guy in a way, but he was one of those very technically talented guys. I knew he'd be able to handle *Doctor Who* so I tried to persuade him to come to the BBC. To leave ATV, go freelance, come do a *Doctor Who*. But he said no, because being a staff director at an ITV company, he was financially made for life. These directors were getting paid oodles of money and all had brand new BMWs in the car park. There was this huge divide in pay between ITV and the BBC, which meant people just couldn't afford to go away from that just to do a four-part *Doctor Who* for me.

* * * *

It was especially important to have good directors at the start, as I was developing my approach to the show, making it slightly older, darker, giving it a bit more of a 'mysterioso' atmosphere. Both David and Douggie especially responded to that – and they were very good location film directors – and they spread that understanding of my needs and ideas into their designers and cameramen and so on. Which was great for people like Roger Murray-Leach who designed so much of that first season's stories. I never had enough time at the start to get to know everyone as much as I'd've liked, but I could see on screen that Roger bought into my vision and also brought his own, adding enormously to the finished shows. I think that he was fed up with doing Light Entertainment shows so this was an opportunity I'm not sure he'd had before to show everyone what he could do. He was the type of designer who relished *Doctor Who*'s challenges. As a designer, he thought like a film director and so made a big impact.

Sometimes, of course we had failures, noble failures perhaps because of the good intentions behind them, but failures all the same. The Skarasen, for example, was my inexperience showing. I hadn't ever had anything to do with stop-motion animation at all – I knew literally nothing about it other than what I'd seen in Ray Harryhausen films but knew it could be very effective. What I hadn't realised was how long and how complicated the process is, and to get enough coverage, you need to spend a lot of time doing it. Therefore it was my inexperience which led me to believe the special effects guys could do this – of course they could have, *if* they'd had five times the time, the budget and the facilities to match our collective imaginations. I know they would have been able to construct a film sequence that would have been believable – but we didn't have enough time or money. Therefore we had this stop-motion monster crossing the moors very unconvincingly and then, worse still because it was using a monster shot on film against video in the studio, we stupidly put the Skarasen coming up out of the Thames. It wasn't exactly a success."

the ANDROID INVASION

THE NON-TELEVISION STORIES OF PHILIP HINCHCLIFFE

KENNY SMITH

This isn't Earth. This isn't real wood. It's some kind of artificial material like plastic. These are not real trees. And you're not the real Sarah.

THE *Android Invasion* is arguably the least Philip Hinchcliffe-like story of the entire period during which he was producer.

Thematically, it shares much of its DNA with the years that former-producer Barry Letts was in charge of *Doctor Who*, and whilst has a fair bit in common with the Season Thirteen opener *Terror of the Zygons* (a remote village, UNIT, locals acting strangely and the Doctor and Sarah in a pub), it definitely feels more like a story of the previous producer's era in terms of its pacing and visuals. The presence of a certain Mr Letts as its director probably has a particular significance in this being the case.

The story would quite possibly have surprised many at the time, given that Terry Nation's name was attached to the script. Since 1973, he had been writing one Dalek story per year, so there would no doubt have been a reasonable expectation that this story would feature the most famous of his creations. But no. Instead, Nation crafted a story with a contemporary setting, with strange goings on in an English village, more akin to his work on *The Avengers* or *The Champions*.

So, if we accept that this story was transmitted at pretty much the halfway point of his entire stewardship of *Doctor Who*, we find ourselves asking what was Philip Hinchcliffe's view of *Doctor Who* as it should be? What can we see of it in its purest form, without the influences of writers, directors and actors? Perhaps most importantly, without his friend and script editor, Robert Holmes? When asked what the tone of the Hinchcliffe era on television was, many fans would suggest something akin to Hammer and other classic horror films of the 1950s and 1960s, with doses of science-fiction literature, as well as nods to Victorian Gothic texts.

Since 2009, *Doctor Who* audio producers Big Finish have been releasing *The Lost Stories*, adaptations of scripts and storylines originally planned for television, but never made. It was during the discussions for *Foe from the Future*, the Robert Banks Stewart script originally planned for the conclusion of Season Fourteen but ultimately replaced by *The Talons of Weng-Chiang*, that producer David Richardson received a telephone call.

Philip had been talking with Banks Stewart when the adaptation of *Foe from the Future* came up in conversation. Philip then remembered his outline for *The Valley of Death*, a story which he had proposed to his successor Graham Williams. He offered Big Finish his original pitch from 1978, which ran to around two-and-a-half pages. The document contained details regarding the story's premise and background, although not so much on what would happen on an episode-by-episode, scene-by-scene basis. Big Finish readily accepted it.

What was apparent from this plot is that it had very clear literary influences, with the jungle setting evoking the adventurous spirit of H. Rider Haggard, or even Arthur Conan Doyle's *The Lost World*, by taking a British explorer and pitting them against the unknown. *The Valley of Death* featured a character called Godrin as the main enemy, a short, yellow-skinned Luron, whose people captured their own sun for use as a power source, then discovered its radiation had corrupted their minds.

Whilst the original outline came from Hinchcliffe, the resultant 21st-century version came from experienced Big Finish writer Jonathan Morris. In the finished script, the narrative skipped forward two years in the middle of the story, moving from the then-contemporaneous 1977, to 1979, which

allowed Morris to write the first two episodes in the more serious style of the Hinchcliffe era, before lightening the tone to suit the Williams period in 1979. The script was developed with little direct input from Philip Hinchcliffe, so it's not a pure distillation of the original writer's vision. This was to change in subsequent productions.

It was during the recording of the third season of *Fourth Doctor Adventures* in 2012 that the idea for what was to become *Philip Hinchcliffe Presents* was born. Philip had come along to the Audio Sorcery studios in Tunbridge Wells, to listen to his old friends Tom Baker and Louise Jameson recording their latest run of adventures. When he spoke with David Richardson and executive producer Nicholas Briggs, Philip pitched the idea of doing a set of stories of the kind he would have hoped to have done, *had* he stayed on to produce the

series for longer. It was an instant yes from Big Finish.

Philip told issue 67 of Big Finish's *Vortex* magazine, in September 2014, "I got a sense of Big Finish and what they did from *The Valley of Death*, and when talking to David Richardson, got discussing other stories. I think he was hoping I had a big treasure box full of unmade story ideas that hadn't seen the light of day, but sadly, that wasn't the case.

"Instead, I thought about what myself and Bob Holmes would have done if we'd done a fourth series together. I think [Bob and I] talked about it for maybe a week, before I realised I wasn't going to be there to produce it, as I would be moving on. There were possibilities and trends about where the show could have gone, and I told David there were a few things I'd had in mind.

"I went away and had a think, and although there were no stories written down, I put myself back into the frame of mind, as best I could, that I would have been in back then and what we would have done with that fourth series.

"What I have done, to some extent, is replicate the sort of stories that we *would* have done. They wouldn't really have appeared in the fourth season, as in some ways they are perhaps too similar to the stories we had done before, but after forty years, I thought it would be nice for the fans to have stories that feel like Hinchcliffe/Holmes adventures."

To bring the stories to life, Philip was this time paired with Marc Platt, who had television experience of *Doctor Who* via *Ghost Light* during the Seventh Doctor's era, as well as numerous original novels and audios. Philip provided storylines, as well as a substantial amount of character details, tone and plotting. Marc would expand these details, adding subsidiary characters of his own. These ideas were then returned to Philip, and discussions would ensue to bring the scripts to a form which the former producer wanted.

The initial result was a box set containing two stories, *The Ghosts of Gralstead* and *The Devil's Armada*, both starring Tom Baker and Louise Jameson.

The Ghosts of Gralstead saw the Doctor and Leela return to Victorian London, in the year 1860, thirty years earlier than the period which Hinchcliffe and Holmes had previously touched upon with *The Talons of Weng-Chiang* and presented here with the addition of an *Elephant Man*-like tone. Rather than the fun and joy of watching a music hall show, the Doctor and Leela visited a freakshow, where they witnessed a man cure a child's crushed hand. The story also featured bodysnatchers, and later, the resurrected corpses of the dead.

The feel of the story was pure Hinchcliffe/Holmes – it captured that darker tone prevalent throughout Season Fourteen but pushed it even further into territory that might have given Mary Whitehouse and her associates at the National Viewers and Listeners' Association coronary arrests if it had aired on television. Freakshows were a staple of Victorian life, featuring people with genetic abnormalities and disabilities, and brought together for the purpose of entertaining the masses – all part of the dark underbelly of life to which whimsical variety television shows like *The Good Old Days* could never have alluded.

There was also a trip to very unfamiliar territory for *Doctor Who* when the Doctor and friends travelled to Africa. This involved meeting some local people, one of whom, Abasi, was an exiled prince, whose father was murdered by the bloodthirsty Obingo, to become leader of the Wengalu Tribe. Visualising this on a 1970s television budget would have been especially hard to do, but it pushed the series in a different way, with a H. Rider Haggard atmosphere. How the depiction of race would have been done in 1970s British television also raises a few questions.

One other character of note is Mordrega, originally conceived by Hinchcliffe as being male, but Platt suggested a change of gender, to differentiate her from Magnus Greel. Stories in the Hinchcliffe era rarely tended to feature strong female characters, aside from Sarah Jane Smith and Leela, so having a female villain was a huge break from the television tradition – and it worked all the better for that.

The Ghosts of Gralstead was released along with *The Devil's Armada*, another story set in the past – something of huge appeal to Hinchcliffe, who had encountered resistance from his script editor when trying to do so on television.

The Devil's Armada took the TARDIS to the 16th century, where Catholic priests were hunted, so-called witches were drowned, and something was lurking in the shadows. Straight away, it's clear to see that this may have been problematic had it been shown on television, given the sensitivities around the IRA (Irish Republican Army) at the time. This was probably because the story was partly inspired by events earlier in Hinchcliffe's career, when he was a budding writer and story editor working at ITV. He had been interested in the Jesuit Mission in Elizabethan England and set out to create an adventure story in that period for children, but ultimately, it was never produced due to the Troubles and the religious context of the story.

As the Seventies continued, there was no resolution to the conflict, so it's unlikely the BBC would have wanted *Doctor Who* to look at the issue of faith in this context.

The story featured a threat of impending danger and espionage, and unlike contemporary spy stories which tended to be set during the Cold War and, invariably, Russia or China, this kept things closer to home by having spies from Spain.

The Devil's Armada is another story which would no doubt have had Mary Whitehouse on the telephone to the BBC straight away, given that the adventure featured the Doctor being tortured, and later had a noose placed around his neck, an idea which evokes the controversial drowning of the Doctor in *The Deadly Assassin.* There's also the devil-like figure who proclaimed themself to be Satan (although the Doctor recognised the horned species as a Vituperon) as well as diabolical imps. However, quite how a sea battle in the English Channel would have been realised is one which could have gone either way – with model work like the Eternals' vessels in *Enlightenment*, it could quite possibly have been pulled off, but with obvious cuts from filmed model shots to studio recordings on video. Again, it was a natural extension of what was seen on television at the time, taking familiar elements from broadcast episodes and pushing them into new territory. It tapped into familiar British folklore (with the aforementioned elements of witches, imps and the devil) for a satisfying conclusion to this set.

If these first two adventures tapped into the popular pseudo-historical formula that was so beloved in *Doctor Who*, for the third release, *The Genesis Chamber*, Philip turned back to his childhood reading for his starting point.

Hinchcliffe created a seven-page outline with his basic ideas for the story, including the themes, location, groups of characters and their backgrounds. In his notes for Marc, Philip noted: "Babies are manufactured artificially according to eugenic principles and to their required function and station in society." *The Genesis Chamber* is very much in the mould of Aldous Huxley's *Brave New World*, where people were created as genetically modified in the titular device, but here, there's a little of Shakespeare's *Romeo and Juliet* thrown in too, with a romance between two people who should never have met.

On first listen, the tone of the adventure feels akin to *The Face of Evil*, with human colonists on an alien world and, after clashes amongst themselves, a breakaway group leaving the safety of an enclosed city to go live in the wilds. However, things begin to get complicated due to the indigenous population of the planet too, whose very existence is unknown to any of the human colonists.

There are elements of class at play too, with Hinchcliffe having suggested the colonists of Newjing City were modelled on Chinese society. The lowly proletariat was governed by an elite group of privileged princelings, forever tussling for power, whilst the *Romeo and Juliet* element gave rise to a mafia threat and powerful families, with a touch of *I, Claudius* too. The creation of a realistic society to which the listener could relate gives this story some depth, perhaps in a way that some *Doctor Who* stories on television didn't, when it came to creating cultures on other worlds. Also raised is the issue of refugees, given that the planet already had a populace before humanity arrived, looking for their new home.

There's also the all-controlling computer system, Inscape, upon which the citizens became dangerously reliant, drawing parallels with our own 21st century reliance on the internet for everything from shopping to music to the actual company of others. The idea of using the Genesis Chamber to create an army of soldiers is a constant worry – especially in an age where scientific advances in cloning and genetic manipulation are regularly reported in the news today. If broadcast in the 1970s, this would have been perceived as being ahead of its time, but these days feels especially relevant.

It's hard not to picture the city as being BBC studio sets, as it's the first of these stories that one can most easily imagine being produced. The exterior jungle settings would most likely have been realised in studio, no doubt with a little exterior filming for inserts. The atmosphere is tense and claustrophobic at times, especially in the colonists's city, and this is very much one that could have worked well on screen.

If *The Genesis Chamber* is the story most akin to a television story of the releases so far, then the fourth adventure, *The Helm of Awe*, was the most different.

It brought the Doctor and Leela to a remote Scottish island in 1977, on the trail of an ancient stolen artefact invested with mysterious powers, which had been brought to this bleak location. Here, the travellers encountered Vikings at the real-life Norse fire festival of Up Helly Aa! In this instance, Marc Platt was presented with the idea of a story set in the Shetland Islands, linked to Up Helly Aa!, and the Shetland Bus, a secret World War II operation that ran weapons and refugees across the North Sea to and from Norway. He also added aliens into the mix as well. This story feels different from the others, perhaps due to featuring

Leela in a contemporary setting, something which only happened once on television, albeit not during Hinchcliffe's time on the show.

It's hard to imagine this as a broadcast story, particularly as the Doctor and Leela come under attack at different times from a U-Boat, a horde of Vikings, plus the alien Barbezzan (a being akin to a jellyfish) – on top of which, the story ends with a volcanic eruption, all of which might have stretched a BBC budget beyond what was achievable.

The Scottish island-setting offers comparisons with 1973 British horror film *The Wicker Man*, especially given there's a celebration of an ancient burning ritual. However, imagining all the required effects, studio sets and location work on a 1970s *Doctor Who* budget isn't something that's easily done, and whilst tapping into Norse mythology felt faithful to Hinchcliffe's era, this is definitely the most unusual of the releases.

The final release was *The God of Phantoms*, and in many ways was a greatest hits package of the whole Hinchcliffe era, both on television and audio. It featured several familiar elements – a colony world where a once advanced society has fallen into a more primitive state, whilst an old foe of the Doctor returns from the shadows having been contained within a mountain. In this case, the enemy is someone the Doctor has previously defeated off-screen.

The setting felt more filmic, as the society on this world, Cresta Serene, appeared more like colonial America, rather than a primitive English village, evoking *The Last of the Mohicans*, *The Crucible* and *The Revenant* rather than something akin to *Terror of the Zygons* or *The Android Invasion*. *The God of Phantoms* showed the settlers resorting to mining for their existence, reverting to a primitive way of living as the energies needed for technology runs out. There was a feeling of tiredness and world-weariness which permeated the story, with people exhausted mentally and physically by the dry heat. Interestingly, there's an inversion of the standard six-part formula for a television story, as here, it begins at a slower pace then really picks up from the third part, rather than a traditional high-energy beginning before slowing down and resuming speed for a dramatic conclusion when the villain of the piece is revealed. *The God of Phantoms* has an atypical story element with the Time Lord involvement (Leela meets one of the Doctor's people, an emissary who gives her hints as to what is happening), bearing in mind Hinchcliffe and Holmes's reluctance to use the Doctor's heritage as part of the ongoing series on television, bar *The Deadly Assassin*.

Something to note in all five of these stories is the lack of an obvious 'monster of the week', akin to the Zygons, Krynoids or Kraals, or even a returning creature from the past. As with the majority of Hinchcliffe's stories on television, the biggest monsters of all are the people – antagonists such as Hieronymous, Solon, Harrison Chase and Magnus Greel were far more scary than the aliens. In the case of *The God of Phantoms*, the would-be deity Flindor fills that part, and has a booming, theatrical feel, constantly stating "I, Flindor ..." – giving them an ego, presence and sense of self-importance.

Philip Hinchcliffe Presents is five stories, comprising twenty-six episodes, the equivalent of a full series of *Doctor Who* on television at the time he was in charge. Each story basically feels true to the period, whilst pushing the envelope slightly further than would have been likely back then. You can feel the hand of Hinchcliffe throughout, as the range very much accomplishes precisely what it set out to do.

Philip chats about writing *Doctor Who*

"I think the strength of *Doctor Who* is that it doesn't have a formula in the way it's made. Sometimes you have a story with loads of film location work. Other stories are shot solely in the video studio at TV Centre. Others are a healthy mix of film on location or at Ealing and then the VT stuff. But that always raised the question of how exactly do you tell an adventure story in a small television studio? Well, I had the good fortune to have a script editor and writer who understood this – it was Bob Holmes's natural bent because he came from that era of television drama when it was all in four walls with hardly any location work. *Doctor Who* writers had to be able to construct stories that worked *despite* those restrictions. You create a contained world, ideally, and you set up the tensions and the conflicts and you play it out with a limited number of characters. Bob Holmes was the master of that. Writers like Bob Baker and Dave Martin and Terry Nation preferred really to write for film, and they were always excellent writers – I did other series with them later which Bob Holmes might not have been able to do in the same way they did. A sort of energetic bravura. But you couldn't often do that in *Doctor Who*. So the classic formula for us was the closed world; thus you needed writers who could create suspense, development and enough characterisation within those constraints. Which led to stories that were entirely studio-based, be it Ealing or TV Centre, such as *Planet of Evil*, *The Brain of Morbius* and *The Ark in Space*. What doesn't work is if you try to make stories out of just running around corridors or through woods being chased by a silly monster, which means that the story just dissipates any build-up of suspense. We always did our best to hold stuff back and to have enough elements other than just a monster, and that's what I liked about the stories we did.

* * * *

Occasionally a script would come in from a really brilliant writer who knew the show backwards – and yet it still didn't work. *The Brain of Morbius* was one of those. I can't remember in detail what went wrong, but I think it just wasn't achieving what Bob and I were trying to do. This often happens in television – you get script editors who are very, very careful with the writers who are working for them and make sure there's a dramatic unity, saying the writer can only have so much of this and this and they can't do that. But when they're let loose as writers, they suddenly ignore all these things they used to say – welcome to *The Brain of Morbius*! Terrance Dicks's script had lots of stuff with a Frankenstein-style robot, which was far too complicated for the story that he was telling. I remember talking to the all the key people who would have had to make this robot, who were telling us they couldn't do it realistically or practically on the budget and allotted time. I can't remember exactly who but probably the visual effects team, plus the set and costume designers. It needed to be mostly done on CSO because of the way Terrance had written it but it couldn't just be someone in a suit. It just was too difficult to do. The thing I liked the most about the original idea was that it was the *Frankenstein* story but made new within a science-fiction treatment with a robot being pieced together. It's a brilliant notion, making a robot from whatever's lying around and trying to bring it to life. However when the script came in, it hadn't fulfilled that potential. I can understand where Terrance was coming from, but I think he'd forgotten what he'd have said to any other writer who delivered the impossible when he was script editor on the series. Bob finally decided it wasn't going to work with a robot and he'd rewrite it himself because Terrance had delivered and gone off on holiday or something. What I was then told was that we needed to do it with an actor in a costume, making instead a monster out of funny arms, animal bodies and shells rather than a robot. I said, right, we'll go with that and I left Bob alone to get on with it. He still set it on another planet, even though he knew it was all studio-based with no location work, and took it even further towards the original *Frankenstein* story than Terrance had, which I was wary about because that's what I'd always said I really didn't want. However, time was short and the designers and everyone just went for it with a spooky castle, and the witches chasing the monster with burning torches. For me, the final production came out as this rather strange, rather repulsive at times, creation. Yet the script itself was really very powerful with some wonderful stuff in it – Bob's final script is one of the wittiest scripts over the entire series and is brilliant. Really, it is. Despite my fears, all the dancing witches, the elixir of life and all that did work. But it wasn't science-fiction enough to be the way I wanted it originally and it was a bit over the top when the brain falls onto the floor and bounces around, which I didn't like. That was a bit *too* dark and I was having to pull things back a bit … but still probably not enough. Then again, it's a popular story with the fans and had big viewing figures, so maybe my instincts weren't always right after all."

the BRAIN *of* MORBIUS

REAL SCIENCE vs FANTASY SCIENCE

MICK SCHUBERT

There was an accident. Morbius's brain on the floor.
I don't know what damage has been done.

"NO, that won't do. The cranium's too narrow; the cerebrum undeveloped. That is an insect! Even a half-witted cannibal like you can see it won't do!"

Of course, any half-witted cannibal knows that the main factor – scientifically speaking – that prevents the successful transplantation of an insect's head onto a humanoid body is the shape of its cranium. In this, as in other aspects of science, Philip Hinchcliffe's *Doctor Who* is ahead of its time.

To really dig into the science of *Doctor Who*, where better to begin than with *The Brain of Morbius*? A post-modern Prometheus fantasy with more Gothic horror than scientific fact, the story simultaneously denounces the perversion of science and celebrates its triumph over hubris and mythology. But which side is truer to life – and how long does humanity have before we need to call on the Doctor to save us from a horror of our own making?

"I can see nothing, feel nothing. You have locked me into hell for eternity. If this is all there is for me, I would sooner die now."

So, what if you want to reanimate Morbius? Well, first, you'll need a (living) brain in a jar. Although a convenient thought experiment, the idea becomes far less practical when you're actually tasked with keeping it alive. The first challenge arises at an even earlier stage: contrary to popular belief, brains (at least, human ones) are soft. So soft, in fact, that it can be difficult to pick one up intact, let alone manoeuvre it into a jar and hook it up to a series of tubes and connections. The realistic probability of a brain teleportation device is somewhat beyond the scope of our investigation, but let's assume for the sake of convenience that Solon's unparalleled surgical skills extend to the problem-free transport and manipulation of a brain – or that Time Lord brains are much more durable than ours.

In aspects of science, Philip Hinchcliffe's Doctor Who is ahead of its time.

Now that you have your jar of brain, you face a much greater challenge – keeping it alive long enough to find an appropriate receptacle. Brains demand a substantial and ideally uninterrupted supply of energy and resources. In humans (and, therefore, likely in Time Lords as well), the brain makes up only about two per cent of body mass – but consumes about twenty per cent of the body's energy. About one quarter of that energy is expended just to keep the brain alive; the rest goes to thinking and acting. Fortunately for Solon, Morbius may need less energy than the average brain because, after all, he has no body to operate. No eyes to steer, no skin to monitor, no pancreas to regulate – but plenty of time for the brain's most energy-hungry function: thinking. (And, somehow, hearing – but this is a necessary scientific sacrifice on the altar of narrative; with no way to express the horror of its existence or the evil of its plans, what would we have to fear from a jellied brain?)

Whether the green liquid surrounding Morbius is food or environment is a mystery for the ages, but whatever he consumes – perhaps the Elixir of Life itself – will presumably supply him with an array of essential amino acids, vitamins, minerals, proteins, fats, and sugar. This may be enough to

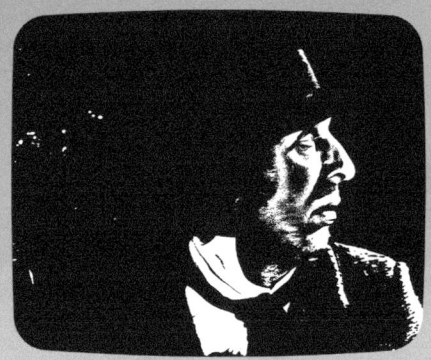

keep him alive, but for how long? If the brain goes on functioning, it goes on ageing, and that means it goes on undergoing processes that ultimately result in a reduced ability to learn, remember, and survive. As brains age, they shrink; their structure changes; their blood flow reduces; even the speed at which signals transmit grows slower with time. How long has Morbius been floating in his vat? How much memory does he have left? And how fast do Time Lord brains age?

"Every part of this, every organ is mine, with my own hands. And it's functioning perfectly, exactly to the required standard."

The brain may be an integral part of any Frankenstein equation, but without an appropriate body, its odds of survival are low. So what does it take to make a man out of Morbius? In this case, the answer appears to be "whatever you can get." It's possible to argue that Solon wanted nothing but the best for his body – as many different functions as possible (pincers, fingers, inexplicable patches of fur) – but an honest evaluation suggests that perhaps that was more aspirational than achievable. Options were probably quite limited on Karn and a parts-sourcing method that involves crashing alien spaceships into the planet is unlikely to have yielded top-quality outcomes. As a result, the body built for Morbius has some fatal flaws – not just the lack of a head, but also massively imbalanced arms, significant range of motion issues, and hair that clearly grows into and under suture lines, which is never a pleasant sensation even when it isn't creating a fast-track entry route for opportunistic infections. It's no surprise that Morbius is less than pleased with the final product.

That said, the body apparently does have some unusual bells and whistles – methane filters in the lungs, for instance, to protect against cyanide gas poisoning. A handy feature in the presence of concentrated methane (which, when inhaled by a human, can replace normal air in the lungs and cause oxygen deprivation), these filters are unfortunately much less useful when it comes to inhaling hydrogen cyanide gas due to its total lack of methane. It's possible that the lungs have a universal gas filtration system capable of removing both, and the Birastrop who donated them is simply known for its methane-heavy homeworld – but it's also possible that Solon's grasp of organic chemistry falls somewhat short of his expertise in microsurgery and tissue transplantation. At last, a television expert who doesn't fall victim to the "omnidisciplinary scientist" trope!

Whichever way you slice it – and slice Solon does – the long-suffering Morbius eventually ends up with a makeshift housing for his mighty consciousness. Minus the head, that is. We know that the Mutt's head is rejected for this purpose because of its narrow cranium (not so much the undeveloped cerebrum; one presumes this is of little importance given that it will be Morbius's cerebrum that occupies the head). We also know that Sarah Jane's head is unacceptable for the same reason – "the female braincase is too small." Why Condo's head has remained safely atop his spinal column for years while Solon searches for an appropriate substitute is a mystery, unless Morbius is pickier about his haircuts than his limbs, but eventually the Frankenstein process reaches its inevitable conclusion: the brain discontentedly floating in its jar must be given its body – and the body must be given life.

"A head such as this, a head that will soon command the universe, must be taken with care and skill. Every step must be planned. Every suture, every small incision has to be perfect. Any third-rate hack can fix an arm, but a head, the centre of the nervous system, that takes more than just skill. That takes genius."

There are two ways to pair brain with body: via head (ideal, as long as the cranium suffices) or via artificial braincase (formidable problems). Each comes with its own unique challenges.

To use a head, you first need to find a suitable one. Morbius's brain is a particularly robust specimen – it's no wonder Solon struggled to find an adequate housing – and would still need enough space for a substantial protective cushion of cerebrospinal fluid. In this case, given Morbius's propensity for physically attacking his enemies (when he can) and the importance of intelligence and mental fortitude among the Time Lords, there's no such thing as too much protection for a brain whose ultimate goal is universal domination.

But where might such a head come from? Fortunately for Morbius, the Doctor's fourth incarnation boasts an impressive hat size that makes him an excellent candidate (to say nothing of the species compatibility). Had the Doctor not come along, however, Solon might have faced a long wait for another alien with an appropriate cranial volume. But although skull size is a vital first consideration, the challenges of head fitting extend much further. For instance, does the donor species have a spinal cord (or, indeed, a spine at all)? Are there blood vessels that can be matched to both the brain of Morbius and the borrowed neck on which the head will sit? Does it have all of the senses Morbius's original body possessed and can they be appropriately hooked up? Are there extra senses or functions that Morbius, with his Time Lord brain, will be unable to operate? Simply installing a head with a magnetic field detector won't give Morbius the ability to navigate without a compass – because, without the corresponding region in the sensory cortex, those organs will be useless.

But, all things considered, Solon's somewhat questionable construction is not – from a brain's perspective – all that different to a Time Lord's body. It has two legs, two arms, a torso, walks upright … everything a bipedal humanoid needs to be happy. That is, presuming Solon has a plan for intensive rehabilitation as Morbius learns everything from how to walk to how to excrete to how to operate his shiny new pincer. Fortunately, brains are adept at reorganising how they work to cope with change – and, although controlling a new head, body and set of senses is a little more intense than learning to work around a stroke or injury, the conditions are similar enough that Morbius should eventually be able to operate Solon's monstrosity about as well as the Doctor operates under the influence of Solon's special wine.

A braincase, however, is a somewhat different prospect. Solon has thoughtfully provided Morbius with sensory input – "eyes" on stalks (a clumsy attempt to replicate one of nature's most complex systems), some hardwired sensors presumably intended as ears – but his skill in the construction of artificial organs clearly doesn't compare to his tissue transplantation abilities. Although technology has doubtlessly advanced since the 21st century, poor Morbius is likely operating with limited vision, confusing auditory signals, and an uncertain amount of sensation. He can't smell, taste, speak or even walk fully upright – a far cry from the physiological triumph Solon promised. No wonder he can't safely navigate a laboratory full of fragile glassware and open flames. No wonder he isn't pleased with whatever fuzzy, distorted outline of himself he sees in the mirror. No wonder Solon considers madness a likely outcome. Morbius has no mouth, but he must scream.

It's unfortunate, however, that Solon has deemed it impossible to address the issue of static electricity build-up within the braincase. Although no system is perfect, he could have experimented with chemical coatings, ionisers, special tubes and fittings, insulating pads, grounding cables … the more one considers the options, the more it seems as though Solon simply couldn't be bothered with safety precautions – or perhaps his solitary science-and-wine existence was simply too enjoyable to cut short with a successful recorporealisation.

"When I said I could create life, they laughed at me, they mocked me. Only Morbius had the faith to believe in me."

As many human researchers have discovered throughout the years, simply attaching a brain to a body is not enough to create life. Twenty-first century advances in surgical tools, techniques and treatments have meant that we can successfully

attach heads to bodies (and keep both halves alive), reconnect severed spinal cords (and restore some level of sensory and motor function), and even bypass damaged areas of the spinal cord with brain-computer interfaces. But the challenge of re-establishing every function of the brain – from autonomic functions like breathing and digestion to high-level neurological demands like playing the piano or commanding the universe – remains well beyond the grasp of science. Fortunately for all involved, Solon's grasp doesn't seem to extend much farther; between his inability to build a working artificial braincase, his repeated failures to properly connect Morbius's brain (not to mention its brief sojourn on the floor), and the "efficient" body he apparently based on a child's crayon art, Morbius's long-term prospects remain grim.

Perhaps Solon's somewhat desultory efforts at a Morbius Potato Head have some advantages, though. After all, he appears to have given little thought to the potential for tissue rejection. How long will the patchwork parts of Morbius's new body continue to work well together? How long will the body tolerate the brain? If Solon's many oversights and omissions included providing Morbius with a functioning immune system, perhaps rejection would never have been a concern. So was this lapse by dereliction or design? The exercise is left to the viewer …

One final note on life – or, rather, on capturing and bottling it. What is the mysterious Elixir of Life that everyone on Karn seems to take for granted? The Doctor notes that it regenerates tissues (Sarah Jane's retinas would agree), and in this the Elixir is not completely out of touch with modern science. We may not yet be able to regrow a human retina inside the eye (one of many ways in which we are inferior to newts), but it's far from an impossible dream; we can grow retinal cells in a test tube, transplant them into living eyes, and even teach stem cells to turn into new retinal cells. By applying the right combinations of factors, we can convince undifferentiated stem cells to become all manner of organs and tissues – but only under controlled conditions and with careful supervision. Could the Elixir of Life provide the factors a body might need to regrow its own organs? It's unlikely, given that those include a wide range of proteins and other organic compounds not often found in oxidised rock. It's even more unlikely that it would contain elements compatible with both human and Gallifreyan biology. Most importantly, though, if the Elixir of Life can truly regenerate any tissue, why not simply bathe Morbius's brain in it and give him back the body he once had? Again, we are forced to draw the only possible conclusion – that Solon has no great desire to do a swap with the Sisterhood and share his supply of wine.

"Please, listen. Why don't you listen? This could explain why I've been sent here. You need scientific advice!"

Humanity's fascination with life – its creation, its manipulation, its destruction – is a delightful playground for enthusiasts in science-fiction, horror, and the human condition. *Doctor Who* is no exception. From cyborgs to cryostasis,

 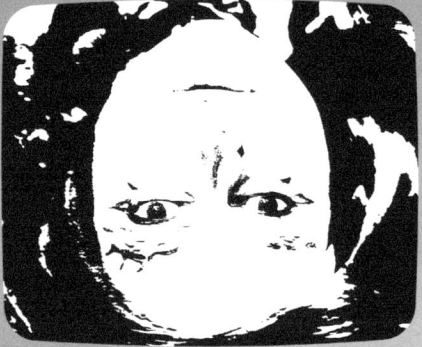 

split personalities to sentient living energy, the Hinchcliffe years are filled with intriguing explorations of what happens when one's reach exceeds one's grasp.

For instance, consider *The Ark in Space*. Why do humans fear cryopreservation – is it the risk that, having once gone under, we might never wake up again? Is it the vulnerability of lying unconscious and exposed for decades, centuries, even millennia? Is it the uncertainty of what we might wake up to when those millennia have passed? Combine this with humanity's inherent horror of insects (possibly a trait evolved to protect us from danger – or possibly one we have learnt from parents, books and films) and you have a perfect recipe for existential terror. Not only that, but a remarkably likely terror; even on our planet, there are plenty of arthropods that willingly deposit their eggs inside human bodies and that number is likely to increase as we continue to destroy the ecosystems that currently provide suitable alternative hatch sites. Fortunately, although we're pretty good at freezing and thawing individual cells and even embryos, science is still a long way from reviving whole frozen adult humans – so if you do end up as an alien egg case, you're unlikely ever to find out.

This is a recurring theme in the Hinchcliffe years (and in the classic horror that inspired many of the stories) – the juxtaposition of our human curiosity against our fear of the unknown. There will always be those who want to push the boundaries of our knowledge, whether it involves

> **The Hinchcliffe years are filled with intriguing explorations of what happens when one's reach exceeds one's grasp.**

aliens testing human resistance to torture or a mad computer bent on eugenics. But, in science, it's often impossible to spot the edge of the cliff until you're already falling – and it's beyond the edge of this precipice that most of Hinchcliffe's stories lie. Afraid of monsters, especially those who can hide in plain sight? *Terror of the Zygons* is for you. Grew up in the Cold War years under the shadow of the bomb? Try *The Hand of Fear*, a new take on the threat of nuclear radiation. Mistrustful of robots or computers? The world is your oyster, from *The Android Invasion* to *The Robots of Death*. No matter your deepest fears, somewhere, they have been given life on film – and it's no stretch to assume that many of them were brought to life on *Doctor Who* by Philip Hinchcliffe.

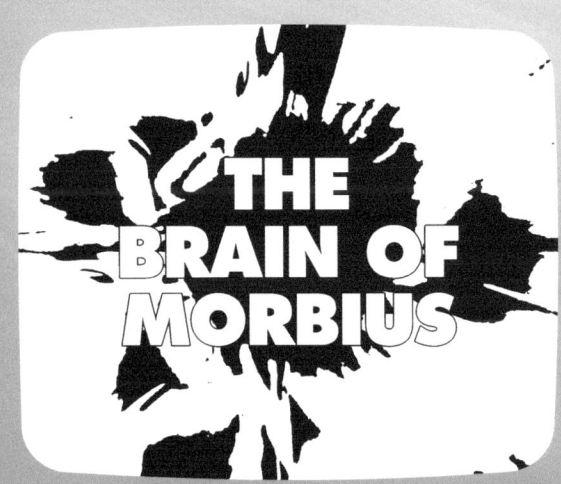

Philip chats about writing *Doctor Who* outside the BBC

"Part of me was quite itching to get involved in creating stuff during my time on the programme, but I didn't really have time to write scripts and they wouldn't have been as good as Bob Holmes's. My creative juices were pretty much satisfied by all the input that I was having as producer. However I'd noticed that since he'd left the show Terrance Dicks was doing all these books. I can't remember whether Target came to me or whether I went to them, but I think they probably approached me and asked if I would like to do one. I quickly said yes and because *The Seeds of Doom* was so fresh in my mind, I reckoned I could do that easily, because you work from the scripts. I'd never written a novel, and it was quite a challenge to write prose and see what I could do it. I really enjoyed it and it didn't take me very long, so when they asked if I'd do another one, I said I'd like to do *The Masque of Mandragora* because it had such a great setting. They didn't pay a lot, but were good fun to do and as I had finished on *Doctor Who* by then, there was no conflict of interest (the BBC had very strict rules about what freelance writing you could do while producing a show). Each book was done and finished within three weeks. I could never have done it while making the series though. Time was too short, and we were all too busy.

✶ ✶ ✶ ✶

I remember Tom, with Ian Marter, had decided to write a *Doctor Who* film script, which Bob Holmes and I thought was a bit … odd. I don't think we were particularly worried – to be honest we didn't think it would ever really happen. I vaguely remember that we thought, "Hang about a minute, Tom's got enough to do being the Doctor on the series." It all happened without me being consulted or brought into it or talked to by the filmmakers who commissioned Tom and Ian. I knew they had forged a good friendship while they were working together so whilst I was a bit surprised, I wouldn't go as far as saying I felt any disloyalty on Tom's part, because in a way it was typical Tom, trying to expand the franchise. The thing is, if you're going to do a movie, you need top talents to write it, especially if it's got to succeed in America. You really had to get a writer who understood the global markets, and they would spin it that way. You could understand a producer hiring that kind of writer. But you wouldn't entrust it to the leading actor, and one of the supporting actors to write the script. So, it sounded a bit amateurish as a project, and I don't whether they had been talking to BBC Enterprises or found outside finance. Perhaps they were just doing a kind of spec script, but I stayed well out of it."

the SEEDS of DOOM

ON TARGET!
DAVID J HOWE

Now I shall play you my requiem. My Floriana Requiem, dedicated to Linnaeus.
You know, Doctor, I could play all day in my green cathedral.

He was a tall curly-haired man of indeterminate age with sparkling blue eyes and a beaming smile. He was dressed rather curiously in tweed trousers and a long red-velvet frockcoat. Round his neck he wore a very long woollen scarf of many colours which trailed on the ground behind him.

Philip Hinchcliffe,
Doctor Who and the Masque of Mandragora, 1977

YOU can tell the quality of a writer by the way they describe the Doctor. Some are content to let the reader's 'race memory' fill in whichever character they think they are reading about. Letting the reader do the work. Others, like the auteur of the art form, author Terrance Dicks, have the art down pat, being able to describe the iconic character with a single phrase which leaves no doubt as to who's (excuse the grammar) company we are in for the course of the coming adventure.

Philip Hinchcliffe prefers to go the expressive route, tackling the Doctor as a multidimensional character, and filling in his appearance over a few sentences. What is interesting, is that while in *Doctor Who and the Masque of Mandragora*, he does this in one paragraph, in the novelisation of *The Seeds of Doom*, there is no single, snappy description. Instead we are introduced to the Doctor via a number of vignettes, totally following the literary 'rule' of 'show, don't tell'. Thus the Doctor is seen from the point of view of the frosty businessman Dunbar, deputy of the World Ecology Bureau (WEB). He 'invades' his office in a flurry of red velvet coat, floppy hat and long scarf. He plonks himself in Dunbar's office chair and puts his feet on the table. This is classic Fourth Doctor behaviour, and Hinchcliffe nails it.

Of course, for *Doctor Who and the Seeds of Doom* he had some great source material in Robert Banks Stewart's scripts, and Hinchcliffe makes the most of this story of alien possession and change.

The Seeds of Doom was a six episode adventure on television, but told in two distinct parts. This structure works excellently as the opening shows what happens to Antarctic scientist Winlett when he becomes infected by the alien Krynoid, and then later on, we repeat the sequence, initially with Sarah Jane Smith as the intended victim, but ultimately it's one of Chase's staff, Keeler, who becomes the plant-creature instead.

The story is perfect fare to close the thirteenth season, a year of *Doctor Who* which had, rather more than any before or since, drawn on horror film tropes to power the storytelling. For *The Seeds of Doom*, we're in 'monster frozen in the ice' territory, and *Doctor Who*'s take on the idea mixes horror in with the science-fiction and presents a tale which touched on all the elements which Hinchcliffe and his script editor, Robert Holmes, loved and knew would make a thrilling 1976 TV adventure.

The main element of horror here (aside from being fed into a manure composting machine!) is one of being changed into an alien being. The concept of loss of self/humanity is an area that Hinchcliffe and Holmes explored time and again during Hinchcliffe's time on *Doctor Who*.

Director of *The Seeds of Doom*, Douglas Camfield, had a theory about *Doctor Who* producers, as he explained in 1979 to Gary Hopkins for the fanzine *Doctor Who Review*: "Producers are primarily 'Hawks' or 'Doves', depending on how they see the show. This dictates the whole ethos of the thing. The 'Hawk' is a pioneering, to-hell-with-it innovator who regards

Doctor Who as an adult programme that children watch. He champions bold, breathtaking concepts, and won't shirk dark mysteries and horror. The 'Dove' is a conservative producer who prefers to stay on Earth for his stories and avoids anything really frightening. He regards *Doctor Who* as a children's programme – and the true Gothic worries him as much as it does [Seventies morality campaigner] Mary Whitehouse. Take, for example, Philip Hinchcliffe. Philip was the ultimate 'Hawk'."

This certainly seems to define the approach that Hinchcliffe took on *Doctor Who*. His stories are brave, complex, and not afraid to go where others might have turned the cameras away from.

What is interesting, however, is that when Hinchcliffe had the chance to go the whole hog in the novelisation, *Doctor Who and the Seeds of Doom*, he chose not to.

There's a scene in the story where Keeler is being changed into a plant, and as Hinchcliffe explained to J Jeremy Bentham in 1983 for the *Doctor Who Magazine Winter Special 1983/4*, they had to be careful: "We had [a] scene we had to chop down, where the guy is being turned green by a plant infection. You see, it all has to do with the portrayal of human pain, which, curiously enough, does not worry many children but does worry a lot of adults. If you have a good actor who is made up to look horrible and who is really putting everything into portraying pain, anguish and torment, then it does convey very strongly across to the audience."

The equivalent scene in the novelisation runs as follows:

Inside, the cottage was dark, apart from a glimmer of candlelight overhead. Sarah groped her way to the foot of the stairs. All at once she heard a sound, a pitiful inhuman moan, which chilled her spine. Shaking, she mounted the steps. At the top stood a closed wooden door. She raised the latch and entered.

The sight in the room transfixed her with horror. A monstrous, hybrid creature lay on the bed, half human, half vegetable.

'You should be glad,' it croaked. 'This might have been you.'

Sarah could not speak as the hideous picture swam before her eyes.

Philip Hinchcliffe,
Doctor Who and the Seeds of Doom, 1977

It's interesting how, given the opportunity to explore just what is happening here, Hinchcliffe chooses to actually look away. Part of this may have been the requirement to tell the story in only around thirty thousand words. This necessitated some cutting back of material, most notably the vast majority of the scenes involving the artist Amelia Ducat.

On television, Ducat is one of the joys of the story: a dotty botanic painter, who comes into the story in order to lead the Doctor and Sarah to Harrison Chase, the plant-obsessed millionaire who had bought – but not paid for – one of her paintings.

In the novelisation, Ducat is present for just one short scene, all her subsequent appearances having been jettisoned presumably in order to cut the length back. This is a shame as it would have been fascinating to see how Hinchcliffe handled a strong female character (other than Sarah Jane) in print.

Hinchcliffe came to the Target book novelisations during a period where Terrance Dicks was pretty much dominating the schedules, and working on the vast majority of *Doctor Who* adaptations for the Target range. In fact, for the 1977 schedule of eleven titles, Dicks penned all but three: one was by former *Doctor Who* companion actor Ian Marter, and two were by Hinchcliffe.

It was Barry Letts, former producer of *Doctor Who*, and the man who Hinchcliffe took over from, that suggested that Hinchcliffe should approach the publishers about doing some

adaptations as they were looking to bring more writers to the range. "Barry had written his book and knew the Target editors quite well and he mentioned to me that they were looking around for competent writers who could take some of the burden off the shoulders of Terrance Dicks," Hinchcliffe explained to the *Doctor Who Winter Special* magazine in 1981. "I had never written a book before, but decided I would rather like to try. I did *The Seeds of Doom* first and Target liked it and said they would be happy for me to do others."

Doctor Who and the Seeds of Doom was published in February 1977, and was followed by

Doctor Who and the Masque of Mandragora in December the same year.

Doctor Who and the Masque of Mandragora was another adaptation of a story that Hinchcliffe had produced for the show. Written by Louis Marks and originally called *Doom of Destiny* and then *Catacombs of Death* before gaining its transmitted title, it told the story of an alien incursion on Earth back in 15th-century Italy. Many of the familiar Hinchcliffe tropes are present here. We have an alien intelligence trying to gain a foothold on Earth (cf *The Ark in Space, Terror of the Zygons, Pyramids of Mars, The Android Invasion, The Seeds of Doom*), and there's again possession of a human to become a vessel of the alien intelligence, but the story manages to be fresh and to feel original due to the incredible work of designer Barry Newbery, and the use of the architectural 'folly' village Portmeirion in North Wales as the location (it was also used to great acclaim in the Sixties series *The Prisoner*).

The novelisation again makes good use of some of the horror tropes, especially in the scenes where the Mandragora energy, having 'hitched a lift' in the TARDIS, emerges and kills first a farmer, and then a soldier.

Here's how Hinchcliffe describes the death of the soldier:

As the soldier was about to slip through the narrowing gap his attention was caught by a strange shrieking noise. He stopped and turned. It seemed to be coming from the air above him. He looked upwards and his whole body froze with horror. Swooping down towards him from the sky was a blinding ball of fire about ten feet in diameter. He drew his sword but it grew white hot and burst into flames. Screaming he scrabbled at the city gates trying to find the opening but they had already shut behind him. He was trapped. As he cowered against the archway the ball of fire descended upon him and engulfed his body in a blaze of dazzling light. Seconds later the light disappeared. All that remained was the hideously shrivelled form of the hapless soldier, like a piece of scarred wood struck by lightning.

Philip Hinchcliffe,
Doctor Who and the Masque of Mandragora, 1977

Sometimes, it's perhaps best not to 'cut away' but even here there is less than was seen on television, as the corpses of those 'touched' by the Mandragora energy ended up coloured with eerie copper blue markings and burns, rather than black.

"I enjoyed writing *Mandragora* as it had been a good television story with good, strong characters against an interesting background," Hinchcliffe told the *Doctor Who Winter Special* magazine.

Hinchcliffe's final foray into the world of the novelisation was something of an outlier choice. *Doctor Who and the Keys of Marinus*, published in August 1980, an adaptation of a 1964 adventure, which had starred William Hartnell as the Doctor.

This final book came about because the publishers were aware of the problems that having just one author handling all the books might cause, and so during 1979 had approached Hinchcliffe about doing more of the titles.

As with the two titles from his own era, Hinchcliffe approaches the narrative with great gusto. There is much to admire in writer Terry Nation's second script for the series, which is often overshadowed by his first, which introduced the Daleks to the world.

The Keys of Marinus is one of the most ambitious shows that *Doctor Who* attempted in its first year, presenting a quest for the Doctor and his companions across the planet Marinus in search of four keys of power for a Conscience Machine which was designed to keep all the inhabitants calm and docile, but which is inactive. These have been hidden around the planet to stop them falling into the hands of the evil Yartek, leader of the Voord, who wants to use the Machine for his own purposes, but now that the Machine has been modified to affect the Voord as well, they need to be retrieved.

Thus the stage is set for multiple capsule adventures in many different settings: from snowy wastes where a lecherous trapper is out to capture the Doctor's companion Barbara for his own ends and frozen Ice Soldiers which slowly revive, to a city ruled by disembodied brains who project visions of wealth and luxury into the minds of those who visit, to a laboratory overcome by plants, and finally to a city where the legal rule is 'guilty until proven innocent' … and it's the Doctor's companion Ian who is accused of killing one of the inhabitants …

Hinchcliffe does well with this varied base material, and kicks off with an excellent description of the Doctor as played by William Hartnell.

> He was an old man with an upright, alert stance, and a dignified expression. He had flowing white hair and mischievous blue eyes. He was dressed like an eccentric Victorian professor (dark frock-coat, winged collar and tie, checked waistcoat and trousers). He carried a wooden walking stick which he shook vigorously in the air when arguing, which was often. He was known as "the Doctor".
>
> Philip Hinchcliffe,
> *Doctor Who and the Keys of Marinus*, 1980

As with Hinchcliffe's description of the Fourth Doctor earlier, readers are in no doubt as to how to picture the character this time.

Hinchcliffe is not afraid to explore some of the emotions which run high as the adventure progresses. Here's the Doctor's granddaughter Susan arriving in the area controlled by plants:

> Susan stood silently, taking all this in. It was so quiet she could hear her heart thumping. A faint singing began in her ears and the forest rustled and stirred around her. She thought she heard talking and whispering, first coming from behind the creepers on the wall, then off to her left, or was it her right? Her senses were playing tricks in the silence. But no, there was a noise. It grew louder and louder, wrapping around her like a howling wind, piercing her eardrums.
>
> 'Stop it! Stop it!' she heard herself cry, her voice distant and muffled. The loud, harsh screeching pervaded her entire being.
>
> Philip Hinchcliffe,
> *Doctor Who and the Keys of Marinus*, 1980

And here's Barbara being tormented by Vasor, the trapper:

> The trapper sat at the wooden table, peering suspiciously at Barbara. She was seated by the fire.
>
> Suddenly he rose without a word and halted a yard from her, a foolish grin on his ugly face. 'There's nowhere you can run.'
>
> 'Keep away!' Barbara snatched a hot poker from the smoking logs and held it before her. 'Don't you dare come near me.'
>
> 'All right,' Vasor said. He retreated to the table. 'I'm in no hurry. There's no-one coming to help you.' He leered at her lasciviously.
>
> Barbara gripped the poker tightly.
>
> Philip Hinchcliffe,
> *Doctor Who and the Keys of Marinus*, 1980

It's the economy of words which makes the tension racket up, and as a television producer with similar concerns around what you can and cannot show, and how much or how little you can get away with, Hinchcliffe does well with the adaptation. Even Vasor's dishonourable intentions for Barbara are well handled, never crossing the line from 'horror' into 'creepy'.

"*The Keys of Marinus* was not my choice for a novel," Hinchcliffe told the *Doctor Who Winter Special* magazine, "and I did not enjoy writing it so much. There are no good characters who stand out in the story aside from the Doctor, and he only really comes into it towards the end during the trial sequences."

It's the economy of words which makes the tension racket up.

One actually wonders how *The Keys of Marinus* might have turned out had it had Hinchcliffe as producer rather than Verity Lambert. Certainly a bigger budget than Sixties *Doctor Who* could command would only have been a benefit, but it is telling that *Doctor Who* tends to generally shy away from this sort of multiple location/character adventure, however it's interesting to see it still being used in modern-day adventures like the Thirteenth Doctor's *Flux* sequence.

Returning to Hinchcliffe's penmanship, and, aside from his descriptions of the Doctor, another way to consider the impact on the range of novelisations is how he handles the various arrivals and departures of the Doctor's own timeship, the TARDIS. While the descriptions in *Doctor Who and the Seeds of Doom* and *Doctor Who and the Keys of Marinus* are fairly perfunctory, *Doctor Who and the Masque of Mandragora* delivers a classic description which seems to sum up the essence of the Doctor's machine:

The strange blue box began to emit a peculiar trumpeting noise like a wounded animal. Simultaneously, the little white light on top started flashing and the whole contraption slowly faded into thin air.

Philip Hinchcliffe,
Doctor Who and the Masque of Mandragora, 1977

At the end of *Doctor Who and the Keys of Marinus*, the Machine explodes as Yartek has been tricked and one of the eponymous keys is actually a fake. Hinchcliffe's description of this sequence is magnificent.

The gleaming, crystalline structure began to hum and quiver like a glass bell. A red glow appeared at the centre, growing in intensity as the humming sound grew louder. Then, spokes of purple light radiated outwards along the delicate metal connectors until the entire structure blazed like a giant catherine wheel. Suddenly, the entire machine burst apart with the force of an exploding sun. In one millionth of a second Yartek's flesh was seared to the bone, and the bone reduced to ash. The room, the guard, and two hundred feet of surrounding masonry were simply scorched out of existence within the blink of an eye.

Philip Hinchcliffe,
Doctor Who and the Keys of Marinus, 1980

With prose and imagination like this, there's little wonder that Philip Hinchcliffe's era of *Doctor Who* is revered and appreciated by fans.

Doctor Who and the Keys of Marinus would be Hinchcliffe's last contribution to the Target book range, and the three *Doctor Who* titles form the only published paperback fiction from Hinchcliffe to date. Which is a great shame, as he writes convincingly and seemingly effortlessly, capturing on the page, the *Doctor Who* that was adored on television.

Hinchcliffe understood what the show was all about, and that in order to entertain, you need to instil a sense of wonder … and sometimes to scare the living daylights out of the viewers.

Philip chats about historical trappings

PHILIP CHATS ABOUT HISTORICAL TRAPPINGS

"Between seasons I think we probably got a little rest – poor Bob *had* to have a rest. But we had no notes or post-mortems with our Head of Serials, Bill Slater. Conversations about that third season were held just between Bob and I really and we were always generating bits of ideas, bits of this, bits of that. There was always a bit of stuff left over that we hadn't used, just sort of notions, scraps of ideas. We used to go round to a boring little restaurant in Shepherd's Bush and just chew the cud, and sound one another out. Bob would say, "I've been thinking something like this idea might be good" or "I'm bringing on this Chris Boucher chap". Chris was the only new writer we ever sounded out and Bob was championing him a lot. Normally we went back to the writers we knew but Bob really had a rapport with Chris ... Meanwhile, I'd be saying, "I'd like to do something about this old idea from a book, or this point in history ..." so nuggets of ideas would evolve between us and I remember thinking that we'd got the historical feel right in *Pyramids of Mars.*

* * * *

I happened to be watching television one night and there was Roger Corman's *The Masque of the Red Death* which I'd never seen before but thought "We should do something like that." I immediately thought about filming it in Portmeirion – not because I'd seen *The Prisoner*, because I hadn't, so I didn't associate it with that. But I'd been to Portmeirion as a student when I'd worked as a travel courier and taken a group of Americans on a tour – they were visiting cathedrals and old churches all around the British Isles. I said to Bob we should do an Italian story, filmed there, based around Machiavelli and the Renaissance. It wasn't Louis Marks coming in saying, "Would you like an Italian story?"

Bob meanwhile would come up with ideas like the mummy story or the re-animated hand. He had a little library of memories in his head of all these films which I'd never seen ... So, we had a relatively leisurely brainstorming session for that last season, just the two of us. We'd always done that – I remember right back at the start he had the notion of a Jekyll and Hyde story but I said we couldn't just do that – why not make the planet itself the Jekyll and Hyde character. And then next thing he's developing with Louis Marks this idea about a dangerous planet with dark anti-matter and the two elements worked well together. For *The Masque of Mandragora* we gave Louis the Machiavelli framework because Renaissance Italy and science versus superstition is just absolute gold dust, especially when you marry in these wonderful characters like Federico and Hieronymus. Federico is just a wonderful, writ large, horrible despot, set against these two lovely princes with their interest in the new science, Galileo and all that. Bob understood that those kinds of characters worked in *Doctor Who*, he just got it.

Louis was a real pro like Bob Banks Stewart and Terry Nation. We knew we'd get a very workable script from him on this subject because he was an historian and knew all about Italy – I think he was a Doctor of Philosophy as well. It was one of those scripts that really worked well. Bob of course did a little bit of tidying up and amplifying a few characters. He would look at the trappings of that period and make sure everything was as real as it could be within our show's limitations.

Ironically, doing historical stories was totally against Bob's wishes to begin with. *Doctor Who* had a lot of them I believe, back in the black and white days – but I had never seen any of those stories. Bob always said to me, "Oh, no, you know, they don't work." He thought they were dreary, awful stories. But I said they would be fine if he wrote them! I was fascinated by the collision between a period in history and something totally inexplicable from the future. It's such a clever formula because viewers can then see both sides of it which is just wonderful.

The BBC was always so good at creating period pieces, so that gave us a strength we could build on. That was what I liked about playing with history, even if Bob didn't at first: it provided a setting the audience instinctively already knew, or thought it did. They certainly knew enough that it gave them a shorthand introduction to the setting for *The Masque of Mandragora*, and it felt familiar enough that they'd instantly accept a little alien fireball coming across the lake and suddenly exploding and killing a peasant. It's simple, accessible storytelling and doesn't require a horrible rubber-faced monster and it's just not one-dimensional. It gives you a simple through-line in the script. Even if it's utilising pseudo science, pseudo history or pseudo logic, you had to *have* a logic to make the story believable within that setting. Bob was adamant about that, and I was a quick convert too. You can do the fantastic in both science-fiction or history, but the internal logic has to work or the whole thing falls apart. You couldn't always dot all the i's and cross the t's, but in the moment that the story was unfurling, it had to feel right, logically. That gave our stories a kind of rigour as well.

* * * *

Pyramids of Mars had been a page one rewrite of Lewis Greifer's script by Bob and much to his surprise, he pulled it off and enjoyed the historical setting. I loved Bob's writing in *Pyramids of Mars* – there's a moment with a machine that's been built, detecting radio waves from Mars. As the viewer, because the Doctor has said it works, you accept it works and Bob always made sure there was enough logic that you believed in it working. Just enough broad brushstrokes, so we can buy into it. That moment was Bob and the art of writing *Doctor Who* in a nutshell."

the MASQUE *of* MANDRAGORA

SPARKING THE IMAGINATION
ROBIN INCE

Well, I've taken you to some strange places before and you've never asked how you understood the local language. It's a Time Lord's gift I allow you to share.

I START with a disclaimer. I am not a *Doctor Who* expert, but *Doctor Who* made my childhood existence considerably better than it might have been and it remains a show very dear to me. I was an anxious child, full of nightmares and uncomfortable at school, but from the first moment of hearing the theme tune on Saturday night, I knew I would happy and excited for the next twenty-four minutes and it was the Philip Hinchcliffe years that remain most important to me. (I should make it clear that it was nothing to do with ogres as parents or other such things, my parents were full of love but I think a car accident that I was in just before my third birthday made the world more terrifying to me and also made me very anxious of causing harm as, being three years-old, I decided I must have been the reason for the crash.) The many universes of *Doctor Who* are catalogued by people who have spent their lives researching and unearthing, so this is not an essay of Gallifreyan academia, but some words of appreciation.

Looking across my shelves of horror movie books, a collection that began when I was eight years old, I realise that it was Philip Hinchcliffe who began my obsession with Hammer films, Boris Karloff and Edgar Allan Poe. Here was *The Curse of Frankenstein* as *The Brain of Morbius*, *The Mummy's Hand* as *Pyramids of Mars* and *The Murders in the Rue Morgue* as *The Talons of Weng-Chiang*. I am being a little fast and loose with the comparisons, but you get the idea and I think this is one of the reasons that the Hinchcliffe years have aged so well. Many of the stories are not locked into imagined futures that can fade fast as we move forward into a future of our own, but they are embedded in the notions of a gothic past.

Perhaps it was my burgeoning love of the horror movie that meant *The Masque of Mandragora* didn't stick with me in the way that *The Seeds of Doom* or *Horror of Fang Rock* did.

My tastes have changed now. When I returned to the Hinchcliffe years one Christmas, my fondness for *The Brain of Morbius* ebbed away, despite Philip Madoc's splendid turn, and my fascination with *The Masque of Mandragora* blossomed instead. In the interim. I had spent less time at horror conventions and more time with sceptics; my intrigue had moved on from the vampiric and other undeads to psychic mediums and charlatan hacks.

As well as being about the improbability of using a woollen scarf as an effective weapon, *The Masque of Mandragora* is about the power that comes from relentless bamboozlement and the weapon of evidence-based thinking that can combat it. How delightful it would be to say that that weapon had triumphed in the interim centuries, but as we see from the contemporary political landscape of the USA and the UK, those with the power that comes with money still have a strong manipulating grip and numerous toadying allies. But before we get onto that, we can dwell on the interior design of the TARDIS.

Whenever I see a walk-in model of a TARDIS, a little bit of me still imagines that there is a possibility that, when I walk in, it really will be much bigger on the inside. With all the possible universes that exist, perhaps one of me one day really will find *that* TARDIS. The tour of the TARDIS was the perfect way to open a new series after we had been waiting so long. Remember, nine months to a 7-year-old is the equivalent of a decade to a 54-year-old. We are a species that always wants to know what lies behind any trap door or

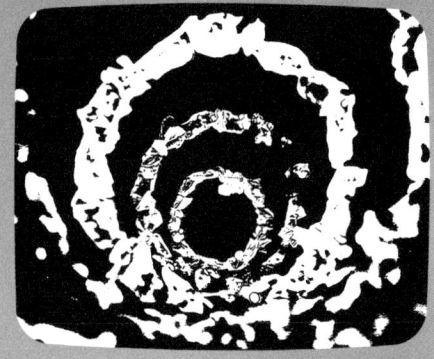  

boarded window. There is the possibility of treasure everywhere. We wander past the boot-room and eventually into a beautiful other control room with 19th century veneer that reminds us of HG Wells's *The Time Machine*.

What the best children's television frequently does is place words and ideas inside children without worrying about what the audience will understand. They are giving us the seeds and it may only be many years later that we realise what they grew into. I think of Eric Thompson's brilliant scripts for *The Magic Roundabout*. He had no fear of putting in references that no 4-year-old would understand – it didn't matter, because they were captivated by the entire spectacle rather than demanding transparency in every phrase. In one story, Dougal the Dog is trying to make a film. As he battles with his cast, he declares, "I bet this never happened to Sergei Eisenstein!" Pre-school me was not full of umbrage due to being unaware of *Battleship Potemkin*, I just delighted in the chaos. Later, Dougal states, "I am a camera." I had no idea that this was the name of the play that would be adapted into the musical *Cabaret*, just as I had no idea that Professor Yaffle in *Bagpuss* was inspired by Bertrand Russell, but what delight there was when I grew up and discovered these links.

Therefore, the TARDIS was our first introduction to Einstein and the idea of relativity, though at the time we would have had no idea if it was general or special. In those early days, scientific accuracy was not as vital to a child as scientific intrigue. We now believe that time-travel is only possible in one direction, the direction you are moving in now as your eyes move across this sentence femtosecond by femtosecond. What is so important in much science-fiction is the whatiffery of it. I still think of the TARDIS when I contemplate how time cannot exist without space, and space cannot exist without time and how space tells objects how to move and objects tell space how to curve.

My friend Fay Dowker is a brilliant science lecturer. I experienced her third-year introductory lecture about relativity and it was riveting. What was delightful is how excited she was to give this lecture, to officially introduce her students to general relativity.

When I asked her what the TARDIS meant to her, she replied, "Emotionally: bright! safe!"

When we move on to something bigger on the inside than the outside, Fay talks of "traversable wormholes". We do not know if wormholes exist as they require exotic forms of matter, but the uncertainty of their existence does not mean that they cannot be studied.

Here are Fay's instructions to construct a wormhole in your mind that will take you from wherever you are now to the Royal Albert Hall (apologies if you are in the Royal Albert Hall now, if so, just use the stairs instead).

"1. Remove a 3D solid ball of space of diameter 2 metres from your attic. There is *nothing* in the hole created, *not even space*. So, if you were to throw a book, a let's say *Gravity's Rainbow*, across the edge of the hole and into the hole it would disappear from reality entirely.

2. Remove a similar 3D solid ball of space from the RAH.
3. Each of the two holes has a spherical 'edge'. Glue the two edges together so that they are now one and the *same* sphere.

Now when you throw *Gravity's Rainbow*, as it crosses the edge of your hole (and leaves your attic), it enters the RAH. Now we have the wormhole, you can leave your attic yourself by walking across the edge and finding yourself in the RAH. Let's say the RAH is the interior of the TARDIS. In your attic, you are looking at a two metre diameter spherical edge thingy – that's the exterior of the TARDIS. Just to make it more TARDIS-like, you can enclose that sphere in a two metre cubical box with a door in one side only. Go in that door, across the spherical edge inside and find yourself in the Royal Albert Hall where someone with a puzzled expression has started to read *Gravity's Rainbow* …

Astronomer Chris Lintott told me that the TARDIS must be manipulating gravity and reminds me of *Star Trek* creator Gene Roddenberry's answer to the question, "how exactly do the Heisenberg compensators on the USS Enterprise work?"

"Very well, thank you."

Janna Levin interprets the TARDIS as a black hole in her *The Black Hole Survival Guide* and Helen Czerski suggests a sensory illusion. One thing that all these serious scientists have in common is no loss in fascination when dealing with what we imagine to be real and what we presume is purely from the imagination.

This importance of the imagination divides up those who sneer at the low budget effects of *Doctor Who* and those who see those effects as a placeholder for what our imagination can fill in. The boot-room we see is a flat, almost blurred image, but that is just the starting point for us. This is part of the joy of BBC special effects. A big movie budget effect does everything for us and may well underwhelm because its magnificence leaves no room for us to use our own imaginations. I think this is also why the BBC television adaptation of *The Hitchhiker's Guide to the Galaxy* is more fulfilling, to me at least, than the cinematic version.

Now the 'Elle Interiors' section of *The Masque of Mandragora* is over, we find ourselves viewing a wonder of the universe. With reverence, the Doctor speaks of the Mandragora Helix as "a spiral of pure energy that radiates outwards [though] at its centre there's a controlling intelligence". Fortunately, it is also summed up as something that behaves "in ways that no one understands".

Of all the Doctor's incarnations, I delight in the Fourth's way with the terminology of scientific mechanisms the most. Tom Baker has a particular way with his lines that is in a superposition of both being utterly reverential and utterly irreverent. He knows it is all pretend, but he also persuades you it most definitely is very real. I think this approach is now described as meta-modernism, but I will let you do the research on that.

After some brief jeopardy from helix energy and a demonic laugh, we find ourselves in the land of the 15th century – and uncertain supporting players. As simple folk with a hay cart are

bludgeoned by uniformed men with swords, there is one of my favourite 'I don't think they have thought this through' moments. As the peasants are slaughtered, one of them decides that rather than flee, he should concentrate in gathering the spilt hay before his own inevitable murder (although my favourite underwhelming reaction to carnage and chaos remains the television producer in 1971's *The Daemons* who, after the unleashing of terror, just packs up his stuff and thanks everyone with the sort of goodbye you might offer after sharing fruitcake with a distant relative).

To you all I say, forget the hay when the Count's men come slaughtering, live on to dry grass another day.

The Masque of Mandragora tells the story of the battle between the mystical and pseudoscientific, in this case astrology, and its diminishment due to the creation of lenses that allowed humans to truly start interrogating the skies and the increasing use of a scientific method. The advantage of the pseudo scientific is that it can be bent to your will and manipulated to fit your desires or lust for power, but rigorous research by experiment and evidence means however flat you want Earth to be, when your gyroscope keeps countering that, you must eventually bow to the results or ignore them for the purposes of your belief. If you have seen *Behind the Curve*, a documentary on Flat-Earthers, you will see the sad sight of smart people blaming their instruments for their refusal to offer the result they demand.

Reason in the story is represented by Giuliano, a little bit Galileo and a little bit Hamlet. When Ian Charleson played Hamlet on stage, he perpetually carried a book with him, a sign that knowledge was the real weapon, the sunshine needed to bleach out the balderdash and bigotry that can be so useful to the dictator and the zealot. I read that the Vatican's dislike of the telescope was that it confounded the notion that Heaven was up in the sky but we couldn't see quite far enough to spot the angels plucking tunes out of their harps. Once the lenses had been ground and adapted and the sky magnified, it seemed Heaven was a little further away than first posited.

Our villain is Hieronymous, an astrologer hungry for power and happy to assist in murder. He foretells of Giuliano's death having already prophesied the death of his father accurately (though accurately only by the assistance of a little poison). Fortunately (initially), unfortunately (eventually), Mandragora energy arrives to enthuse his murderousness.

The story is one of skullduggery and the need for a human sacrifice by astrological occultists who may be even more than they seem. Unsurprisingly, Sarah Jane is the winner of that audition and we prepare ourselves for another altar bludgeoning to assuage the gods or flirt with the aliens.

More than any other story of the Hinchcliffe years, there are reminders of the original intentions of *Doctor Who*; the concept of these time-travel adventures as a history lesson. *The Masque of Mandragora* is a good starting point for a discussion on the battle between codswallop and cosmology, and some of the blurred areas in between, that – via Copernicus, Galileo and Francis Bacon – led to the scientific method. The history of the scriptwriter reveals why this should be so clear.

This was Louis Marks's last outing for *Doctor Who*, his previous stories had included *Planet of Giants* and *Day of the Daleks*. *The Masque of Mandragora* was his most personal script, having studied the Italian Renaissance in Florence after a history degree at Balliol College, Oxford. You can see his learning in the script and the Machiavellian outing, combined with some tip top BBC wigs which shine as if in a 1960s advert for Silvikrin shampoo, gives this story a real sense of style. Alerted to Marks's education, I wondered if the cult of Demnos had any basis in actual history, but on asking the internet, it suggested that I just wanted to know if Demis Roussos was married – for those of you unaware, Demis Roussos was an unlikely sexy pop-star pin up of the 1970s, the closest thing to a soprano werewolf to reach the UK's top five. He was immortalised in the play *Abigail's Party* as the sort of music to be played in suburbia whenever vol-au-vents were nearby.

The Masque of Mandragora is also my favourite for the canny use of big curly wigs on the stuntman/fight arranger, Terry Walsh, alongside some beautifully choreographed sword fighting and horseplay. Terry Walsh was the master of obscuring his facial features and he also popped up in a variety of roles in other stories including a window cleaner in *The Time Monster* and a man with a boat in *Planet of the Spiders*. This is not to say Tom Baker was not capable of handling himself and there is an impressively high-kick to disable Hieronymous and a few other moves which could count as warm-ups for his meeting with Magnus Greel at the end of this season but I am afraid to say that I find his scarf work to topple an executioner remains improbable – though it left me wondering, can a Time Lord regenerate if beheaded?

In the end, I think the message of *The Masque of Mandragora* is make sure you educate yourself thoroughly, leave the hay cart sooner rather than later once swords are drawn, and don't trust astrologers, whether they are trying to harness evil or just fleece you with an overpriced astro prediction phone line. As the astronomer Carl Sagan said of fate being predicted by the pull of celestial bodies at our birth, "the gravitational influence of the obstetrician was much larger than the gravitational influence of Mars".

The Doctor's instruction to keep an open mind echoes the words of Professor Walter Kotschnig in a 1940 address to the students at Mount Holyoke College. He told them to keep an open mind, "but not so open that your brains fall out." Well-used, doubt is not only a great ally in navigating the world around us (especially when evil tries to use cosmological power to rule said world) but also as we watch the heartless, clumsy, greedy buffoons trample on so many. Writing this at a time where the UK government is trying to distract us from their crimes and destruction by stoking culture wars that will victimise the powerless and the struggling, we have grown up and discovered that the monsters we are facing have turned out not to be sentient flora or brains with crab claws, but monstrous human egos savaging humanity for money.

I am reminded of the part Philip Hinchcliffe's *Doctor Who* years played in helping to shape openness to otherness, our own and other people's; something we see so stealthily in the work of Russell T Davies too. *Doctor Who* was not just a comfort blanket (even if it was a terrifying comfort blanket at times too), those blankets helped build our armour and our compassion.

Finally, I cannot leave without an appreciation for Elisabeth Sladen. I don't think anyone in the news media was ready for how deeply affected so many people from so many generations would be when she died back in 2011. One story after this one, in *The Hand of Fear*, Sarah Jane Smith finally left the Doctor and the TARDIS and what struck me most when I watched that again was how perfectly underplayed it was. Twenty-first century *Doctor Who* wears its heart on its sleeve and, in the case of David Tennant's first departure, pretty much everywhere else. Sarah Jane's departure is the departure of a different generation and a different time, but it gets me every time – its impact comes from its seeming slightness. Few things are likely to bring me closer to tears than Tom Baker remembering the little nudges the last few times he and Elisabeth Sladen met up with one another and how perfectly he sums up that melancholy when we lose someone we love: "poor us, eh".

Philip chats about companions

"Elisabeth Sladen and Ian Marter were terrific actors. You could argue that I could have had Ian Marter on the show for longer because Bob Holmes gave him a lovely old-fashioned, humorous sort of persona, which was really delightful and worked well with Lis and Tom – they all bounced off each other. But I'd always had this feeling from when I first saw the show that when you've got a number of juvenile assistants around your main character, it kind of felt like a kids show. I knew I didn't want that element in my version of the programme. It was nothing to do with Ian as an actor or the way he played the part, which I thought was very, very good, I just thought having two companions wasn't the way I wanted the show to go.

As well as Harry Sullivan, I also chose to get rid of UNIT, or lessen their regularity at least. We planned on giving the Brigadier one last story, in Terry Nation's android story. When we did *Terror of the Zygons* one at the end of the first season, I didn't just say "That's it, no more UNIT" but it felt right, natural really, because obviously we weren't doing stories set on modern day Earth. And because he didn't go on trips with the Doctor, the Brigadier just quietly vanished. I'm sure Nicholas Courtney was very disappointed when the work dried up for UNIT, but when we asked him to come back and do the android story, he simply wasn't available. It would have been nice to see him one final time. It wasn't that I wanted to kill off UNIT so much as there was no need for them any longer. Added to that, the chemistry between just Tom and Lis was terrific. When I look at my episodes now I see … I wouldn't say the word 'depth', but there was a lot going on in that relationship, an extra texture. I think I was very lucky that they hit it off straight away. Maybe she and Tom both being from Liverpool meant they shared the wellspring of Scouse sarcasm. Plus Tom and Lis together had scored highly with viewing figures and audience appreciation indexes and there was a kind of buzz around from one's peers at the BBC about their success. Bob and I were thinking, "Okay, this all seems to be going right".

Lis was so good at what she did. Particularly when she was possessed or hypnotised or under an alien influence. She acted that so well. I remember Barry and Terrance telling me the Sarah character was a modern woman, an independent spirit. Feminism had probably emerged during the late Sixties. On television, there was Honor Blackman and then Diana Rigg in *The Avengers* – strong-minded women who could do karate and stuff like that. It began to seep into *Doctor Who* a bit later and so when Barry talked to me about Sarah Jane Smith as one of these new women, I could see what he was doing. Of course, under Bob and I, Sarah didn't do nearly as many modern-day Earth-based stories as under Barry and Terrance and as a result our stories didn't help her be the inquisitive journalist, going off on her own and finding stuff. So it took her away a bit from that early conception of Sarah Jane that I think quite rightly was a good one for her.

In Elisabeth Sladen's autobiography, she talks about her leaving the show, saying she started thinking about it a bit earlier than when she finally went. I recall that it was while she was doing *The Seeds of Doom* she says something in her book about wanting to jump before being pushed. She thought I was thinking along those lines too, being, in her eyes, still the new boss. She says that when she broke the news to me that she wanted to go, her suspicions were confirmed as, apparently, I just said, "Okay, Lis, if that's what you want." She believed that she was saving me the difficulty of asking her to leave and that I asked her to stay a bit longer so she could have a proper send-off. Now, I think it's pretty accurate in terms of what happened, but she absolutely misconstrued what I was feeling, what I was thinking. I think she had made *her* mind up that it was going to happen, and whatever I had said in that moment, she would probably have interpreted it the way she did. Nevertheless, I *was* surprised and whilst I might very well have said those words, I don't think she read my tone. She was certainly wrong to assume that I'd been thinking along the lines of losing her – I hadn't really thought about her leaving at all. I mean obviously I must have assumed she would probably go at some point, but I genuinely hoped not yet because I was such an admirer. I just thought the best I could do was to persuade her to stay on as long as possible. I was very sad and very disappointed that she was leaving, and maybe I didn't say, "Oh, gosh, you've got to stay" out loud or quickly enough or whatever. I was just alarmed: "Oh, my God, I'm losing Sarah Jane".

The poor writers of *The Hand of Fear*, Bob Baker and Dave Martin, had no idea when they started that this was her farewell story. I suspect at that stage, we hadn't decided on the final running order of stories but once we got our ducks in a row, it just meant a bit of last-minute rejigging for them to write her out. They sort of had five minutes to write a scene, which Tom and Lis both felt was falling short. And I suspect Bob had quite a large hand in writing that of course because it led directly into his Time Lord story. Nevertheless, Tom, Lis and I believed this was not a proper farewell for such a good character in the series. They said, "Look, we think we can do something here". Tom and Lis went away and gave us a really good spin on it – one of those rare occasions where the actors really knew what was at stake and what that scene needed to deliver. They found the text, the words to build on what was already there and made it into a much better scene. The downside of this was it created another issue – which was Tom saying, "You know, do I really *need* a companion?" Well, we knew, of course, the Doctor still had to have one, but I thought we could humour Tom and also do something a bit different and do a story, just one, without a companion just to be different. So that's what we did with *The Deadly Assassin*.

By then we also knew we had Chris Boucher and Robert Banks Stewart in the frame to write us a couple of stories and in one of them we could introduce Bob Holmes's choice of new companion, a sort of Victorian Eliza Doolittle. Now I have to say, that was never my idea, at least nothing so on the nose – my idea wasn't an Eliza Doolittle specifically, that was just a reference point I used to describe a sort of uncivilised character that the Doctor had to take under his wing. It wasn't anything to do with *My Fair Lady* and George Bernard Shaw. It was just a notion that I had that it would be really interesting to have a companion that was a real handful. Combined with that was something I had noticed about girls in our audience. I had a neighbour, a little girl who always watched *Doctor Who*. One day I very casually asked her what it was she liked about the programme and who her favourite characters were. What emerged was that she really only identified with the Doctor – she's a little girl, but she was relating to the male protagonist not the female one. I thought it would be nice to have a stronger role model, a female that the girls could also follow but in a different way to the Doctor. This led to the idea of an Amazonian – not too physically strong but mentally so, and at the same time a bit of a handful. There'd be a lot of conflict and fun, but I feel we never fully mined that scenario enough, although we did get some of it. So, this person merged into the Leela character that Chris Boucher had written for *The Face of Evil*.

Now we had to cast it. Finding somebody new made my heart sink. How would we find someone as good as Lis Sladen? We had a list drawn up of potential actresses. It was mostly Pennant Roberts's list because he was directing the first story with Leela in it. He was a prolific television director and obviously knew a lot more actresses than I did. Pennant was very friendly with Louise Jameson, and he was pushing hard for her. Rightly so. Louise had a warmth and a great directness and she didn't look like a typical conveyor-belt modern kind of young actress of that era; there was something special about her – she was striking and I really liked her. She had that certain something which suggested that she could carry on beyond one story, that extra ingredient. She was utterly perfect.

Louise was playing the role of a 'primitive' descended from human colonists whose society had regressed over the ages, so she needed a suitably primitive costume. I went to the first costume fitting and got a bit of a shock – Louise looked like Raquel Welch in *One Million Years B.C.*

I said, "You'll have to lengthen it."

They said, "We have lengthened it!"

I said, "I'm glad I didn't see the first version … you'll have to lengthen it more!"

It wasn't our intention to turn Louise into a pin-up girl but the popular press jumped on her appearance and boosted interest in the show …

Louise made Leela a refreshing foil to Tom's Doctor and galvanised the series. The way she portrayed the character's strength, intelligence and straightforwardness came, I think, from similar qualities she actually has herself. She is a lovely, open-hearted person, good fun but firm when needed and very hard working – a joy to be around. She brought something very special to the programme."

the HAND *of* FEAR

FEMALE COMPANIONSHIP
IAN WINTERTON

Now you are King, as was your wish. I salute you from the dead.
Hail, Eldrad, King of nothing.

"WELL, I quite liked her, but I couldn't stand him."

So says Sarah Jane Smith reflecting on the two incarnations – one male, one female – of Eldrad, the crystalline villain she and the Doctor face in The Hand of Fear. Spoken during Sarah's final exchange with the Fourth Doctor, it's a particularly fitting sentiment for the farewell scene of a character brought into Doctor Who in 1973 to reflect the growing women's liberation movement.

In the story, Sarah picks up the titular fossilised hand and becomes possessed by Eldrad, its undead owner, obliterated by his own people 150 million years before. Unable to say little more than "Eldrad must live!" for the rest of the episode, Sarah is compelled to take Eldrad's hand to a nearby nuclear power station. There, exposed to radiation from the nuclear core, Eldrad grows a new – female – body based on Sarah's physiology, although, played by the statuesque Judith Paris, significantly taller than Elisabeth Sladen's modest 1.62m. Once the Doctor and Sarah have transported this version of Eldrad to her native planet of Kastria, the villain is soon transformed into his true, male form, with Stephen Thorne taking on the role.

That Sarah finds the female version of Eldrad more sympathetic is down to both the writing – Bob Baker and Dave Martin's script made her a more complex character – and Paris's interpretation, which is compelling and nuanced. Contrasted with this is Thorne's Eldrad: a shouty, though undeniably enjoyable, megalomaniac of a kind seen many times before and since on Doctor Who.

Progressive female representation placed in traditional male-skewing adventure stories has been part of the DNA of Doctor Who since its inception. Indeed, it could be argued that by embracing this tension between old fashioned – but reassuring – story modes and progressive attitudes (including proto- and then actual feminism), that the show embodied the spirit of the age. This perhaps further added to Doctor Who's undoubted appeal as this ethos, perhaps unintended by the programme makers, chimed on a subconscious level with audiences. Furthermore, Hinchcliffe's era is the apotheosis of this creative tension and his ability to hold these opposing forces in check is one reason, amongst so many, that his tenure is widely regarded as the high benchmark for Doctor Who.

As Hinchcliffe would be the first to point out, the foundations for his success on Doctor Who lay on the secure foundations he inherited. Over a decade old, and firmly embedded in the consciousness of the viewing public (in Britain and beyond), Doctor Who, following a slight ratings dip during Patrick Troughton's final season, had been reinvigorated thanks to producer Barry Letts and script editor Terrance Dicks. Having sent Troughton out on a high with The War Games (where the Doctor's race, the Time Lords, were first identified), Dicks, along with Letts, then returned Doctor Who to the centre of popular culture with Jon Pertwee's dandyish Third Doctor – and now in colour, no less!

As well as high ratings and an adoring audience, Hinchcliffe – thanks to the Doctor being exiled to Earth for much of Pertwee's run – was also bequeathed the semi-permanent setting of UNIT HQ. The Doctor even had a job – Scientific Advisor – and an on-site laboratory. Though some of his writers moaned that having the Doctor stranded on Earth meant they were reduced to running two types of story – alien invasion and mad scientist – Dicks made the narrative constraints a boon. Not only did the Doctor have a ready-made reason to investigate

strange goings-on, but the audience got to spend time with recurring characters such as the Brigadier, Sergeant Benton and Captain Yates. Occasionally, as with Yates, we even got to see character development.

Though the Third Doctor's exile had been ended by the Time Lords as a reward for defeating the villain, Omega, in *The Three Doctors*, allowing him to resume adventuring throughout the cosmos once more, he was still very much tied to UNIT. And, when the time came for Pertwee to regenerate into Tom Baker, it was in his laboratory that he did so. Present at the Doctor's side, with the Brigadier looking on, was Sarah. And it was at UNIT HQ that Tom Baker's inaugural season began with *Robot*, scripted by Dicks and produced by Letts, which also added UNIT doctor Harry Sullivan to the TARDIS crew.

Hinchcliffe, putting his stamp on the show, quickly severed ties with UNIT, not returning until *Terror of the Zygons* in which he booted poor Harry out of the TARDIS, while the Brigadier doesn't return until Season Twenty's *Mawdryn Undead*. It's also telling that, until broadcast was pushed back to allow the show to shift its transmission schedule from a January to September start, *Terror of the Zygons* was initially planned to end Hinchcliffe's inaugural season, his intention clearly being to commence Season Thirteen with a distillation of the show down to its essence: the Doctor, the TARDIS, and one companion, a role still filled by Sarah Jane Smith.

How the character of Sarah developed over Seasons Twelve and Thirteen serves as an example of Hinchcliffe's era as a whole, particularly in regard to the aforementioned cultural balancing act. Created by Letts and Dicks, as a foil to the paternalistic Pertwee, Sarah in some ways was an amalgamation of the Third Doctor's other female companions, marrying Liz Shaw's brainy boffin with Jo Grant who, though spirited, was often the screaming damsel in distress. Like Liz, Sarah had an actual profession, but was still out of her depth when it came to matters of advanced science – meaning she worked as the necessary proxy for the audience as the Doctor explained what exactly the aliens were up to each week.

Sarah was, of course, written as a 'women's libber', and would have been immediately recognisable as such to a contemporary audience. Letts, an unabashed progressive, was keen to reflect societal change in the show but, though his intentions were admirable, creating Sarah as a feminist archetype feels rather forced, even tokenistic, and – as is so often the way with well-meaning, middle class, male liberals – mildly patronising.

That this wasn't as noticeable as it might otherwise have been is, of course, down to Elisabeth Sladen, whose wonderful portrayal of Sarah elevated the character from the outset. By the time of Pertwee's exit, Sladen was so thoroughly embedded in the show that having her stay on to travel with the Fourth Doctor must have been the easiest decision Barry Letts ever made.

But the choice to retain Sarah beyond Season Twelve – until, in fact, Sladen herself opted to leave – was Hinchcliffe's. Indicative of Sarah's popularity with the audience, yes, but it also demonstrates what a canny producer Hinchcliffe was. Not for him the new broom approach; he instinctively knew that the secret to *Doctor Who* is change, but that this change must be gradual. Some years later, Season Seventeen's script editor Douglas Adams even put a number on it, decreeing that *Doctor Who* could only bear to alter by up to 15 per cent series to series.

By respecting the world set up by his predecessors, Hinchcliffe took the audience established by Letts, consolidated it, and added more to the number.

For Sarah, it guaranteed her place as possibly the most popular companion in *Doctor Who*'s initial 1963–1989 run. Tellingly, when Russell T Davies brought the show back in the 21st century, Sarah Jane Smith was the first classic era companion to be reunited with the Doctor, and Elisabeth Sladen went on to front the highly successful spin-off *The Sarah Jane Adventures*.

This astounding popularity would not, it could be argued, have come about without Sarah's time with Tom Baker's Doctor, when Philip Hinchcliffe was steering the show. Though relatively young when he took up the post, Hinchcliffe was a far less radical figure than Letts and veered very much towards tradition and societal conservatism. It was this outlook, one could argue, that was key to the fulfilling of Sarah's potential as a character – and of Hinchcliffe's era more generally.

This seems counterintuitive in light of the fact Hinchcliffe – as well as outraging Mary Whitehouse and her ilk – was key to establishing Tom Baker's bohemian, free-wheeling rebellious Doctor; until one considers that the opposite was true of Letts's *Doctor Who*. Letts, holding left-of-centre views, placed Pertwee's Doctor on a military base, surrounded by soldiers and effectively working for the government. Hinchcliffe's era was the inverse of this and yet the show still thrived because the dichotomy at the heart of *Doctor Who* – tradition vs progress, past vs future, stability vs flux – remained. And, with Hinchcliffe apparently keen to downplay

the on-the-nose women's lib aspect of Sarah Jane, he enabled the character to transcend her clichéd roots and become a fully-rounded character who happened to also be a woman.

This inadvertent progressiveness remained in play when Hinchcliffe and Holmes were creating Sarah's replacement. With any creative decision, especially in the chaotic and fast-moving world of television, myriad factors come into play, each vying with one another. It is through this process that stories and characters are dreamt up that, with even the people involved unsure how the final product came about, feel organic and – magically – real.

This was certainly the case with Leela – jungle-dwelling warrior of the Sevateem – who, fiercely intelligent and deadly with her dagger or venom-tipped Janus thorn, could be a leading contender for the programme's strongest female character. Except … clad in animal skins and baring more flesh than was usual during tea-time viewing, it was clear – as Hinchcliffe freely admits – that uppermost in his mind was that *Doctor Who* aired on BBC1 directly after the football. As Hinchcliffe says, on *The Robots of Death* DVD commentary: "[Leela] was certainly very popular with the dads."

But, as with most creative ventures, the story behind the character's creation was more nuanced. Leela's genesis lay, not in a cynical ploy to boost viewing figures among adult men, but – according to Hinchcliffe – in a conversation he had with a young girl who lived next door. Asking her which character she most identified with, the girl answered, "The Doctor" rather than, as Hinchcliffe had expected, Sarah. Inspired to rectify this, Hinchcliffe decided to make the next female companion more proactive.

At the same time, Robert Holmes was planning to set a story in Victorian London, and came up with the idea of a young, 19th century woman in the mould of Eliza Doolittle from *Pygmalion*, feisty but in need of education, with the Doctor taking on the Professor Higgins role. The proof of this idea would have been in its execution but, in basic form, it seems somewhat flawed – not only because its dynamic risked falling very easily into sexism, but because it was too direct a lift from Bernard Shaw's play.

Happily, the drama gods intervened and Holmes's workload meant he had to postpone his Victorian script (it was re-purposed to end the season as *The Talons of Weng-Chiang*) and so Hinchcliffe took the kernel of Holmes's idea to writer Chris Boucher, and it was he who transposed the Eliza Doolittle template onto Leela. The result – a primitive savage in the far future who's descended from the survivors of a starship crash – is brilliant science-fiction. And perfect *Doctor Who*.

In Leela, wherever the TARDIS took us, we had a constant reminder of the show's unique format. We always had the Doctor, of course, to reminiscence about meeting Lord Nelson or Shakespeare, or to darkly equate the human race to a virus, but he almost always knew everything about everywhere he visited; with Leela, even Earth became an alien world. "Doctor – blue guards!" she cried in *The Talons of Weng-Chiang*, when the local bobbies came calling.

In addition, Leela's ignorance wasn't stupidity but lack of education. When the Doctor explained the science to her, it didn't feel patronising as it so often had before. Furthermore, through Leela's uniquely innocent lack of guile we're given the opportunity to look at everything through a slightly different lens. See, for instance, how her presence in *The Robots of Death* added colour that few other companions could; not only was her phrase for the Vocs – "mechanical men" – wonderfully evocative, but her naïvely questioning why the people of Kaldor City would want robots labouring for them – let alone why they would want machines to appear and behave like humans – worked as a commentary on the story that, coming as it did naturally from Leela as a character, felt all the more chilling.

Leela's unique perspective was a driver for humour, too, as her violent threats – "Silence! You

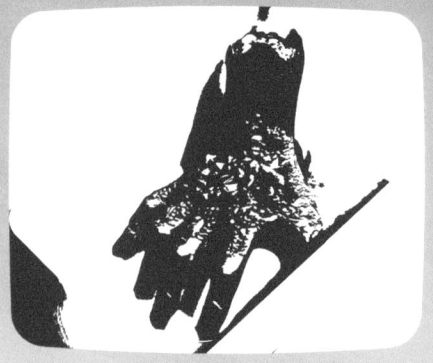  

will do as the Doctor instructs, or I will cut out your heart" – or earnestly naïve reactions to remarkable events all added an extra layer to scenes. Most of all, Leela was fantastic at undercutting the Doctor's pomposity and, by extension, that of the show. In particular, her bewilderment in the face of what we – the audience – knew to be preposterous pseudo science enabled the writers to wryly bring us in on the joke. The epitome of this function of Leela's character was surely when the Doctor tried explaining the TARDIS' dimensional transcendental technology, using two boxes, one larger than the other. When the Doctor moved the smaller one closer, so it appeared bigger, Leela sensibly insisted that the one further away remained the larger, to which the Doctor replied: "If you could keep that exactly that distance away and have it here, the large one would fit inside the small one."

And Leela's response? "That's silly."

It's a perfect little scene that encapsulates much that's brilliant about Leela. That Louise Jameson cites this as her favourite moment indicates that she understands exactly what it was that made Leela work. And, lest we forget – as with Elisabeth Sladen and Sarah Jane Smith – it is the actress behind such a character who truly makes them come to life. With Jameson as Leela, the negative inspiration for her creation – appealing to the dads – fell into the background and our overriding impression of Leela derives from Hinchcliffe's infinitely more laudable goal: to create a strong female character who'd appeal to his young neighbour and millions of girls just like her. That he succeeded – due in no small part to Jameson, Boucher and Holmes – is not in doubt, but there remains, as with Sarah Jane's emancipation, an element of chance at play. There's no escaping the fact that Leela was born from some retrograde impulses on the production team's part; aside from the skimpy outfit, there's the fact that the initial conception for Leela was that her flesh should be darkened. This may very well stem from the scenario in *The Face of Evil* – Leela's tribe lived in a jungle on a hot planet – but it hints all the same at an unconscious equation of the colonial notion of the "savage" with dark skin.

Thankfully the make-up tests of Leela's intended appearance were less than satisfactory, so Leela was spared the same opprobrium that – quite rightly – the 'yellow-face' of *The Talons of Weng-Chiang* later elicited. That this is accidental rather than deliberate reinforces once again the arbitrary nature of productions such as these. Chance plays a large part in television drama, and there is much that is beyond the production team's control. This includes, to some extent, the times in which a piece is made. Not necessarily to forgive Hinchcliffe and co's apparent latent sexism and racial insensitivity, but to understand the society which instilled it in him, look no further than his predecessor Barry Letts and his casting of white Australian actor Kevin Lindsay to play seemingly-Tibetan monk Cho-Je in Jon Pertwee's final story, *Planet of the Spiders*.

What really counts in television – as in life – is intention. Hinchcliffe, above all, had a clear idea for the direction he wanted the show to go in: solid adventure stories with an emphasis on strong characterisation. The strength of

Hinchcliffe's vision and his ability to deliver it – even in the tumultuous world of BBC programme-making – resulted in one of the finest eras of *Doctor Who*. It makes the fact that, while shooting on *The Talons of Weng-Chiang* was coming to an end, Hinchcliffe was informed he'd be moving on – by his replacement, Graham Williams – even more egregious.

This represented a shamefully missed opportunity for the show (imagine another season or two with Hinchcliffe at the helm!), no less so than with regards to Leela. The delicate character development and plans for a gentle, *Pygmalion*-style education story arc fell by the wayside. Of course, Leela in the Graham Williams era was still captivating, but thanks more often than not to Jameson's performance than the writing. Because of Jameson, Leela, forged as she was by a collision of Hinchcliffe and Holmes's overt, albeit mild, contemporary sexism and covert – nigh on subconscious – feminism, was never quite reduced to the screaming damsel, but her vitality was damped down. The way she exited the show says it all: married off to Andred, a character with whom we're expected to believe she's fallen in love – despite the fact they'd barely shared any screen time.

It wouldn't have happened under Hinchcliffe, which brings us back – by way of comparison – to *The Hand of Fear*, and Sarah's exit. When Sladen confirmed to Hinchcliffe that she thought it was time for Sarah to leave, the producer ensured that she featured heavily in her final adventure. He did this not out of any sense of feminism – though it was a feminist act – but because it was what the story demanded.

Thus it turns out, Bob Baker and Dave Martin gave Sarah a fantastic last story. She's possessed by Eldrad – something Sladen conveyed with chilling brilliance – and had some lovely moments of connection with the female Eldrad. Finally, she's the one who decided she wanted to leave the TARDIS and duly went off to pack a bag. Returning to the console room, she discovered the Doctor had been instructed by the Time Lords to return to Gallifrey and Sarah couldn't go as humans weren't permitted (that this rule is so easily broken in *The Invasion of Time* in the next season is yet another mark against Leela's exit). With Sarah now having second thoughts about leaving, Sladen's subtle portrayal of this internal conflict was quietly moving.

This being television drama, there are many reasons why this small scene works so well, but behind it all is Hinchcliffe who, as producer, provided the optimal conditions in which his team could fashion outstanding stories. He did this not by analysing the times in which he was living, but simply by moving forward with one clear-eyed purpose: to keep story at the heart of *Doctor Who*. Placed into the crucible of the show's inherent dichotomy – the struggle between unchanging narrative traditions and a society forever evolving – from this one simple dictum all else followed.

Including, of course, the characters, some of which were amongst British television's most memorable and beloved fictional creations. And, purely incidentally – in what may be a lesson to all well-meaning, middle class, male liberals – the best of them happened to be women.

Philip chats about the NVLA

"When I started on *Doctor Who*, I hadn't produced any serious drama. I hadn't been involved in any real, what shall I say, powerful acting, really. This meant I didn't have the ability to predict how, in the hands of a good actor, a scene could play. When I read a scene on the page, I couldn't always predict how it would play on screen. For instance there was a sequence in *The Ark in Space* I was a bit concerned about it when I saw it in the script. But when I saw Kenton Moore giving it his all on the recording, it became a very highly charged scene; he's asking the woman he loves to kill him because that's better than becoming a Wirrn. Well, that's a very adult drama situation for children to be exposed to. Usually you got around this by not dwelling on it for too long and the hero would make a quick quip or whatever – but we didn't have our hero there, the scene wasn't with the Doctor. This was a learning experience for me about the power generated by good performance, and it put me on guard, really, about things that were too strong to stomach by the younger audience members.

We had a similar situation in *The Brain of Morbius*, when the manservant was shot in the stomach with a standard modern gun, not a science-fiction one. Chris Barry used a blood bag exploding in that, which was very unusual for *Doctor Who*. We had Mary Whitehouse and her National Viewers' and Listeners' Association plaguing the BBC a lot around this time, and she personally had a particular issue with *Doctor Who* – I think Barry Letts mentioned that they'd had a couple of run-ins. Most of her complaints were confusing violence with the sort of 'monstrous' stuff. However, that gunshot was an act of violence. It's the only violent thing I can recall, quite frankly. You might say holding the Doctor under the water in *The Deadly Assassin* was violence, and I suppose it is but only up to a point. The rest of the stuff she complained about was just more about monsters and nasty faces and things like that. We sailed close to the edge, but that's good drama. If there were no scares, nothing at all, *Doctor Who* just wouldn't work.

Another story she objected to was *The Seeds of Doom*, which I liked a lot. Robert Banks Stewart wasn't really a traditional *Doctor Who* writer. We were importing a writer who had lots of skills but whose motifs and story proclivities weren't naturally the same as ours. The well-worked out plot and nice atmosphere and funny old ladies were the sort of filigree work he had to lay over a traditional *Doctor Who* monster story, so we were shoehorning him into our show. Bob Holmes and I thought this was exactly right though, because we were in danger of becoming too 'samey', not in individual stories but in the outlook of the writers we had. Robert Banks Stewart came in both here and with the Loch Ness story to shake the other writers up a bit. Well, I hope that's what they felt. In a way, *The Seeds of Doom* is another take on *Quatermass*, very much in the British science-fiction tradition, if there *is* such a thing as a British science-fiction tradition. That said, I recall that the dark bits that Mary Whitehouse didn't like, people being minced up in a giant machine and stuff like that, were suggested by Bob Holmes and myself. I can't imagine that Robert Banks Stewart would ever have come up with that left to his own devices. I think he was pushed by Bob Holmes to make things darker. Take that scene where the butler takes the raw meat supper to the poor soul who's half a tree by then …

One place where Banks Stewart's writing was more prevalent than Holmes was the creation of the old painter lady, Amelia Ducat as a light-hearted counterpoint to the darker elements. That's the kind of eccentric character Bob Banks Stewart loved writing, whereas if Bob Holmes had been writing the story alone, we'd have had far more people turning into plants and being chucked into giant shredding machines.

★ ★ ★ ★

No one at the BBC was making a big deal about Mary Whitehouse, at least not to me; nobody came along and said, "What are you doing? What's going on? We've had Mary Whitehouse on the phone." However, thinking about my final season, there might have been an accumulating sense of unease, somewhere in the upper echelons but as we were delivering dazzling ratings for a Saturday night, the BBC1 controllers weren't too fussed, and said they could keep Mary Whitehouse at bay, and we should carry on."

> Throug...
> Lord...
> of peace a... otect...
> from...d th... sser
> civilisat...ns by
>
> ... Suddenly
> ...e Lords
> ...gerous
> ...istory ...

the DEADLY ASSASSIN

USING THE SHOW'S HERITAGE
MATTHEW TOFFOLO

You weak fool! You craven-hearted, spineless poltroon. You failed me ...

"I'VE received the call, and as a Time Lord I must obey" – this was the hook from *The Hand of Fear* into *The Deadly Assassin* that promised viewers they were about to get a new look at the Doctor's homeworld the following Saturday. It is hard to imagine how exciting the prospect of visiting Gallifrey was for fans at the time – I first watched it on VHS in the early Nineties as a toddler, and alas the significance of this story was lost on me until years later. It has remained a firm favourite of mine ever since, so much so that I was shocked to discover it received some heavy criticism at the time. What makes the story and the Hinchcliffe era so significant is not just its impact on the series, such as securing the look and culture of Time Lord society, but the way in which it reinvents and subverts the heritage of *Doctor Who* up to that point. In fact, I would argue it is partly that which makes the Philip Hinchcliffe era so successful: the way in which it subverts our expectations – not just with *Doctor Who*'s heritage, but also with the wider influence of literature and film.

Before their return in *The Deadly Assassin*, the Time Lords are presented as omnipotent figures. In their first appearance, in *The War Games*, they are able to manipulate time itself, erase the memories of the Doctor's companions, and force him to regenerate. Later, they can control the Doctor's TARDIS by crippling it or hijacking it for their own purposes (*Colony in Space)*, and even break the laws of time by having the Doctor meet his earlier selves (*The Three Doctors*). In *Genesis of the Daleks,* from the start of Hinchcliffe's era, the Time Lords are shown to appear at will and are able to transport the Doctor and his companions across space and time. Even the physical appearance of John Franklyn-Robbins as the Time Lord who gives the Doctor his mission, adorned in his high collar black robe amongst the swirling mists of Skaro, gives the impression of a wizard with limitless power. It is also noteworthy that, while James Acheson was not behind the costume design for *Genesis of the Daleks*, Barbara Kidd almost preempts his own iconic design for the Time Lords by incorporating a similar high collar and skullcap like hood. It gives Franklyn-Robbins a sinister Grim Reaper like quality, as if the Time Lords are figures to be feared and not taken lightly, which is particularly apt given that the task the Time Lords have set is that of committing genocide.

With this in mind, fans of the series may have been surprised when tuning in for *The Deadly Assassin*, if they expected this characterisation to continue. Under writer Robert Holmes, any sense of the Time Lords's past omnipotence is stripped away, as they are presented as far more fallible and, arguably, more relatable characters. This is our first example of the story subverting our expectations from what had come before. Holmes presents the Time Lords as a dusty, antiquated race, steeped in tradition and ceremony. Their powers are now limited, in as much as they require the use of a security force in the form of the Chancellery Guards, and are armed with traditional science-fiction laser guns. This was one of several elements of the story that incensed Jan Vincent-Rudzki (co-founder of the *Doctor Who* Appreciation Society), who famously argued against the apparent impotence of the Time Lords in *TARDIS Magazine* Vol 2 Issue 1. Referencing this and further alterations to the Time Lords from previous stories, he mockingly refers to the serial as the "Deadly Continuity". Here the Time Lords are concerned with meaningless bureaucracy: the Doctor has decided to park his

TARDIS on the Gallifreyan equivalent of double yellow lines, whereupon the Castellan informs Hildred to "impound the machine" – like some sort of intergalactic traffic warden towing away a mis-parked car. The Chancellery Guards themselves are a bit hopeless, like most guards in *Doctor Who*, fooled by a coat and hat hung on the back of a chair in a dimly-lit, smoky room.

These examples stress the fact that the Time Lords have, to some extent, become an indolent race, one so sure of their age-old-power that they no longer have the necessity to show it. During the Presidential resignation ceremony, the fanciful robes and Dudley Simpson's organ music harken back to the powerful figures of *The War Games*, and it is easy to imagine that the two representations are consistent with each other. However, what *The Deadly Assassin* does so cleverly, is pull back the curtain to show that this pomp and circumstance is merely window dressing. In fact, we see this in the literal sense when the Doctor pulls back the curtain on two elderly Time Lords fussing about trying to get into their robes. While it is a comical scene, it makes an important point that the Time Lords are not what they seem and equally makes them more relatable. They can get a bit doddery, as we had already seen at times with the First Doctor, and much like the Doctor, they are fallible. Later, we notice it in the way that they have forgotten the true nature, and in fact the very existence, of the Eye of Harmony. Even aspects of their Matrix technology, which to them seems state-of-the-art, is snubbed by the Doctor as being primitive compared to other worlds. It further exemplifies that, in the case of both the Doctor and the Master, they have become wiser and more capable than their stay-at-home leaders through their experiences in the wider universe.

The most significant change comes in the lack of a companion in this story. After Elisabeth Sladen departed the series, it has been suggested that Tom Baker believed he did not require a replacement. Considering that the companion role was a part of the make-up of *Doctor Who* from the start, this was a bold claim. Hinchcliffe himself argued against it, noting that a companion is necessary to "split the plots into different routes … and that [Tom] needed someone to talk to". Robert Holmes rose to the challenge to prove Tom wrong, and in the process wrote one of the most successful serials in the show's history. Part of the reason why it works so well is that it raises the stakes because the Doctor is isolated by not having the familiar comfort of his best friend present. A side-effect of this however, is that there is a distinct lack of women in this serial (with the exception of Helen Blatch as the voice of a computer, who incidentally goes uncredited on-screen). Looking back from a 21st century perspective, where diversity plays such a key component in television production in order to paint an accurate and believable picture of society, it seems mad that there is not a single female face on Gallifrey, and narratively it doesn't make an awful lot of sense either. While the lack of Time Ladies is consistent with the previous appearances of the Time Lords, at the very least it does make you wonder how Time Tots are made? It would not be until *The Invasion of Time* that we would meet our first Time Lady, and unfortunately her role is initially reduced to that of the Gallifreyan equivalent of a switchboard operator.

While the lack of companion only lasted for one story, it was not the only change to the female companion role Hinchcliffe would make. The following story, *The Face of Evil*, introduces the noble savage, Leela, who was a direct attempt to tackle the types of companions previously seen in the series. Hinchcliffe likened them to the damsels of silent films such as *The Perils of Pauline,* and was keen to have a female lead that could hold her own in moments of danger, sometimes using deadly force, much to the Doctor's disapproval. The intention to give the character an arc in which she would develop from a person of pure instinct to one more contemplative and considered, due to the Doctor's influence in a *Pygmalion*-like fashion, was a marked departure from the companion role. That is not to say previous companions did not develop over the course of their time on the programme, but here a decision was made during her creation that there was a goal for her development, something that would continue with several companions post the Hinchcliffe era.

It was not only the Doctor's allies that changed; the Master's return marks a departure from his last appearance in *The Frontier in Space*. Having been played with such acclaim by Roger Delgado, the choice to recast the Master could not have been a decision taken lightly. Instead, Hinchcliffe and Holmes go in a significantly different direction with the character. If audiences were anticipating a Master along the lines of Delgado, who was urbane and refined, they were in for a shock when the new Master was revealed as a decaying husk. Here the Master finds his influence in Gothic horror, like so much of this period of the show. He is now a monstrous figure skulking in the shadows, akin to the titular *The Phantom of the Opera*. The character's motivations are also different, and while he still wants dominion over the universe his main goal at this point is survival. The Master here seems more ruthless and deranged than ever, possibly because he no longer has the handsome appearance of Roger Delgado to hide behind, and so his raw villainy is exposed as are his wounds. This motivation would continue beyond the Hinchcliffe era both in the classic series, *The TV Movie*, and the modern series, becoming an integral aspect of the Master's character. Hinchcliffe explained that this "darker take" on the Master was a deliberate attempt to move away from a character that he saw as something of a pantomime villain: "There was no way I wanted that [...] It's got to be very different and it's got to work on this deeper level". This perfectly sums up his use of heritage characters and storylines in his *Doctor Who* – in order to keep these things fresh and new they must have a different take on them, or a total redesign, as with the Master.

However, it would be unfair to say that it was all change with *The Deadly Assassin*. The Doctor's school master, Borusa, played by Angus MacKay, infuses the role with a similar pomposity that Holmes had written into the Time Lord played by David Garth five years earlier in *Terror of the Autons*. Even the casting of Bernard Horsfall as Chancellor Goth seems to be a callback, on director David Maloney's part, to having been previously cast, again by Maloney, as one of the Time Lord judges in *The War Games* back in 1969. On the surface, Horsfall retains the same lofty performance as before, but that only better hides his corrupt machinations in his servitude to the Master. Holmes himself admitted that this was part of a wider plan to build on what had already gone before with the Time Lords, citing that there had been so many "galactic lunatics" born from their society that it "didn't square with the perceived notion that the Time Lords were a bunch of omnipotent do-gooders". This concept follows the real-world adage of Lord Acton, that absolute power corrupts absolutely, and when a race is as mythically powerful as the Time Lords it makes sense that some of them would go a bit bonkers. And doesn't that make them more interesting? Who wants to see a planet filled with old goody two-shoes? It also further strengthens the idea as to why the Doctor had to get away from Gallifrey. He did not want to end up like one of them and, as we see in 21st century stories like *The Waters of Mars* and *Hell Bent*, even the Doctor is susceptible to the temptation of power. He is only a Time Lord after all.

The story also introduces the CIA, the Celestial Intervention Agency, put in place to handle the Time Lords's dirty work, contravening their strict rule of not interfering in the affairs of other species. Again, this story simply puts a name to the powers who had previously been pulling the Doctor's strings during the Pertwee era, and within the Hinchcliffe era's own *The Brain of Morbius*. Unfortunately, this fell flat with Seventies nascent *Doctor Who* fandom, and it seems they perhaps missed the point of the

story and indeed Hinchcliffe's era as a whole. The CIA also being an acronym used on Earth is a not-so-subtle wink at the story's inspiration of political thrillers, in particular, *The Manchurian Candidate*. It strengthens the conversation the show is having with its audience by saying "you've seen these things before, well here is our take on it". It is no different to the use of Condo, the hunchbacked manservant, and his mad scientist boss in *The Brain of Morbius*, who are building a monster in a castle on a dark and stormy night. In that case the audience knows *Doctor Who* is doing *Frankenstein*, and that's part of the fun. These stories are not simply pastiches of other works, they take the recognisable elements and turn them into something different and distinctly *Doctor Who* – Egyptian mummies are robots, the Loch Ness monster is a cybernetic dinosaur and the mad scientist's monster is another of those megalomaniacal Time Lords that Robert Holmes mentioned earlier. *Doctor Who* as a series has always been a reflection of the time in which it is made, playing on what is bubbling away in the current zeitgeist, and, in the case of the mid-Seventies, Victoriana and Hammer Horror was amongst them. All of which find themselves as part of the make-up of Hinchcliffe's *Doctor Who*.

It is not just *The Deadly Assassin* that subverts our expectations of *Doctor Who*'s heritage at this point in the show's history. *Genesis of the Daleks* puts a new spin on the previously understood history of a *Doctor Who* icon: the Daleks. Here, they gain a new origin that keeps elements of what has gone before – a war between the Thals and the Dals that led to the mutation of both species with the Dals becoming the Daleks – but under Hinchcliffe the Dals become the Kaleds and the creation of the Daleks is the solution to winning the never ending war with the Thals. Nazi imagery is adapted into the look of their ancestors, with the Kaleds adorned in black SS-style uniforms and insignia. Of course, it is the inclusion of Davros, the creator of the Daleks, that really adds to the their established history. Perhaps because the characterisation of the Daleks and the world surrounding them was relatively consistent with what had been seen before, it has not come under the same scrutiny as *The Deadly Assassin* over the years. So popular was Davros that he has returned throughout the classic and modern series, with the Kaled war becoming a permanent fixture of *Doctor Who* lore. In that same season, the TARDIS, the most consistent piece of iconography from the programme, all but disappears until the closing moments of the final story, *Revenge of the Cybermen*. While the TARDIS normally acts as the gateway to the wonderful adventures the Doctor and his friends find themselves on, here it is reimagined as the ultimate prize of those adventures, as the TARDIS crew go on a quest to retrieve it. Even UNIT, a mainstay of the programme since the start of the Jon Pertwee era, is fizzled out so that the series can return to its roots as nomadic travels in space and time. When UNIT do appear however, they are subject to alien invasions by body-snatchers and doppelgangers (*Terror of the Zygons* and *The Android Invasion*). To have familiar faces like Harry Sullivan and RSM Benton suddenly turn threatening subverts the cosy familiarity of the UNIT set-up.

Finally, it is important to note the legacy that *The Deadly Assassin,* and other stories from this period, has had on the future of the series. Rassilon, architect of the Time Lords, was first mentioned here and became a key part of the Time Lord mythology going forwards, continually referenced throughout the classic series before appearing in *The Five Doctors,* as well as appearing in the modern series as a villain on a number of occasions. Borusa would continue to appear before turning evil and meeting his end in *The Five Doctors*, very much following Holmes's suggestion that Time Lords go a little mad. Perhaps that is the curse of living for so long? The iconic look of the Time Lord headdresses and robes, designed by James Acheson, has remained relatively untouched since their debut in *The Deadly Assassin*. While these original costumes would be recycled throughout the rest of the classic run, they would return with embellishments and new colour schemes under Russell T Davies, Steven Moffat and Chris Chibnall. Likewise, the Chancellery Guards and the Castellan would return, with the ceremonial armour being revamped but retaining their original hues in *The Day of the Doctor* and *Hell Bent*. Even the Time Lord motif, designed by Roger Murray-Leach (originally for the Vogan society seen in *Revenge of the Cybermen*), found its way back to Gallifrey under each of the modern showrunners. So popular was its design that it was plastered all over the cathedral-like TARDIS of *The TV Movie,* giving it an almost venerated quasi-religious quality, adorning buttresses, staffs, and the Eye of Harmony (which again, debuted in *The Deadly Assassin*, albeit under different circumstances). Even Rassilon's head gets an unnamed cameo sculpted on the top of a staff. These elements have become so iconic and a part of the recognisable fabric of *Doctor Who*, that during the coronation of King Charles III in 2023, *Doctor Who* fans on Twitter likened the event and its ceremonial pomp-and-circumstance, to that seen on Gallifrey.

While *The Deadly Assassin* might have caused an uproar with fans at the time, another aspect of the Hinchcliffe era has found itself back in the fray of fan conversation. During *The Brain of Morbius* it is suggested that the Doctor had several regenerations before the first televised Doctor, William Hartnell, through a series of faces appearing in a mind-bending contest against the villainous Time Lord, Morbius. This was a conscious decision by Hinchcliffe and Holmes to add further mystique to the Doctor's character, their own faces being among those of the BBC production staff chosen to represent these unseen incarnations. However, when *The Deadly Assassin* explained that Time Lords could only regenerate twelve times (giving them thirteen lives), the suggestion of previously unseen incarnations was all but dismissed by fans, who instead attributed the faces to Morbius. Fast-forward to 2020, and showrunner Chris Chibnall re-introduces the idea of the Doctor having had regenerations pre-William Hartnell, and among the faces chosen to represent this are those previously shown in *The Brain of Morbius*. Likewise, the Sisterhood of Karn and the Elixir of Life also found themselves playing a significant part in the series under Steven Moffat, when both were used to usher in the regeneration of Paul McGann's Eighth Doctor into John Hurt's War Doctor. The reaction from fans to the 'Timeless Doctors' was a mixture of intrigue and controversy. It goes to show how even the seemingly forgotten elements of the Hinchcliffe era continue to find new life forty years later.

It is clear that the Hinchcliffe/Holmes team's ability to reimagine aspects of *Doctor Who*'s history not only kept the storytelling fresh but was also influential on the series writers and designers that followed. It is hard to think of the Time Lords today without linking it back to the stories told under Philip Hinchcliffe's time as producer. This influence has not been without its detractors, such as that famously put forward by Jan Vincent-Rudzki in that *TARDIS Magazine* review. But let us return to his argument that the Time Lords featured in *The Deadly Assassin* are "petty, squabbling, feeble-minded, doddering old fools", almost to the point that they behave just like humans. This characterisation has remained fairly consistent since, and arguably it works far better than the lofty, untouchable monoliths introduced in *The War Games*. While those Time Lords certainly have their place, and continued to do so under Russell T Davies's introduction of the Time War, the humanised, relatable Time Lords of *The Deadly Assassin* also help us to better understand the Doctor himself. In their petty squabbling we can equate this to real world politicians, the adornments of robes and trinkets remind us of the superficial lavishness of the British Royal Family or the Church. These are exactly the aspects of the society that motivated the Doctor to run away and start his adventures in the first place, and although the Doctor tries to avoid being one of this elitist race, we do see elements of their characteristics reflected in him. For all of their good points, in a number of regenerations, the Doctor has been shown to be petty, prone to squabbling, and even a little doddery. So even if the apple didn't necessarily fall far from the tree, it is important that the Time Lords are always there to remind us of what it is that the Doctor is trying to get away from.

Philip chats about being a producer in television drama

PHILIP CHATS ABOUT BEING A PRODUCER IN TELEVISION DRAMA

"Television became mainstream in the 1970s, nearly everyone had a set in their living room, which hadn't been the case ten years earlier. I wouldn't describe it as a renaissance, but I think it was just a natural evolution as television was getting up to date – there had already been a lot of really good programmes in the Sixties, many of which were truly ground-breaking. It was a bit of a golden era when I joined *Doctor Who* and I was feeling that zeitgeist. Before I landed the job at the BBC, I felt trapped in ATV, which was a trailblazer with big Light Entertainment shows but for somebody who wanted to do drama, it wasn't great. Whereas at the BBC, you felt people were pushing the envelope, things were moving forward and you could do more and be a bit more daring. Something in the air. There was this feeling of being in an industry that was forward-looking and willing to try new things. There was always something happening in British television when I joined the BBC – we didn't always know what, but it was exciting to be swept along with it.

* * * *

As a drama producer, your mind is always on the budgets – no matter what you and the other creative people do, my job was to be the person who had to remind everyone about the numbers. I think I was quite good at striking that balance, so everyone felt they were making a good show, without having people knocking on my door from upstairs, telling me I'd overspent. I believe recently Louise Jameson said something about that in an interview she did for *Radio Times*. She said she remembers me back in 1977, being young, determined and visionary. I quite like that. But then she said something that threw me. She said, "I think the thing about Phillip is that he's not a compromiser. He has an incredibly clear vision, and he just keeps whittling away until that vision is realised." Then she goes on to add that I never had an eye on the budget like the other producers did. Well, I did of course although we did go over slightly budget on *The Talons of Weng-Chiang*. But I really appreciated "He has an incredibly clear vision, and he just keeps whittling away until that vision is realised." That's a good way of explaining what a drama producer does. With people like Bob, Tom and Louise and the directors and the crew, it was my job to command their respect and cooperation because they wanted to help it to happen as much as I did. Although I was young, I think if you're confident and you truly know what you want, you find a way to get people to buy into your vision and still bring their own thing to it. I never considered myself as very charismatic or anything like that, it's not my in my nature, although maybe there was a sort of confidence and sense of fun and a bit of bravura. Perhaps that gave *them* confidence too."

the FACE of EVIL

REVEALING THE DANGERS OF ORTHODOXY

TREY KORTE

When it woke, it had a complete personality. Mine – it thought I was itself. Then it began to develop another separate self, its own self. And that's when it started to go mad.

THE Evil One eats babies – or at least that's what the Tribe of the Sevateem believe about the Evil One (aka the Doctor). Whether this belief stems from the Doctor eating Jelly Babies on his prior visit to the Mordee expedition or is just completely invented propaganda from Xoanon isn't clear. But while this early scene in *The Face of Evil* is played mainly for laughs when the Doctor offers his new friend Leela a Jelly Baby, it hints at something much darker – the historical need of the establishment to discredit minority groups and independent thinkers, painting them as a threat to children in the most visceral and horrific way. From the antisemitic blood libel which has throughout history falsely accused Jewish people of murdering children for ritualistic purposes to the current moral panic about Drag Queen Story Hours to the QAnon belief that Hillary Clinton and other American Democrats were operating a child trafficking operation from a Washington DC pizza parlour, exploiting parents' primal fears about their children's welfare and opening up centuries-old prejudices in the process has been a favourite tool of ideologically-driven bigots and fearmongers throughout history. So, yes, of course Neeva and the religion of the Sevateem would teach that "the Evil One eats babies."

There's a pertinent coincidence here. While *The Face of Evil* was first being broadcast in the UK in January of 1977, during that same month, the US state of Florida passed an ordinance that protected LGBT people from employment and housing discrimination; this spawned an evangelical Christian movement called Save Our Children – the first organised political movement opposing gay and lesbian rights post-Stonewall – because American Christian groups were fearful that LGBT teachers would *not* be fired for being LGBT and would, thus, have "access" to children. Anita Bryant, an orange juice spokeswoman and former Miss America, became the public face of this movement which set into motion the culture wars involving government-funded schools, religious freedom, and concerns about "secular humanism" indoctrinating the nation's schoolchildren. Today's current controversies related to LGBT representation in American education can, in many ways, be traced back to this moment in January 1977 just when *The Face of Evil* was exposing how religious orthodoxy is threatened by education; and where the hero of the story teaches a young woman to firmly reject the faith and society in which she has been raised.

Because that's just what happens in *The Face of Evil*; the Doctor encourages the already doubtful Leela to question her upbringing further, mocking her whole society's belief system. The introduction of Leela as a companion allows the series to interrogate religious upbringing and belief systems in a way that wouldn't have been socially feasible before, at least not with any Earth-based companion with a religion viewers might actually practise.

With the exception of Susan, all the Doctor's previous companions originated from Earth. The majority of them were from 20th century England, where you'd expect at least one of them to be standard Church of England. Yet no companion's religious lives or upbringing are ever mentioned so we can only speculate how their adventures with the Doctor might have impacted their faith or religious belief had they been particularly devout. One would imagine that irrefutable proof of alien life would challenge a religious person's belief that humans are God's special creations, made in His image. Certainly a fundamentalist who believes in Young Earth Creationism would most likely experience a crisis of sorts were the Doctor to take them back to the Cretaceous Age. Having been raised in an evangelical household, I was always curious how travelling with the Doctor would affect someone's religious beliefs – but the series always steered well clear of companions expressing any religious belief or background.

That is, until Leela arrives.

And Leela provided me – and perhaps many others – an example of how to live both truthfully to your own independent beliefs whilst respecting and honouring your own heritage. Because I was raised to be a proud American man by my army officer father, encouraged to be a dutiful Lutheran boy by my highly religious mother, and groomed to be a flag-waving, piously patriotic soldier in the struggle against 'secular humanism' by my faith-based schooling, I understand firsthand how difficult it is to break through those years of social conditioning. I knew the litanies, I could cite the stories, and I could offer the rehearsed explanations for why my faith was the right one and all others were false. But like Leela, I harboured doubts. I remember vividly watching her defiant claim of "There is no Xoanon" and wishing I could have a similar moment in my religious education classes – but I also knew that I'd be subjected to our version of the Test of the Horda.

The admirable thing about Leela is that she manages to formulate her own ideas and her own beliefs while still being terribly proud of her tribal origins. Whether it's dispensing proverbs while bandaging Toos on Storm Mine 4 or still insisting on a pouch of Janis thorns for the Doctor's inauguration, Leela remains a proud member of the Sevateem and its traditions. Similarly, while I may reject the beliefs of my parents's religion or politics, I can still be proud of my American heritage and my family's military service. Leela's example helped me to reconcile these different forces in my own religious upbringing, and I'd like to think other fans have been helped similarly.

Leela's journey from superstitious savage to independent-thinking woman who thinks "it is better to believe in science" speaks to the Doctor being the catalyst for change as he embarks on educating Leela. *The Face of Evil* then, allows the series under Philip Hinchcliffe to create a manifesto of sorts regarding faith, religion, and belief which we can then see permeates his tenure as producer. While the series at this point might not be 'educational' in the didactic "Hey kids, let's learn about Marco Polo and condensation!" style of the Sixties episodes, its instructive ethos is front and centre, putting it on a direct collision course with religious orthodoxy. Perhaps this reveals why religious groups are so often threatened, not only by schools and education, but family entertainment like *Doctor Who*.

But first, we must ask "What is education? And how is *Doctor Who* educational in this era?" As a high school English teacher, I often hear that education is simply about job training or career preparation. However in my discipline, education is often about teaching people to question – as the Doctor says in *The Face of Evil*, "answers

  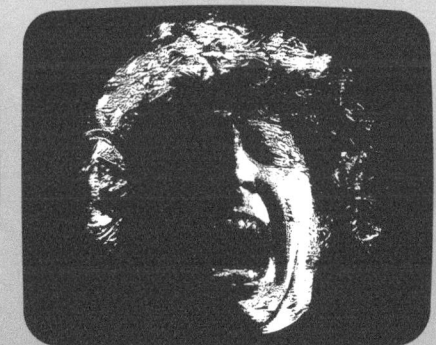

are easy, it's asking the right questions that is hard". Classic liberal arts education is all about introducing doubt into established beliefs and then proving claims with evidence and reasoning. In fact, when teaching my students, I have shown the moment from *The Face of Evil* where the Doctor claims "The very powerful and very stupid have one thing in common; they don't alter their view to fit the facts. They alter the facts to fit their views." Classic liberal arts education encourages scholars to avoid this cognitive dissonance, to separate our identities and biases from the pursuit of truth and facts, no matter how threatening or inconvenient. It also reveals the difference between teaching and educating. Leela's tribe have taught her the litanies regarding Xoanon and the Tesh to the point of rote memory – but it is the Doctor who educates her about what it all means. When Leela finally meets Xoanon, she asks him the question most of us would ask of our deity: why?

So, if *The Face of Evil* offers a manifesto of the Hinchcliffe era's ideas about faith, what can we conclude from this? There are several angles worth exploring.

Let's begin with the title. The Doctor's face is the titular face of evil. What does this mean? Consider again, the perspective of a conservative religious fundamentalist whose whole life – whose whole identity – depends on the belief being true. The Doctor then, may indeed be 'evil'. He might not be smiting villages or actively hurting anyone, but he commits the worst sin: he creates doubt and encourages self-belief, which, in turn, threatens the whole religious belief system. He asks the right questions and dismisses pieties as silly nonsense, making true believers look like fools. If we go back to the Garden of Eden story, the serpent, representing the Devil, encourages Eve to eat of the fruit of knowledge of good and evil, therefore allowing her to be like God and decide for herself what is right and wrong. At least that is what I was taught in Bible school and youth group. Satan was never

the horned beast with a pitchfork, but rather the friendly science teacher at your public high school who would convince you that evolution was real and make you doubt the Biblical account of Genesis, and once that was in doubt, then the other stories could be in doubt, and the whole thing could potentially collapse.

Could the Doctor be a fallen angel like Lucifer? We know from *The Deadly Assassin* that he's been cast out of Time Lord society, itself reminiscent of the Vatican with its robes and cardinals and pomp. What was the Doctor's main crime? Interference with the affairs of lesser races. Like Prometheus, he brings others his technical gifts and knowledge, regardless of the consequences and regardless of whether they are ready for it. Unlike Prometheus, however, he is seldom actively punished for this arguable recklessness – but when he is, it's by his own people. If the Doctor is a role model for children watching at home, he is certainly one to encourage them to think for themselves based upon the available evidence rather than blindly accepting whatever their parents and society have taught them – and this is threatening for communities that insist on conforming to an established set of unproven beliefs.

Tom Baker's Doctor does not have time for ceremony and ritual.

From this vantage point, it's easy to see why a religious conservative like Mary Whitehouse had issues with the series. Much like the book bans we see today that are nominally about protecting children from sexually and violently explicit passages, but are much more about shielding children from alternative viewpoints, one wonders if Mrs Whitehouse really had that much concern about the graphic violence of the Hinchcliffe era itself but rather had issue with its overall irreverence towards faith and belief. The Doctor himself encourages the audience, including children, to question their society and that's enough to be a corrupting influence in the eyes of a social traditionalist.

But the Doctor doesn't stop there. Throughout the Hinchcliffe era, religious ritual itself is presented as silly and annoying, even when the situation is quite dangerous. Both Namin's organ music in *Pyramids of Mars* and the Sisterhood's chanting in *The Brain of Morbius* are called out by other characters as being unpleasant to listen to despite the sincere devotion to the performance. It's not just the Doctor who does this either; in *Planet of Evil*, Vishinsky's reaction to Morelli's Morestran Orthodox religion is disdainful when he says "One of those" before switching off the audio to the funeral music. And Neeva's gyrating, hip-shaking ritual involving "cleansing" the Doctor with the ultrabeam accelerator is both hilarious and highly reminiscent of Charismatic churches. The Doctor, though threatened with execution, behaves more amused at the display of silliness and conviction that the true believers exhibit. His interactions with Hieronymus and Federico in *The Masque of Mandragora* also demonstrate his contempt for astrology.

Put simply, Tom Baker's Doctor does not have time for ceremony and ritual. He's impatient with it, he's bemused by it, he makes it seem ridiculous. It's worth remembering Tom Baker had considered a life of similar ritual as a priest before rejecting it, and certainly the irreverence and impatience comes across more through Baker's acting choices rather than the lines themselves. Baker's disillusionment with the Catholic church could certainly inform how he plays these scenes, influencing the Doctor's dismissive attitude towards the theatricality of ritual. This tendency to poke fun at religious ritual, to delight in irreverence, is a radical and refreshing one, especially for American audiences.

In America, but also in many Western societies, we are taught that while we might not share a religious belief, we ought to always *respect* a religious belief if it's sincere, no matter the quality of belief. But during Philip Hinchcliffe's time on *Doctor Who*, an erroneous belief is an erroneous belief, regardless of whether it's a religious or a scientific one and both individuals and societies who blindly follow an erroneous belief inevitably suffer for it.

Take *The Robots of Death*, a story which, at first glance, is steeped in 'hard' science-fiction ideas and there's no ancient evil or supernatural-type power at work. Yet, faith and belief play a major role in the conflict. None of the sandminer crew can even conceive that a robot could harm a human. The reverential way they speak about such rules with phrases like "It is forbidden" suggests religious overtones, almost like a litany of sorts. Poul, a rationalist, logical agent, is the one whose worldview (and sense of self) is most threatened by the possibility of robots killing people. His vehement refusal to entertain the thought initially, first with scoffing humour and then by defensive anger is similar to how many religious individuals react when presented with ideas that challenge their worldview. Therefore when confronted with much more visceral and undeniable proof that the robots are doing the killing, Poul loses his grip on reality – in a very similar vein to Neeva in the previous story when his faith in Xoanon is shattered. On a larger scale, when Leela asks about the implications if the strangler is a robot, the Doctor responds that it's probably the end of that particular civilisation – all because it had become an article of faith that robots can't harm humans. The true threat isn't a handful of reprogrammed robots but rather the *idea* that they can be reprogrammed in the first place. *The Robots of Death* serves as a metaphor then for what can happen to ideological adherents when confronted with worldview-shattering facts – and explains why so many ideologues double down on their slogans and litanies even when confronted with irrefutable evidence.

This actually helps us understand so many of the 'culture wars' waged by religious organisations against "secular humanism". Why do some churches spend so much time on LGBT issues? Or why do some go to great lengths to convince their followers that Earth is young and humans must've walked with dinosaurs? Because fundamentalism doesn't allow for ambiguity. Things that challenge the worldview – a loving and kind gay couple/the fossil record/incriminating evidence – can result in a loss of identity similar to Poul's robophobia, Guy Crayford's realisation that he never lost an eye, or Neeva's fugue state; it could even mean the end of the belief system itself.

This is why it's important to consider the less-remembered part of the Doctor's famous line about the powerful and the stupid altering facts which "can be very uncomfortable if you're one of the facts that needs altering." To just use one of many examples across the globe, LGBT people living in America's Bible Belt are often seen as that: walking facts that need altering in order for fundamentalists to have a more comfortable and secure worldview.

So, the Hinchcliffe era doesn't seem to offer much in the way of patience or respect for fundamentalism of any sort be it religious or secular but even the secular ideologues seem to mimic religiosity. Harrison Chase plays a *Hymn of the Plants* in his 'Green Cathedral' (and again, we have characters commenting on how awful the music is) while Taren Capel behaves like a charismatic cult leader in the presence of his robots. Both of these characters represent another truth that is revealed throughout the Hinchcliffe era: that fundamentalists, epitomised in real life by people such as David Koresh, are often destroyed by either the objects of their worship or their own creations, forged by their beliefs.

Consider this list: Taren Capel is killed by his own reprogrammed robots; Harrison Chase

falls into his own composting machine; Li H'Sen Chang is killed by Greel whom he worshipped, who in turn falls victim to his own misguided Zygma machine; Hieronymous is consumed by the Mandragora energy; Namin is killed by Sutekh's messenger; and, finally, Davros, like many a crazed fanatic, is deemed not worthy enough by the movement he created and is exterminated by his own Daleks.

If, according to the Hinchcliffe stories, ritual is a joke, fundamentalism is misguided, and even secular beliefs can become warped, what *should* we believe in? The Doctor offers this insight to Leela in *The Robots of Death*: "To the rational mind, nothing is inexplicable, only unexplained." This simple statement allows the rationalist to still believe in wondrous things such as dimensional transcendentalism, and, perhaps surprisingly, what we might view as irrational.

Louis Marks's two stories during this period both explore the possibility of the irrational. *Planet of Evil* suggests that the antimatter universe does not obey the laws of our universe whatsoever. The opaque nothingness of the black pool suggests something like Tartarus or the Catholic idea of Hell (eternal separation from God) while the story itself makes tangible the importance of intangible ideas like promises. And the threat in *The Masque of Mandragora* is that superstition and astrology will take control as an alternative to the pursuit of rationalism the Renaissance represented. The message here doesn't seem to be "Science is more real than magic" but rather "Rational scientific inquiry is preferable to magic" since magic and superstition will only enslave us.

All of this may suggest a rather cynical view of faith and belief in Philip Hinchcliffe and Robert Holmes's guardianship of the show. Whilst it may discourage us from worshipping ancient alien gods, misguided ideologies, or war criminal cults, it very much *does* encourage us to place our faith in each other. We are an invincible, indomitable species, and whether it's believing that Sarah can make it through that ventilation shaft, her ability to shoot a small target at an Egyptian rocket site, or Leela's intuition, the Doctor demonstrates that faith in our friends and loved ones is worthwhile. In return, the companions don't lose faith in the Doctor.

Perhaps the ultimate test of faith for the Doctor occurs in *Genesis of the Daleks*, where the Doctor ignores the instructions of the Time Lords on moral grounds, refusing to destroy the Daleks at their infancy, and justifies this with the belief that "Out of their evil must come something good." Whether the Doctor's faith here is justified is a matter of debate, but it's important to note that it is a choice based on his own view of right and wrong, his own alien ethics, not some external set of external laws or orders.

It would be wrong to say that the Hinchcliffe era is blanketly critical of faith and belief, but what it is definitely critical of is dogma, fanaticism, and unthinking ritual. The Doctor tends to be a disruptor of orthodoxy, whether it's Kaled ideals of genetic purity, Mandragora's baleful influence, or Xoanon's experiment in eugenics. He questions, he causes others to question, and therefore he truly educates those around him who are willing to be educated and liberate themselves from orthodoxy. Sutekh famously observes, "Your evil is my good", and if the reverse is true, then, in the face of all these fanatical forces, perhaps the Doctor truly deserves the title of "The Evil One".

Philip chats about his early days in television

PHILIP CHATS ABOUT HIS EARLY DAYS IN TELEVISION

"I owe it all to my wife.

I'd spent six months knocking on doors trying to break into television without success. Associated Television, created by Sir Lew Grade was one of the founding ITV companies, serving the Midlands region, known for Light Entertainment spectaculars but also for a handful of dramas, like *The Power Game* and *Emergency Ward 10* and *Crossroads*. They had studios in Birmingham and Elstree but their HQ was based at Marble Arch in London. Which was where my girlfriend (and wife-to-be) had recently started working as PA to an executive there. She heard that there was a job going in the ATV Script Department. So I applied for it – it wasn't the BBC but it was going to get me towards working with writers and scripts. I was interviewed against strong competitors but got the job nine months after leaving university, so I felt lucky to get it.

Renee Goddard was the Head of the Script Department and quite an extraordinary person. She came across as a perfectly cultured Englishwoman but in fact she was a German actress born in Berlin who had worked with Bertolt Brecht before coming to England during the war and then interned on the Isle of Man before continuing her acting career in films and theatre. She married several times, including to Stuart Hood, a former BBC Controller of Programmes. She followed Stella Richman at ATV who had produced single plays for Lew Grade including the very successful *Love Story* anthology before switching to Director of Programmes at LWT. Both had started out as actresses. Stella was an impressive producer in every respect; Renee worked from instinct and intuition, hardly read anything, but soaked up information by inexplicable osmosis. It was now handy for her to have me at her side! She was a born networker and began to introduce me to the Hampstead/Primrose Hill cultural set. I remember meeting Doris Lessing and Fay Weldon among many others. It was an exciting new world for me …

* * * *

All television companies received unsolicited scripts and somebody has to read those, in the very unlikely chance that maybe a good one would be sent in. Of course, not all unsolicited scripts were from Joe Public; agents who had scripts and ideas from their writers wanted to send them in to somebody, usually the BBC. And if that failed, they sent them to regional ITV companies like ATV. So that was my primary job to start with. I began to form good relationships with agents and got to know very quickly the landscape of television drama. I also became a sort of Man Friday around ATV – if anything came up, they'd give it to me to do – research for little films about the Midlands towns or guest acts for the Sunday religious programmes. I was a terrible researcher, but did it until at some point I decided I really wanted to write. I went to the *Crossroads* producer Reg Watson and Peter Ling the storyliner who was very amused to hear that I'd been reading his stories in the *Eagle* comic when I was a boy. I knew *Crossroads* wasn't as good as *Coronation Street*, but it was what ATV had. I asked Reg if I could have a go. He said yes and I got a contract to write twelve episodes which paid for the deposit on my first flat with my new wife!

Meanwhile, I still wanted to get into production as well. I was commandeered to find some new contemporary children's serials rather than remakes of the classics, so I commissioned one from Carey Harrison, son of Rex Harrison – a thriller called *The Jensen Code*. An actress called Charlotte Mitchell brought in an idea called *The Kids From 47A* about a family of kids whose parents were in hospital, leaving them alone to look after themselves. To script it I found John Kane, Gail Renard and an actress called Lynda Marchal, who was beginning to write and later became Lynda La Plante, the creator of *Prime Suspect*!

Finally, I was spotted by a comedy producer, Shaun O'Riordan and became his full-time script editor working on *Girls About Town* amongst others – I was spectacularly unsuited for this role when I look back as I didn't understand comedy enough at the time (I turned down *On the Buses*!). I preferred the children's stuff because it was much more rooted in drama, although a lot of my drama output years later did have a lot of comedy: *The Gravy Train*, *Bust* and *Private Schulz*, even *The Charmer* in a way. Maybe I do have a comic streak in me after all.

During this period, I was contacted by Betty Willingale, the grand dame of the BBC Script Unit who went on to oversee classic serials like *Tinker, Tailor, Soldier, Spy* with Jonathan Powell. She was a great talent spotter. She was very encouraging to would-be writers, many of whom she helped over the years. On two occasions she put me up for script editing jobs, one with Derrick Sherwin on the *Paul Temple* series and the other with Innes Lloyd on *Thirty-Minute Theatre*. The interviews were my first taste of the BBC and without my knowing at the time, with two previous *Doctor Who* producers!

By now I felt I was anchored in the Script Department and there wasn't a clear ladder for somebody like me to climb up to be a producer at ATV as there would be at the BBC.

About this time at ATV I became involved with a new daytime series called *General Hospital* – basically they were trying to do a remake of *Emergency Ward 10*. Whilst I didn't pick the writers per se, I was involved in assembling teams of potential ones with the producer who was a very nice man called Victor Menzies. I must have said to Victor, "Can I be here in some producing capacity on this?" so I became what they called an associate producer. I sat with Victor as he was interviewing actors. I would go down to rehearsals, watch the blocking and then watch the recording and talk to actors on the floor giving them notes, as the producer, for some of the runs. It was a promising step up, but it didn't lead to anything else. *General Hospital* died a death at some point and I knew this was the end of the road for me at ATV. I asked Richard Wakely at Fraser and Dunlop Agency to become my agent. Good move! Then at Christmas this wonderful offer came to join the BBC and produce *Doctor Who*.

This period of my life was a big learning curve of how the industry worked. I was still learning when I finally joined the BBC – I learnt about the importance of the script; I learnt about the relationships between the key people making the programme, writers, directors, designers. I also learnt about the technical difficulties of making a programme with constraints of time and money."

the ROBOTS of DEATH

BUILDING THE WORLDS

PHILIP NEWMAN

You know, you're a classic example of the inverse ratio between
the size of the mouth and the size of the brain.

IN the 21st century, the ambition and scale of production design for television drama – *Doctor Who* included – has drifted ever closer to that of major feature films. Budgets may still be tiny by comparison, but in an age of unforgiving high-definition technology, greater audience expectations and the more fractured way we consume television across a host of devices and time-shifted viewing patterns, the need to compete visually – and narratively – has become ever-more important.

The way dramas are produced and recorded has also moved on, favouring a more filmic, single-camera-orientated approach, and the key creative departments have expanded in size and scope along with it, adopting movie-style production team structures to cope with the additional workload and levels of sophistication required. Where once sets, costumes, make-up and visual effects were each handled by a solitary designer – often working quite independently of each other in different buildings, supported only by a handful of assistants – the creative heads are now backed by comparatively massive art, wardrobe and effects departments deploying every skillset and specialism. Design ideas are shared, discussed and agreed in department-spanning tone meetings alongside writers, directors, producers and executives from the early stages of production, ensuring everyone is "singing from the same hymn sheet" and aware of what the others are doing.

Design is not only valued, it has now become *integral* to the storytelling. But back in 1974, when Philip Hinchcliffe became *Doctor Who*'s seventh producer, this was rarely ever the case. And telling stories is what he was all about.

It's not that design hadn't been considered a vital part of the mix on *Doctor Who* in particular; in a series whose stories spanned time and space in a medium relying on imagery and aesthetics for visual interest and context; it always had. It was simply common practice for producers to leave design decisions to the individual directors and designers assigned to each story. The main exceptions were if, for example, ongoing or important sets like the TARDIS interior (which Hinchcliffe would indeed address himself for his final season) or a costume for a lead character like the Doctor were being re-designed or altered. The unique challenges of producing such a demanding series often precluded much more direct involvement than that in any case.

Doctor Who was, after all, a programme which, despite being treated like any other contemporary serial drama in terms of the production facilities, technology and resources at its disposal, would often stretch the boundaries of what was realistically, technically and financially possible. Hardly surprising that the show sometimes struggled to do justice to the combined ambition and imagination of its creative teams within the confines of the BBC studio system in which it was made! Any one of these factors might have intimidated or fazed any other young, fledgling producer. But not Hinchcliffe. Indeed, as events transpired, he would push those boundaries – narratively, aesthetically and tonally – further than ever before.

In *A New Frontier*, a documentary included on the DVD release of *The Ark in Space*, Hinchcliffe explains, "I loved telling stories and connecting with an audience …(So) having watched the programme, I formed a view of what I'd like to do with it, (which) was basically to take stories away from Earth to other worlds … explore more science-fiction concepts and make it more compellingly gripping and suspenseful. It's not just a kid's show with sets!"

Early on, Hinchcliffe had sensed that some of the team's general approach to the show's stories and production style as being a little too light for his liking, to the extent he sometimes felt they thought of *Doctor Who* as a children's programme. He instinctively knew that his new vision for the show needed to be communicated – and reiterated – to everyone from directors, actors and production staff through to sound and lighting designers, to ensure they all bought into it and went the extra mile. Throughout his tenure, his closest collaborator on this mission to reinvigorate the show would be his recently-appointed script editor Robert Holmes, with whom he formed an immediate creative rapport – creating, in Hinchcliffe's own words, "a marriage of youth and experience". Spending "a lot of time thinking about how to create convincing worlds" in which the story ideas they were developing could take place, together they took the idea of world-building to a whole new level.

Although arguably few in number, there had been a handful of futuristic, largely extra-terrestrial stories which had inspired a sense of world-building by *Doctor Who* designers pre-Hinchcliffe. The show's second-ever story had seen designer Raymond Cusick create a gleaming, angular, metallic Dalek city with long, low ceilinged corridors and doorways specifically built high enough only for the creatures themselves to pass comfortably through. This city was in stark contrast to the more organic, twisted, petrified forest of the landscape beyond. Within a small, ill-equipped studio with meagre resources – and with sets that needed to be assembled and struck on a weekly basis – he accomplished what might have

seemed impossible: the creation of a truly original alien world at once astonishingly atmospheric and claustrophobic yet completely credible. The future Earth Empire trilogy of stories produced during the Pertwee era also attempted thematic links, but whilst both *The Mutants* and *Frontier in Space* featured strong set and costume design work and production values, there was little integration between the two.

Hinchcliffe quickly concluded that to lend atmosphere and an air of credibility to the more far-flung, science-fiction settings they were devising, set design in particular would be of paramount importance. And as good fortune would have it, the designer allocated to work on his first episodes as producer was former architect Roger Murray-Leach, making his debut on the series (although he'd actually been working at the BBC since the mid-1960s). Meeting for the first time, Hinchcliffe recognised Murray-Leach not only as a kindred spirit, but as an inventive and risk-taking creative, and the realisation of what he could do as a designer led to "some very radical conversations". More significantly, it was instrumental in his decision to adopt an unusual and forward-thinking strategy. Instead of following the established pattern of waiting until scripts arrived before passing them on to designers – and thus potentially presenting them with any number of design challenges contained within – Hinchcliffe decided that, by involving designers early on, well in advance of production, they could determine if or how their ideas could be made to work before feeding their conclusions back to the writers with scripts being altered accordingly. The concept of world-building through design on the show had never been so consciously addressed in such a considered way.

This inclusive approach immediately bore fruit with Murray-Leach's much-acclaimed work on *The Ark in Space* which proved to be something of a game-changer in terms of set design on *Doctor Who*. Impressing cast and crew alike when seen in studio for the first time, it encompassed precisely the elements Hinchcliffe was seeking. With its sleek white décor, strikingly tall, circular cryogenic chamber and curved transom corridor, the design employed simple yet imaginative solutions; the use of flexible, modular sections, vac-formed panelling, strategically-placed mirrors and raised walkways helped create a memorable futuristic setting that eschewed many of the traditional sci-fi clichés and rectangular three-walled set layouts so common in drama of the period. Furthermore, it satisfied the main scenic requirements for not one story but two, thereby addressing and allaying budgetary concerns too. Hinchcliffe's vision was beginning to materialise.

The success of the design work on the serial marked the start of a collaboration that would endure for the rest of Hinchcliffe's tenure as producer, with Murray-Leach returning a further four times – more frequently than any other designer – over the next two seasons. And it wasn't to be a case of diminishing returns either. Indeed, for the following season's *Planet of Evil*, he would raise the bar still further, creating an alien landscape which, once again, was devised during

discussions before scripts were written. When asked what kind of planet exterior he thought could be successfully realised in studio that was "different and exciting", Murray-Leach replied, "Well, I can do you a marvellous jungle ... if you give me some filming days!" Resolved to create a dense, swampy alien jungle with its own river, they concluded that the desired scale and quality could never realistically be achieved at TV Centre, not simply due to the restrictions on studio time and use of water and flammable materials, but because they wanted to ensure as far as possible that it didn't *feel* like a studio set at all.

This was a common challenge faced by most production teams of the time as, due to the prevailing recording techniques, exteriors were usually shot on location using 16mm film whilst interiors were recorded on videotape in the studio, unless specific requirements dictated otherwise. Unfortunately, the vast difference in quality and "feel" between the two meant that if the same set needed to be created in both mediums – as with sections of the *Planet of Evil* jungle – trying to get any degree of consistency would be difficult, especially in terms of lighting. On film, each shot could be lit individually, which, though more time-consuming and expensive, also offered greater opportunities to create far more detailed and atmospheric sets complete with uneven floor surfaces; conversely, it was more difficult to create specific dark spaces and shadow in studio because, even though it was generally accepted that brighter lighting made the sets appear less credible, they were often forced to comply with the technical guidelines requiring minimum light levels for the cameras and domestic television sets.

Despite these limitations, Hinchcliffe was convinced that their jungle justified a larger than normal filming quotient for the story and set about adjusting the filming allocation for the rest of the season, redirecting sufficient funds to invest in four dedicated filming days at Ealing Studios. This was an unusual move in and of itself as location filming didn't often require fully-constructed and dressed sets at all. But the results would speak for themselves. Murray-Leach always went to great lengths to base his designs in a relatable context, using imagery that would seem familiar yet when used creatively appear frightening or sinister. The beautifully-crafted jungle of Zeta Minor had tremendous impact, heightened by Brian Clemett's rich lighting design, incorporating deep reds and peacock blues and layered with atmospheric sound effects by Radiophonic Workshop composer Peter Howell. It remains one of the most impressive and convincing alien settings ever seen on *Doctor Who* to this day.

Keen as ever to challenge traditional conventions and practices, Murray-Leach also ensured his designs for the story's Morestran Probe ship differed from the norm too by further developing staging techniques he'd used in *The Ark in Space*. Frustrated that studio sets were so often forced to incorporate the flat, shiny studio floor just so the large pedestal cameras could move around them without obstruction, he deliberately designed both the exterior and interior ship sets with multiple levels to place the actors and action off the floor. This allowed the director far more scope to create diverse, interesting and exciting shots; for instance from low to high, high to low and so on, lending what might otherwise be potentially lacklustre scenes additional visual energy and dynamism. Murray-Leach even installed a glass-topped table on the upper control gantry so the actors could be seen issuing instructions through it from below! These factors may not have been immediately obvious to the audience at home, but they each contributed to the overall atmosphere of the production and the narrative being told.

Of course, Hinchcliffe's vision wasn't limited to futuristic, off-world stories, nor exclusively to the area of set design. It filtered through to all the other creative departments handling costume, hair, make-up and visual effects too. Knowing how skilled the BBC design departments were at recreating periods of Earth history, he and Holmes also decided to move away from the largely contemporary settings favoured by the previous production team and take the show back into the past more often. To that end, they began devising a number of historical tales but with a science-fiction twist. These so-called pseudo-historicals – a type of story attempted only sparingly in the series' past, but one that had recently resurfaced with Holmes' 1973 adventure *The Time Warrior* – also played to the strengths of experienced designers like Barry Newbery and Christine Ruscoe, affording them and costume designers such as James Acheson, John Bloomfield and Barbaras Kidd and Lane, the opportunity to indulge their love and knowledge of history whilst still flexing their creativity devising the look of period characters and alien creatures – and, on occasion, combining the two simultaneously! In conjunction with talented make-up designers such as Jan Harrison, Sylvia James, Jenny Shircore, Jean Steward and Heather Stewart, they responded in kind, producing some of their most imaginative work. Stories such as *Pyramids of Mars*, *The Masque of Mandragora* and *The Talons of Weng-Chiang* are rich in detail and texture, full of visual flair, all departments clearly working together, totally invested in bringing the scripts and characters to life and – also significantly – having fun! In *The Brain of Morbius*, for example, Newbery picked up on the *Frankenstein* and Gothic horror tropes and having decided to incorporate Gothic architectural features such as flying buttresses into his designs for Solon's castle, then subverted them by placing them on the inside instead of the exterior.

Hinchcliffe's foregrounding of design in the show would reach its apotheosis towards the end of what would become his final season as producer with two outstanding productions still hailed as among the best in the programme's history, *The Robots of Death* and *The Talons of Weng-Chiang*. Both stories serve as prime examples of the integrated design strategy he had instigated, with every department coming together to create a greater whole. However, it's particularly interesting to note that in the former story, the memorable Art Deco aesthetic of the Sandminer and its motley crew of humans and Voc robots was conceived without any input from

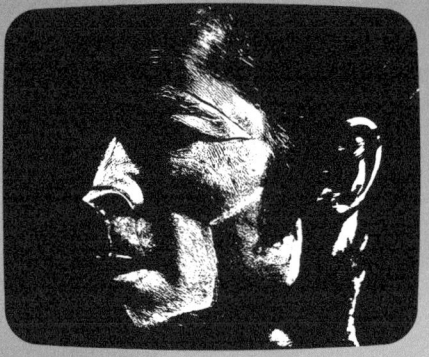

Hinchcliffe at all. Instead, it developed as the result of a conversation between the show's director, Michael E Briant and its designer, Kenneth Sharp on their return from a recce. Unhappy with what they considered a disappointing run-of-the-mill Agatha Christie-style script, they realised that the story needed something extra to lift it from the mundane. Latching on to world-building elements suggested in the dialogue however, they devised the notion of making the Sandminer akin to a luxury liner from the 1920s and 1930s, with decadent prospectors lounging around in inappropriate finery whilst their beautiful robotic manservants fulfilled all the menial tasks and duties. Though initially dubious about this idea himself, Hinchcliffe trusted the talented team of creatives he'd assembled to do their best – and he wouldn't be disappointed. Indeed, that core visual idea was taken, developed and enhanced further by make-up designer Ann Briggs and costume designer Elizabeth Waller, who created not only some of the most extravagant costumes ever seen on *Doctor Who*, using glittery tabards, colourful satins and billowy chiffon for the humans, but also the distinctive, quilted costumes for the Vocs with the elegant, chiselled features of their finely-sculpted – and inherently creepy – masks. These elements all came together to create a truly cohesive, original and memorable look, demonstrating that, even on a programme so often starved of the resources it needed, when striving to be the best, the creativity and resourcefulness of *Doctor Who*'s designers of the time was second to none.

Looking back over the three seasons of *Doctor Who* produced by Philip Hinchcliffe, it's fascinating to observe how clear and focussed his vision for the show and what it could be was, and how successfully and tenaciously he saw that through. Not only did it bring about a rise in the show's general popularity with the public at large, but also marked a significant increase in its production values. The show had never *looked* better. There can be little doubt that this was in no small part inspired by his virtually unprecedented strategy to move towards a more integrated approach in design across all the creative departments working on the show and to encourage the sharing of ideas and communication between them with the aim of making the stories they were telling more visceral and credible. And these things ultimately worked so well because he was an *enabler*. The fact that those stories are still so loved, admired, lauded and celebrated nearly fifty years later, is surely testament to that.

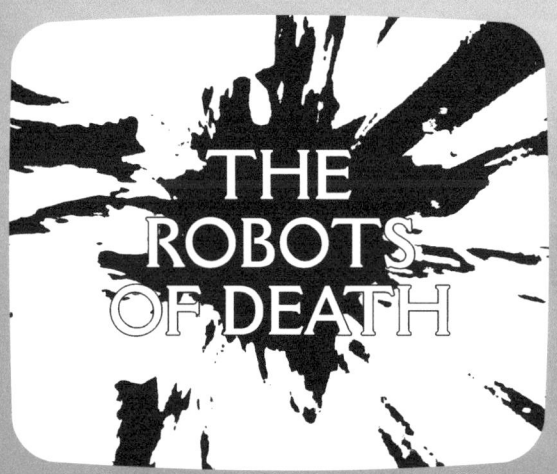

Philip chats about actors

"One of the most important things in *Doctor Who* is villainy, whether human or alien. From my, and Bob Holmes's, point of view making sure our directors cast the parts well was important. It was in Bob's DNA to write scripts that good actors could perform, he knew how to write dialogue and construct scenes they could make the most of. What I intuitively grasped was how to help writers create an atmosphere, an environment, something imaginative and mysterious, strange and alien, even if it's set on Earth. My instinct really was that the horror didn't come from the monster but from the dread, the fear, the suspense. Finding actors that could make the darkness spread out, the darkness that forced the bad guy on, that was very important to us. Possession was such a strong motif in our stories – there's quite a few stories where Bob uses a human who is possessed or taken over and is in conflict between their human side and the alien one. It was something that lent itself to our format because basically you got to tell a really frightening story and if you have a good actor who's playing possessed and has an inner conflict, it's a very efficient way of hooking people. I mean, it's a horrible thing – the idea that someone's human nature is being destroyed – and a good actor could run with that and make it sing.

Human villains have got their own trajectory which has to be headed off by the Doctor. Therefore what you need are strong actors for these parts because it'll be more believable. If you've got really good actors, not 'stars', but really good actors they can make everything believable without camping it up. I mean, maybe Harrison Chase did, but that's okay, because once in a blue moon, there's room for that. Harrison Chase was very much an *Avengers* type of villain because Bob Banks Stewart was part of that era, like Terry Nation who also enjoyed camping the villains up. But on the whole, what you wanted was jolly good actors like John Woodnutt or Bernard Archard or Kenton Moore. These people can act in conflict, even in a comedic way – people like Christopher Benjamin. They are all very adept actors. I understood very early on that that's how we could make these stories more compelling and not be one-dimensional. We always knew that there would be one or two fruity roles like the Freddy Jaeger role in *Planet of Evil*. But you get away with it because you've got other talented actors playing strong characters and they share the storytelling load, contributing to the ups and downs and changes of threats and suspense of the evolving story. You can't just have the Doctor and a companion and a horrible villain – that's when it goes all one-dimensional, so all those other actors in large and small parts just create a richer story.

It's difficult to say who was my favourite guest star, but it would take a lot to top Philip Madoc in *The Brain of Morbius*. Mind you, he did have all the best lines and therefore he's tremendous.

I must give credit to the directors because even by my second season, I didn't have enough of a working knowledge of television actors, and casting was an art the directors had really good instincts for. Either they had worked with these actors before or they knew and admired their work and they knew how to get them to work on *Doctor Who*, which wasn't always easy in those days. Really, a lot of credit should go to them; Douggie Camfield suggested Tony Beckley. Paddy Russell chose Bernard Archard and Chris Barry brought in Philip Madoc. When they've got a good script to offer to a favourite actor or an actor they wanted to work with, they've got a lot of ammo, because who would turn down those scripts?

A number of people have acknowledged how good John Bennett was as Chang in *The Talons of Weng-Chiang* but are also critical of David Maloney's casting him because he wasn't Chinese. I imagine he did look at Chinese actors, but the fact was that back in 1976, the pool was limited. You want an actor that can actually give you the performance you need. John Bennett's performance has got truth because he's a good actor; he rounded the character out, and created real sympathy for him. There were very few oriental actors around the UK to do that. I know now this was a concern to our American audience around this time because in North America there were a lot of great leading Asian actors working there, but that just wasn't the case in the UK. I think that Canada and the US were responding to the sensitivities of this very large minority in those countries, which we didn't have here. And if we *had* had it back then, we would have thought about authentic casting far more carefully."

the TALONS *of* WENG-CHIANG

THE REPRESENTATION OF EAST ASIAN
CHARACTERS IN DOCTOR WHO

EMMA KO

He came like a god. He appeared in a blazing cabinet of fire.
I saw him and helped him. He was tired from his journey.

DOCTOR WHO has never adventured in Hong Kong. Ancient China – yes. But modern day, pre-1997 (or post) handover Hong Kong? Nope. Okay, not strictly true – in the 2020 episode *Praxeus* there are a few shenanigans involving a missing astronaut that take place in a warehouse with some red lanterns dotted around, but had it not been for the words HONG KONG superimposed over a stock plane landing shot, it could just as easily have been a Chinatown theme night in your local bingo hall. So to my original point – the TARDIS has never parked up on the Peak, or Tai Tam reservoir, or a night market in Mongkok. Shame as a *Doctor Who* showdown in a modern Asian city like HK would be lit: the TARDIS glowing under the light show that is the HK skyline; Savile Row-tailored bad guys who have never seen the inside of a dojo, in an e-scooter chase down the bumpy streets of Central. Or Bong Joon Ho-style mutant-seafood monsters exacting revenge on the punters chowing down on them at a Lamma Island restaurant.

I bring this up as I grew up in Hong Kong in the Eighties and Nineties. I think we got *Doctor Who* on HK telly – I knew who the Daleks were, and the theme tune was scarily familiar – but I don't remember watching the show as a child. That's not to say my childhood television memories didn't include British fare: Sunday evening at Family Ko entailed a McDonalds dinner in front of back-to-back classics such as *Worzel Gummidge* followed by *The Muppet Show*. I remember loving *Worzel Gummidge*, imagining England to be a land of green fields and cosy farms where kids had adventures with funny-sounding scarecrows and everything was green and bright. I certainly don't recall any episode where adventures were cut short due to rain. Dramatic licence I guess? In any case, English television programmes to the young me seemed exotic and romantic.

It wasn't until I came to England as a teenager and first watched 'proper' English telly did I come across *Doctor Who* as the very popular television show with its superhero-like main character. I remember seeing the Daleks, hearing their robotic, squeaky voices and thinking they were cute rather than scary. And the episodes I saw depicted a daring, dapper adventurer involved in frenetic, science-fiction stories. There weren't any Chinese characters on screen in those days, let alone in the Whoniverse. I had missed BBC's *The Chinese Detective* – a show featuring David Yip who, in playing this role, was the first ever (and sadly so far last ever) Chinese lead in a UK drama. It didn't occur to me to expect to see myself or other East Asians depicted on UK screens. I was in England, so naturally I would expect to see English people on English telly. If occasionally I caught a pig-tailed, inscrutable (i.e. non-smiling) Chinese character playing a villain on a show, pig-tail flapping as they did kung fu, shouting in mangled English – well, that was just a bit of fun. No one needed to know what their inner landscape and childhood trauma was, they were just there to fulfil a plot line.

Fast-forward twenty-five years. I'm living in London and working as a screenwriter. Diversity is very much a buzz word now. We are – rightly in my opinion – thinking about representation. How nationalities and races are portrayed on our screens. That in a multi-cultural society – especially in our diverse, blended cities – how non-white characters are portrayed has become a

Whilst we wait patiently for a Korean Doctor, or a Vietnamese companion, it's worth looking backwards.

welcome, timely, sometimes heated conversation. And for those of us from ESEA heritages (ESEA being East and South East Asian and includes China, Hong Kong, Japan, Macau, Mongolia, North Korea, South Korea, Taiwan, Cambodia, Laos, Burma/Myanmar, Thailand, Vietnam, Brunei, East Timor, Indonesia, Philippines, Malaysia and Singapore) this means getting past the stereotypes of Chinese and Asian characters depicted on our screens:

- The kung-fu fighting, chopsocky action figures;
- The demure, beautiful women in cheongsams (the tight Chinese dress with slits up the sides), usually prostitutes, always highly sexualised;
- The wily, heavily accented but deeply evil Triad/organised crime boss (special shout out here to James Hong – seen recently and finally getting his due in *Everything Everywhere All At Once* – who got to play a fully-rounded, three dimensional character with an actual name after 70+ years of playing inscrutable Asian bad guys);
- The inscrutable, mystical 'Masters', usually with wispy facial hair and word-mangling accents;
- The nameless, inscrutable (again!) background players, usually restaurant staff, silently serving up dumplings or fortune cookies;
- And last but not least, the hard-working, no-nonsense, nerd – usually at a computer or in a lab coat, sometimes both. Very much a model minority – compliant and hard-working.

This sea change in representation has of course been welcome, and 21st century *Doctor Who* has very much been part of this evolution – we have the very first main cast black Doctor in Ncuti Gatwa (as black actress Jo Martin only played The Fugitive Doctor in various episodes as a guest character), not long after seeing the very first female Doctor – on our screens. Certainly during this modern run of the show, the storylines and companions, episodic characters and settings, have been bold in their breadth and ambitious in their scope. And this includes in the diversity of the stories and characters. We've had the Doctor getting involved in the partition of India in *Demons of the Punjab* (written by Vinay Patel), or making sure Rosa Parks can get on her bus in *Rosa* (co-written by Malorie Blackman, directed by Mark Tonderai). We've had Companions of Colour: Noel Clarke, Freema Agyeman, Velile Tshabalala, Pearl Mackie, Tosin Cole and Mandip Gill – no East Asian companions yet, but never say never! And of course there's Naoko Mori in *Torchwood* – more on her later.

But whilst we wait patiently for a Korean Doctor, or a Vietnamese companion, it's worth looking backwards. Searching out the classic

Doctor Who episodes when there were East Asian characters in the show. Who were they, what episodes were they in, who played them and how were they portrayed? And just how bad were the accents and make-up? Hop in my virtual TARDIS and let's take a gander back in time ...

I was too young to have seen the Hinchcliffe-era *Doctor Who*, and certainly not *The Talons of Weng-Chiang*, but have watched them recently. They seem like a natural starting point to discuss EA representation in the Whoniverse. But not before a quick aside to mention the mostly blink-and-you-miss-them predecessors to *The Talons of Weng-Chiang*, featuring East Asian cast and storylines: In the very first season of *Doctor Who*, there was a 7-part serial called *Marco Polo*, where the Doctor met Kublai Khan. Other than Zienia Merton, who was mixed-race (Burmese/British), the majority of the cast were white despite being set in Asia – though the episode was directed by director of colour Waris Hussein. Then there's an Asian-flavoured villain (dodgy eyebrows, pulled eyelids) Mavic Chen played by British actor Kevin Stoney in Season Three's *The Daleks' Master Plan*. In 1967 there was a serial as part of Season Five called *The Abominable Snowman*, set in a Tibetan Monastery. Almost all the monks were white, with 'yellowface' applied – the practice of using make-up and prosthetics to imitate the appearance of an East Asian – but it's the Snowmen, hulking hairballs on legs, that arguably got a worse deal in the costume department. 1971's *The Mind of Evil* had EA actors Pik Sen Lee – as the uptight, no-nonsense (inscrutable) Captain Chin Lee – and Kristopher Kum in a mind-control storyline.

Jon Pertwee's final story, *Planet of the Spiders*, in 1974, is set in a Buddhist retreat in Berkshire. Amongst the people there are a Tibetan monk and an aged Abbot. Neither are played by East Asian actors (one is an Aussie, the other a rather hammy old Englishman). There's a slight attempt to yellowface the look for the younger monk but not the Abbot. Both turn out to be Time Lords, rather than humans, in disguise, which may have been the reason for not casting authentically. It's a shame as this is the same production team (Barry Letts and Terrance Dicks) that went to such lengths to cast *The Mind of Evil* appropriately in 1971 and makes for an odd backwards step to take at the last minute.

Then in 1977, *The Talons of Weng-Chiang* was aired, a 6-part adventure set in Victorian London where the Fourth Doctor, Tom Baker, visits with his companion Leela. The Doctor and Leela are drawn into a murderous plot involving disappearing women, a stage magician called Li H'sen Chang, a giant sewer rat and a dodgy ventriloquist's dummy who turns out to be a murderous, knife-toting cyborg called Mr Sin. I want to be gentle here, as I know the story is a much-loved, very popular part of the *Doctor Who* canon. So on the plus side: the Doctor is dashing and wry, Leela is surprisingly autonomous and physical for a female character given it was the 1970s, and the comedy duo of Jago and Litefoot provided some thesp-meets-uptight-doc light relief.

But on the downside, and I'm afraid there are many (I think almost every trope listed above

appears!): the magician Chang is not only played by Caucasian actor John Bennett, but the full panoply of yellowface is on display: pulled, heavily lidded eyes; pallid, yellow-skin; wispy facial hair and a Chinese accent so thick and hammy Fu Manchu probably called, wanting a share of the royalties. Background actors – some East Asian, most not – donning a uniform of black hat and pyjamas-style clothes as befitting Chinese Triads (obvs!), leapt out of dark shadows, inflicting chop-socky style moves on the Doctor and Leela. One – portrayed by Chinese actor John Wu but credited only as 'Coolie' – takes the bullet for getting caught and swallows a capsule of poison

from Chang, posing as an interpreter in the police station. Perhaps 'Coolie' mistook Chang's words, mangled as they were, thinking he was saying good morning (早晨, pronounced Joe Sun), rather than "Poe Sun" (... and please top yourself before the police charge me for crimes against English). There's also the liberal use of Chinese slurs including the deeply offensive ch*nks, describing the Chinese as "opium-addicted scum", Leela calling Chang "the yellow one" and one of the police mockingly using the phrase "chinee". The Doctor attempting to speak Chinese is peak "we've given up trying", leaving the DVD subtitles to simply say "speaks Chinese", probably assuming "speaks gobbledygook" would be too on the nose.

Look, it was 1977. The wild spirit and intrepid energy of *Doctor Who* is abundant in *The Talons of Weng-Chiang*. It's a lively set of episodes with a wide array of creepy, quirky and crazy characters. Plus a mutant rat. The representation of the Chinese characters was undoubtedly in keeping with the times in which it was made. But it's hard to watch now, when those very same words have been used so recently against Chinese and East Asian British people in the wake of COVID-19 and Donald Trump's offensive Kung Flu rhetoric. I'm aware the story is adored by fans. But I'm glad we've moved well past that kind of offensive, hokey depiction of Chinese characters. Or have we...?

The next glimpse of an ESEA character in the Whoniverse is in the modern series with Christopher Eccleston as the latest regenerated Doctor. In the episode *Aliens of London*, Dr Toshiko "Tosh" Sato, is introduced as a – you guessed it – scientist! Complete with lab coat *and* computer. She's the science nerd who investigates the dead alien – in actual fact an engineered pig used in a decoy crash to allow the Slitheens to sneak into the Houses of Parliament and take over. Her role in the two-parter is all too brief. We don't see her again once the Doctor and Rose race off to where the action is, presumably leaving her to make sausages from the porcine corpse. However ... based on Naoko Mori's performance, showrunner Russell T Davies revived the character in his spinoff show *Torchwood*, creating a fully rounded, three-dimensional character who got top billing in the main cast and enjoyed excellent, post-watershed adventures (including a brief same-sex relationship with an alien) throughout her time on the series. So yay to that, and thank you to Russell for getting Naoko back and creating a character that's much loved in the Whoniverse, who also happens to be East Asian. And a Scientist.

> The representation of the Chinese characters was undoubtedly in keeping with the times in which it was made.

But back to *Doctor Who* – the next ESEA character appears in the Series Four episode *Turn Left*. David Tennant's Doctor's companion here is Donna, played by Catherine Tate. The pair are strolling through a market on an alien planet, for some reason depicted as a Chinatown-style place

Though it doesn't feature anyone in yellowface it is still pretty egregious in its Orientalism.

– thick accents and coolie hats abound, and those red lanterns get another outing. Donna meets a fortune teller, played by EA actress Chipo Chung, who sends Donna down a parallel timeline where Donna never met the Doctor. This episode – though it doesn't feature anyone in yellowface – is still pretty egregious in its Orientalism. Hokey Chinese-esque music plays, Chipo's fortune teller accent is John-Bennet-as-Chang-level ham and – apart from being the catalyst for the storyline – is given no further character traits or even motivation. The episode itself is great – depicting an alternative reality where, in a world where Donna and the Doctor never meet, everything falls apart. There's a powerful storyline about a non-English family and segregation. If only that care had been taken for the Chinese elements too.

Next up is *The Waters of Mars*, a 2009 winter special. The story revolves around a group of astronauts working on a base in Mars in 2059 who end up fighting a water-based, parasitic life form. One of the astronauts is Gemma Chan – now a huge, global star after her roles in *Crazy Rich Asians* and the Marvel films *Captain Marvel* and *Eternals*. Here, Gemma plays Mia Bennett, the geologist in the team (scientist trope – tick!), who – thanks to the Doctor – escapes with her boyf Yuri from their infected base. Gemma's role is not prominent, she's a key part of the astronaut team, but the action is led mainly by the Doctor and Lindsay Duncan's commander Adelaide Brooks. But she represents more diverse casting as part of an ensemble, and that's always heartening to see when the storyline doesn't require specific race or nationality casting.

A Good Man Goes to War was the seventh episode of Series Six, now with Matt Smith as the Doctor. Mixed race ESEA actress (and now one of the stars of *Star Trek: Strange New Worlds*) Christina Chong plays a soldier with a conscience – Lorna Bucket – part of a villainous army raised by Madame Kovarian. Lorna turns out to have met the Doctor as a child on her home planet, and had joined The Church of the Silence in the hope this would bring her into the Doctor's world again. Happily for her it does (and then sadly as she dies soon after!). This is a main character role, Lorna has agency, a back story, no hokey tropes and is given a heroic journey. She's also the bearer of the startling news that River Song is actually Amy Pond and Rory Williams's daughter. So Lorna becomes part of the *Who* lore, a key cog in the unfolding Whoniverse canon. Which makes her a great character, played emotionally and ably by Christina.

Our next ESEA characters appear in the Twelfth Doctor's episode *Sleep No More*. An eerie, timeline switching story involving found footage, sand monsters, and a gone-dark space station. A crew has been dispatched to investigate, coming across a seemingly deserted station. Very *Aliens 2*. There is plenty of ESEA representation in this

story: the captain of the crew is Nagata, played by Elizabeth Tan. She's accompanied by Paul Courtenay Hyu's Deep Ando. And there's a cutesy hologram singing troupe with Elizabeth Chong and Gracie Lai in the line-up. The rest of the episode cast is equally diverse, with Neet Mohan's Chopra in the search team, and Natasha Patel and Nikita Chadha as the other hologram singers. Apparently, episode writer Mark Gatiss had recently visited both Japan and India, inspiring him to make the cast a mix of both. Whatever the reason, it's refreshing to see such a multi-cultural guest cast, and not a lab coat in sight. Tick!

Series Ten's fourth episode, *Knock Knock* features ESEA actors Colin Ryan and Alice Hewkin as part of a group of student housemates who rent a too-cheap-to-be-good spooky house. It is – as the walls ingest them due to a particularly creepy father-daughter storyline. Colin and Alice do a lot of screaming and running. A fun ep with a very diverse cast.

Also in Series Ten comes *The Pyramid at the End of the World*, where British-Japanese actor Togo Igawa plays the UN Secretary General alongside Daphne Cheung as the representative for the Chinese army, Xioalian (not sure about this name as Chinese names tend to be three, sometimes two words and are more likely to be shortened so this character would be called, for example, Xiao Li An, and shorted to Xiao or Li An in conversation). They, along with reps from Russia and America (spokespeople for the world apparently), join forces with the Doctor and his companion Bill (played by mixed-race actress Pearl Mackie) to deal with a pyramid piloted by some alien monks that have appeared overnight in Turmezistan. Elsewhere, a hungover lab technician botches up a biochemical project. Are the two instances related ... you betcha! Great thing about this episode is there are two people in lab coats and neither is East Asian. Progress. Unfortunately, Togo's character gets reduced to dust, with Xioalian close behind, apparently because they said yes to the alien's demands out of fear. Oops.

Next, we come to 2022's Easter Special *Legend of the Sea Devils*, a smorgasbord of East Asian-ness, centring around the infamous pirate queen Madam Ching – played by Crystal Yu. Set in China in 1807, the opening features a Chinese village under attack by the notorious pirate. Bravely trying to defend the village, and in particular a revered statue, is David Tse's character Ying Wai, who dies in his efforts. The broken statue unleashes a Sea Devil, who sets about slaughtering the entire village before boarding a flying ship and 'fly-sailing' off into the horizon. The Doctor, now regenerated into Thirteenth Doctor Jodie Whittaker, and her companions Yasmin (Mandip Gill) and Dan (John Bishop), arrive in time to save Ying Wai's son Ying Ki (Marlowe Chan-Reeves). Turns out the Sea Devil's ship actually belongs to a 16th century captain called Sin Ji-Hun (Arthur Lee), who died in search of a lost treasure. Or did he? Seems that Ji-Hun is not actually dead, but has been kept in living stasis for tricking the Sea Devils over the whereabouts of something called the Keystone.

> **Nathaniel Curtis played Sir Isaac Newton, much to the pearl-clutching chagrin of The Telegraph.**

Eventually the Sea Devils are overcome due to Ji-Hun's heroic sacrifice. Madame Ching – who had released the Sea Devils so they could lead her to the lost treasure so she can save her captured sons – recruits now-orphaned Ying Ki to her crew and the Doctor chalks up another win.

There's a lot to commend this episode for. The majority cast of Chinese and EA actors is a joy to behold. It's an old-fashioned pirate escapade with some touching moments and big, set-piece fight scenes. The episode was directed by an EA director – Haolu Wang – though written by non-EA scribes Ella Road and Chris Chibnall. A missed opportunity there as I think an EA writer could have brought subtle touches that would have elevated the special to a genuinely authentic piece of drama. The 'ancient Chinese village' scene in particular was tropey and familiar. An EA writer might have included specific touches – for example it's unlikely a Chinese village would not have had numerous small shrines burning incense to deities like Guan Yin and other gods dotted around. But on the whole, from where we were back in 1977 with *The Talons of Weng-Chiang* (not even a Chinese name btw), where the Chinese main character had yellowface eyes and a tongue-mangling accent, *Doctor Who* has come a long *long* way. That's worth celebrating.

That brings us up to the latest episodes, shown to celebrate the show's 60th anniversary in 2023, which have served up a few more diverse castings. These include ESEA actor Jamie Cho as Colonel Chan in *The Star Beast*, alongside other non-white actors Ronak Patani as Major Singh and Dara Lall as Fudge Merchandini. Then in *Wild Blue Yonder*, Nathaniel Curtis – though not ESEA but of South Asian heritage – played Sir Isaac Newton, much to the pearl-clutching chagrin of *The Telegraph*. A heartening sign of progress indeed.

Now all we need is an ESEA Doctor, landing the TARDIS on the rooftop of the Marina Bay Sands in Singapore, brandishing a bubble tea in one hand, the sonic screwdriver in the other, facing off against a slew of slow-hopping Chinese vampires – known as Geung Si 殭屍 in a *Squid Game*-style fight to the death. And if the Doctor does get into a war of words in Chinese, Malay, Vietnamese or Korean, let's hope the subtitles can do better than "speaks gobbledygook".

Philip chats about the show's survial

"Back in the 1970s, there really wasn't much focus work done on television shows, no real attempt to understand what the audience liked or disliked. You had ratings and you had this BBC Audience Appreciation Index and while I'm not a statistician, I thought every kid who wanted to watch *Doctor Who* was bound to be watching anyway. So how could I make the audience grow? I believed that if the programme was marginally more attractive to the slightly older (and perhaps more intelligent, certainly more mature) teen viewers, who I didn't want thinking it was just a stupid kids show, I thought surely that was a no-brainer. If we made it more compelling, a bit more gripping, a bit more interesting and imaginative, you got that audience. All creative people have to be in contact with their inner child, their playful side, however old they are. I wanted the intelligent, imaginative, excitable, young people watching alongside the younger kids and their watchful parents. Make it a family show. I don't know what was in the minds of Barry Letts and the other producers working on the show before me, but the finished show felt like – and I may be doing them injustice – it was mainly for children. I didn't want that. I wanted it to be convincing, to make it more powerfully compulsive and compelling and just a bit more dramatic!

* * * *

Something I possibly kicked against was its place on television. Before I took over *Doctor Who* it was seen as a little British institution. It'd become part of the popular culture scene in a way and people were fond of it, but it was in danger of stagnating, of being taken for granted. British television wasn't the hard thrusting world of network television in America where if the pilot didn't deliver, you were out the window. *Doctor Who*'s audience had a sort of fond indulgence for the programme. It was British, it was idiosyncratic and it was part of people's lives. But that couldn't last forever, it needed a shake up so both it, and the audience, didn't get complacent.

All that said, I don't want to come across as somebody criticising it for what it was, I'm saying I tried to make it what it *wasn't*. At least from my point of view. It had been good (at times, great) but I thought we had an opportunity to make it even better, even more popular. It was enormous fun producing it and it was hard work, but this was the journey we were on. With the right script, the right acting and the good idea, you can create a very gripping, compelling story and entertainment.

I hope that's what we did."

WHOSE PHILIP HINCHCLIFFE

WHAT PHILIP HINCHCLIFFE DID NEXT
MATT DALE

There've been seven producers of Doctor Who in thirteen years and so I'm the seventh and I've been doing it for nearly three years now.

THERE are not many television producers who could successfully drag Hollywood stars like Anthony Hopkins back to the British small screen. Or kickstart the television careers of the likes of Nigel Havers, Pierce Brosnan, Lisa Harrow or some newcomer called Christopher Eccleston. Then chuck into that list a cavalcade of other amazing stars such as James Fox, Leonardo di Caprio, Hugh Grant, Alan Rickman, Pauline Collins, Christoph Waltz … the list is endless. And the person responsible for bringing all those people together of course is Philip Hinchcliffe.

Before all this, of course, Philip had been hard at work on *Doctor Who*. For three seasons he had made the most of the opportunity to shift genre and tone at a whim. It is said that he and his script editor Robert Holmes often borrowed from literary fantasy and whilst there may be some merit to this suggestion, I'd argue it overlooks the fact that he got to play with (real-life) Egyptian gods, 15th century costume-drama, gothic novellas, and the whimsy of futuristic murder/mysteries. Here was a producer desperate to play in the field of classic literature and was bending *Doctor Who* around it.

It's very easy to forget that this was the tail end of a few short years in Philip's first role as a television producer and that his success, personally and professionally with *Doctor Who* is what kicked-off several decades of often critically-acclaimed output across a wide variety of genres. I like to imagine him celebrating his success at this time by idly stretching out on a futuristic chaise lounge, surrounded by (preferably non-deadly) robots serving him. And he would no doubt have been justifiably delighted to be leaving on a such a high note and perhaps this would have been the exact point where he would be looking forward more than he was looking back. He'd now left *Doctor Who*, a young but experienced producer, ready for something new.

In the 2024 retrospective look at the life of his successor on the series, *Darkness & Light: The Life of Graham Williams*, Philip recalls that "Graham appeared in my office and said: 'Oh I'm taking over now' – it was a bit of a surprise." In fact, Philip and his script editor Robert Holmes had been starting to think about their potential fourth series of *Doctor Who* when this happened. Bill Slater, the BBC's Head of Series and serials, and Philip's boss, had made the decision around November 1976, and although the exact reasons are seemingly shrouded in half-truths and mis-remembered conversations, two options certainly seem to hold equal credence. Slater was keen, and probably under pressure from his Sixth-Floor bosses up at TV Centre, to stem the criticisms of *Doctor Who* being regularly paraded

PHILIP HINCHCLIFFE
Producer

around by Mary Whitehouse and her NVLA supporters. But more than that, Slater wanted to keep Philip Hinchcliffe on prestige programming and after three, highly successful years in terms of ratings and audience appreciation (Mrs Whitehouse aside), it made sense to capitalise on his talents elsewhere in Series and Serials.

So as Graham Williams set up camp in the production office, Philip had one final role with *Doctor Who*, as a contributor to the BBC's *The Lively Arts* documentary on the series, *Whose Doctor Who*. In fact, this featured both himself and Graham in situ as producers – the latter holding a script meeting with Terrance Dicks, writer of his first story, *The Vampire Mutation* which, with a dash of irony, ended up not happening, just as his final story *Shada* would not happen three years later.

With equal irony, Philip was asked to produce a show Graham had actually created some months earlier. Graham had worked on a number of police procedural dramas such as *Sutherland's Law* and *Barlow at Large* as script editor and the BBC was ending one of its other crime shows, *Softy Softly: Task Force*, the successor to *Softly Softly*, which itself was a spin-off from that granddaddy of all police series, *Z-Cars* and was looking for something to fill that slot. Williams had come up with the idea of a regional crime squad and came up with a four-part drama series called *Target*. Like *Softly Softly: Task Force* (and indeed *Doctor Who*) this would be made as a standard studio-based series with film location inserts. Williams and his script editor Roderick Graham commissioned former police detective turned writer Kenneth Clark (under his regular pseudonym Ben Bassett) to write the four episodes. After that, Slater put it into the hands of producer Anthony Coburn and script editor Simon Masters to go into production, but Coburn apparently wasn't keen and eventually asked to move off it, taking on the reins of *Poldark*.

Which is where Philip Hinchcliffe entered the scene, seeing the potential in the idea but not Clark's scripts, especially after looking at the success of ITV film dramas such as *The Sweeney*. Philip suggested to Slater's new replacement, Graeme MacDonald, that *Target* follow a similar path, becoming a proper full-on action-based film series of a type the BBC had rarely attempted before. He brought in experienced *The Sweeney* director David Wickes to helm the show and asked his former *Doctor Who* associate George Gallachio to create a budget for nine episodes, while he and Wickes went away and wrote an entirely new pilot episode. Wickes suggested Patrick Mower as the lead, playing Detective Superintendent Steve Hackett, and thus Philip Hinchcliffe's first post-*Doctor Who* project was a huge success. And, much like his time on *Doctor Who*, was often the (excuse the pun) target of Mrs Whitehouse and the British tabloid press. *Target*'s very first episode was broadcast in the week that the Belson Report was published, linking violence in teenaged boys with television and citing such 'contemporary' shows as *The Man from UNCLE*, *Kojak*, *Starsky & Hutch* and of course *The Sweeney* as examples of such violence. With few of those actually being broadcast on television at the time, the press jumped onto the first episode of *Target*, and made it their own scapegoat for violence (it was never mentioned in Belson's report of course). However, it was the kind of front-page tabloid publicity the BBC couldn't buy and backfired on the press as *Target* was ultimately recommissioned for a second season of eight episodes. *Target* takes itself very seriously, and confidently. Looking back, it's all terribly beige and Seventies, and whilst it has the feel of something that's been lampooned to death in the decades since, at the time *Target* must have seemed pretty bold. It certainly looks the part, and that move to shoot on film raises the quality substantially.

Whilst its second run was in production, Philip was doing what all hungry creatives do, looking for his next project, something closer to the kind of thing he would enjoy producing over gritty fist-fighting car-jacking street cops. During this whirlwind of activity, he sought to produce the prestige drama he'd been craving: luckily he had lived for some time in the small Berkshire village of Taplow, with Cliveden House just up the road. Cliveden was famously the home of the Astor family and a recently published biography about them made the idea of a series about Nancy Astor seem very attractive to Philip.

At the point where Philip was casting *Nancy Astor*, intending to go with an American actress, Equity, the British actors' union, stepped in and said for a part as major as this, bringing an American over to the UK was a no-no and whilst ways around this were explored, the show was postponed. At this point, Graeme MacDonald showed Philip a set of scripts by Jack Pullman called *Private Schultz* and asked if he wanted to do that in the meantime. Loving the scripts Philip excitedly said yes, and so that went into production relatively quickly. This gave Hinchcliffe the opportunity to work with acclaimed theatre director Robert Chetwyn (*Bent, There's a Girl in my Soup, What the Butler Saw, Long Day's Journey into Night* etc.) who at that point had only done a handful of television work including a memorable *ITV Playhouse* with Eleanor Bron called *Friends in Space* and some late series episodes of *Crown Court*. Relishing the opportunity to work with such a major theatrical and artistic visionary, who would really understand the comedy and drama combination of *Private Schultz* Philip was no doubt delighted that the series was nominated for two BAFTAs and actor Ian Richardson won an RTS for his role in it.

Nancy Astor, with Lisa Harrow as the lead, alongside James Fox, Nigel Havers and Pierce Brosnan, was finally made after *Private Schultz*. The series was a huge success, nominated for Golden Globes and BAFTAs with Philip himself nominated for an Emmy as producer. As a result, Philip was offered the political drama, *Strangers and Brothers*, a thirteen-part series, in which he cast Anthony Hopkins, Cheri Lunghi and, once again, Nigel Havers, seemingly establishing himself as a regular feature of Philip's productions. Another series he was offered was *Knockback*, based on the novel by Shirley Cooklin about Britain's first convicted murderer after the abolition of the death penalty. This Piers Haggard-directed play, which won a prestigious ACE award for Outstanding Programming Achievement, was part of the inaugural season of BBC's acclaimed *Screen Two* strand and remains the only multi-episode drama across *Screen Two*'s entire decade-long run. After that, Philip optioned Michael Kerr's biography of composer John Ogden, co-written with Ogden's widow Brenda Lucas, and made *Virtuoso*, his second contribution to the *Screen Two* slot, adding more awards to the growing list of those associated with Philip's shows, including an RTS gong for Alfred Molina's portrayal of Ogden. Shortly afterwards, however, Philip presumably saw it was time to move on from the BBC, taking his drive and passion to Nick Elliot, then Executive Producer of Drama at London Weekend Television.

Elliot, it appeared, had two projects he wanted Philip for. Firstly, he asked Philip to look at the early scripts by Allan Prior for another new serial for LWT based on Patrick Hamilton's *The Gorse Saga* and this became *The Charmer*. Once again Nigel Havers found himself starring in one of Philip's shows, albeit this time in the main role of Gorse. After *The Charmer* ended, Philip's next project, both as producer and also as writer, alongside Michael Aitken, was a series named *Bust*, which Elliot saw as a vehicle for entertainer Paul Nicholas. Despite huge viewing figures, *Bust* never went beyond two series, but Philip's next project was already lined up in the wings.

Coming off the high of producing *The Charmer*, Philip was approached to join Portman Productions, who were developing a Jack Rosenthal drama for Tyne Tees TV called *And a Nightingale Sang* which won a Prix Europa for Best Programme from a Regional Broadcasting Organisation. After this Philip produced the RTS-nominated *The Gravy Train*, with writer Malcolm Bradbury, starring a young Christoph Waltz and reuniting him with his friend Ian Richardson, with whom he'd worked on *Private Schultz*. After this Philip brought an idea to Portman, which, utilising his old contacts from his BBC days, became a co-production with BBC Wales. This was *Friday on My Mind*, written by Alick Rowe, directed by Marc Evans and featured a new and exciting young actor called Christopher Eccleston. The series went on to win a number of Welsh BAFTAs.

During this time, Philip (along with Portman Productions) had become very keen to move into theatrical movies. Philip had a long-standing friendship with producer Hilary Heath who had bought the rights to Beryl Bainbridge's novel *An Awfully Big Adventure*. She asked Philip to join her on that venture, with Mike Newell as a director, just before his career sky-rocketed via *Four Weddings and a Funeral*. The success of this, with its box-office stars in Hugh Grant and Alan Rickman, meant Portman had now come into the orbit of European film financiers who looking to do co-productions with British companies. The movie *Total Eclipse*

was one of these, with Christopher Hampton's screenplay (based on his own stage play) about the romance between poets Rimbaud and Verlaine, played by Leonardo di Caprio and David Thewlis. Philip was the English co-producer on this, working with Oscar-nominated Polish director Agneiszka Holland.

After leaving Portman, Philip was snapped up by Scottish Television in the role of Executive Producer of Drama, working to Alistair Moffat. Whilst the drama department at STV had major ongoing success stories like *Taggart* and *McCallum*, for which Philip became Executive Producer, he was clearly very keen to work on new projects with the ITV network. One of these was a thriller called *Seesaw* starring David Suchet, another was groundbreaking male rom-com *Forgive and Forget* with John Simm, and then there was *The Last Musketeer*, which Philip thought was a perfect vehicle for Robson Green. Next, Ian Rankin's *Rebus* novels had been optioned by STV and Philip suggested to Alistair Moffat that they should do it, and put forward John Hannah to play the titular role. This was immediately green-lit and the series was a huge success for both STV and the whole ITV network.

Philip's last job for STV was to commission one of the writers he most admired, Jack Rosenthal, to write a new adaptation of Kingsley Amis' *Lucky Jim* to star Stephen Tompkinson. This would turn out to be Rosenthal's penultimate play and although it actually went into production after Philip had already left STV, his final involvement was to cast Tompkinson in the title role. Philip's time at STV perhaps represented elements of the prestige drama he had often chased in the past, with highly bankable names in lead roles, but with hyper-realistic twists and turns concerning murder and sex, swashbuckling and heroics and just a touch of comfort-food storytelling. A far cry from both giant rats in the sewers and arks in space, for sure.

But of course, there's a glorious postscript here. Whilst *Doctor Who* formed an early and important pivot in Phillip's life, giving him the opportunity to step up to be a serious and well-respected producer, recently he returned to the fold, writing stories for five volumes of Big Finish Productions' Fourth Doctor range. Today Philip Hinchcliffe is, one would hope, incredibly happy to have been involved in so many quality drama programmes across a vastly successful and well-regarded fifty year-career which has demonstrated so very clearly that he was always a little ahead of his time, whether his work was focussed on the distant future, the murky past or the furthest reaches of outer space.

Last Word:
Steven Moffat

Philip's first story, The Ark in Space *is so good, so clever and inventive. It's the* Doctor Who *story you could make with any of* Doctor Who*'s casts. You could do that with Hartnell and Ian and Barbara. You could do it with Jodie and her team. You could just take the script, make whatever little tweaks you have to do and you could just make it.*

When I was running *Doctor Who*, I had a writer called Peter Harness who, like me, was a fan of the series. And when we were discussing how to do something in one of his scripts, I said, "Just Hinchcliffe the shit out of it." Peter, being an old fan knew exactly what I meant, right? Go Hammer horror, go scary because until we've got the big reveal, we've got nothing. Let's have monsters and scares and melodrama and all that stuff. Between *Doctor Who* fans, "Hinchcliffe the shit out of it" just means "make it brilliant".

Philip Hinchcliffe was very good at getting *Doctor Who* as well-made as it could be given the lunatic circumstances in which a show of that kind was being made. And he thought, "Well, you know what I have a big high-profile show. I'm not just getting this done and popping off to the golf course" – because there's certainly a bit of that going on in some mass market shows of that era. He thought of it a prestige show; a flagship show and of great importance to the BBC. And he was right, of course. It's one of the most famous shows in the world, one of the most famous franchises ever. So he held it to the highest standard, even though he was trying to make science-fiction spectacular on virtually no money, in a multi-camera studio better suited to sitcoms and soaps. In a television era when *Z-Cars* struggled to make a convincing car, Philip had to launch spaceships and unleash monsters. Somehow he succeeded – and in the opinion of many, better than anyone else. He seemed determined to make it as well as he humanly could because if he could demonstrate he could make *this* show, people would correctly conclude that he could make *any* show. But I don't think it was just careerism – I think he properly loved it. As a producer, you can have great fun on the show and you can do really cool stuff you'll never get to do again. That's the correct way to think about *Doctor Who*. I think he was being smart, he was being ambitious, and he was doing his level best for a show he adored. We've all heard that old story, that *Doctor Who* was almost used as an internal punishment at the BBC: "You've been bad, so you'll go and design a *Doctor Who* or you'll go and direct a *Doctor Who*". But clearly he never saw it that way, and my God it shows. I mean, look at him – he was a 29-year-old. 29! It was a show for young men then and it's made by such old people now! We're all at twice the age of the people who used to make it!

Philip Hinchcliffe was incredibly good at running *Doctor Who*'s budget too (or as he and I discussed it at a *Doctor Who Magazine* event once, *exceeding* your budget all the time. That's the way you survive on *Doctor Who*. You just spend it and say, "What are you going to do"?) As a result, it's beautifully made show throughout his time. I mean, there are screw-ups because there are always going to be screw-ups in *Doctor Who*, but it is superbly done and endlessly inventive. And because you've got a blisteringly good new producer who's clever and ambitious, and he's got the best ever writer of the show in Robert Holmes becoming his head writer, you get the best from everybody. On top of that, Philip had probably the best companion with Lis Sladen's Sarah Jane Smith at the same time as Tom Baker's blazing Doctor and the brilliant Ian Marter as Harry.

There is plenty of competition for the best ever run of *Doctor Who*, but those three years are truly outstanding.

The *Doctor Who* stories of Philip Hinchcliffe

Editor's Note: These have been listed in Production Order not Transmission Order

Producer: Philip Hinchcliffe
Script Editor: Robert Holmes

Starring
Tom Baker (The Doctor)
Elisabeth Sladen (Sarah Jane Smith)
Ian Marter (Harry Sullivan:)

The Sontaran Experiment

Written by Bob Baker and Dave Martin
Directed by Rodney Bennett

Also starring
Kevin Lindsay (Styre/The Marshal); Donald Douglas (Vural); Glyn Jones (Krans); Peter Walshe (Erak); Peter Rutherford (Roth); Terry Walsh (Zeke); Brian Grellis (Prisoner)

The Ark in Space

Written by Robert Holmes
Directed by Rodney Bennett

Also starring
Kenton Moore (Noah); Wendy Williams (Vira); Richardson Morgan (Rogin); John Gregg (Lycett); Christopher Master (Libri); Brian Jacobs (Dune); Gladys Spencer, Peter Tuddenham (Voices); Nick Hobbs, Stuart Fell (Wirrn Operators)

Revenge of the Cybermen

Written by Gerry Davis
Directed by Michael E. Briant

Also starring
Ronald Leigh-Hunt (Stevenson); William Marlowe (Lester); David Collings (Vorus); Kevin Stoney (Tyrum); Jeremy Wilkin (Kellman); Michael Wisher (Magrik); Alec Wallis (Warner); Brian Grellis (Sheprah); Christopher Robbie (Cyber-Leader); Melville Jones, Tony Lord, Pat Gorman (Cybermen)

Genesis of the Daleks

Written by Terry Nation
Directed by David Maloney

Also starring
Michael Wisher (Davros); Peter Miles (Nyder); Stephen Yardley (Sevrin); Dennis Chinnery (Gharman); James Garbutt (Ronson); Guy Siner (Ravon); Tom Georgeson (Kavell); Harriet Philpin (Bettan); John Franklyn-Robbins (Time Lord); Drew Wood (Tane); Jeremy Chandler (Gerrill); Ivor Roberts (Mogran); Andrew Johns (Kravos); Michael Lynch (Thal Politician); Richard Reeves (Kaled Leader); Pat Gorman, Hilary Minster, Max Faulkner, John Gleeson (Thals); Peter Mantle (Kaled Guard); John Scott Martin, Cy Town, Keith Ashley (Dalek Operators); Roy Skelton (Dalek Voices)

Terror of the Zygons

Written by Robert Banks Stewart
Directed by Douglas Camfield

Guest Starring
Nicholas Courtney (Brigadier Lethbridge-Stewart); John Levene (RSM Benton)

Also starring
John Woodnutt (Broton/the Duke of Forgill); Lillias Walker (Sister Lamont); Angus Lennie (Angus); Robert Russell (The Caber); Tony Sibbald (Huckle); Hugh Martin (Munro); Bernard G. High (Corporal); Bruce Wightman (Radio Operator); Keith Ashley, Ronald Gough (Zygons); Peter Symonds, Barry Summerfield, Alan Clements (UNIT Soldiers)

Starring
Tom Baker (The Doctor)
Elisabeth Sladen (Sarah Jane Smith)

Pyramids of Mars

Written by Robert Holmes (writing as Stephen Harris, incorporating ideas by Lewis Greifer)
Directed by Paddy Russell

Also starring
Bernard Archard (Marcus Scarman); Michael Sheard (Laurence Scarman); Gabriel Woolf (Sutekh); Peter Copley (Warlock); Peter Mayock (Namin); Michael Bilton (Collins); George Tovey (Clements); Vic Tablian (Ahmed); Nick Burnell, Melvyn Bedford, Kevin Selway (Mummies)

Planet of Evil

Written by Louis Marks
Directed by David Maloney

Also starring
Frederick Jaeger (Sorenson); Prentis Hancock (Salamar); Ewen Solon (Vishinsky); Michael Wisher (Morelli); Graham Weston (De Haan); Louis Mahoney (Ponti); Melvyn Bedford (Reig); Haydn Wood (O'Hara); Terence Brook (Braun); Tony McEwan (Baldwin); Mike Lee Lane (Anti-Matter Monster)

The Android Invasion

Written by Terry Nation
Directed by Barry Letts

Guest starring
Ian Marter (Harry Sullivan); John Levene (RSM Benton)

Also starring
Martin Friend (Styggron); Roy Skelton (Chedaki); Milton Johns (Guy Crayford); Patrick Newell (Faraday); Peter Welch (Morgan); Ma Faulkner (Adams); Heather Emmanuel (Tessa); Dave Carter (Grierson); Hugh Lund (Matthews)

The Brain of Morbius

Written by Robert Holmes (writing as Robin Bland, incorporating ideas by Terrance Dicks)
Directed by Christopher Barry

Also starring
Philip Madoc (Solon); Cynthia Grenville (Maren); Michael Spice (Voice of Morbius); Gilly Brown (Ohica); Colin Fay (Condo); Stuart Fell, Alan Crisp (Body of Morbius); John Scott Martin (Kriz); Sue Bishop, Janie Kells, Gabrielle Mowbray, Veronica Ridge, Alison Daumler, Martine Holland, Tobina Mahon-Brown, Karen Burch, Mary Burleigh (Sisterhood of Karn)

The Seeds of Doom

Written by Robert Banks Stewart
Directed by Douglas Camfield

Also starring
Tony Beckley (Harrison Chase); John Challis (Scorby); Mark Jones (Keeler); Kenneth Gilbert (Dunbar); Michael Barrington (Sir Colin Thackeray); Sylvia Coleridge (Amelia Ducat); Seymour Green (Hargreaves); Hubert Rees (Stevenson); Michael McStay (Moberley); John Gleeson (Winlett); Ian Fairbairn (Chester); John Acheson (Beresford); Ray Barron (Henderson); Alan Chuntz (Chauffeur); David Masterman (Guard Leader); Harry Fielder, Pat Gorman, Ian Elliott, Brian Nolan (Guards); Keith Ashley, Ronald Gough (Krynoid)

The Masque of Mandragora

Written by Louis Marks
Directed by Rodney Bennett

Also starring
Norman Jones (Hieronymous); Jon Laurimore (Count Federico); Gareth Armstrong (Guiliano); Tim Piggot-Smith (Marco); Robert James (High Priest); Anthony Carrick (Rossini); Peter Tuddenham (Mandragora Voice); Brian Ellis (Brother); Pat Gorman (Soldier); James Appleby, John Clamp (Guards); Peter Walshe, Jay Neill (Pikemen); Stuart Fell (Entertainer); Peggy Dixon, Jack Edwards, Alistair Fullarton, Michael Reid, Kathy Wolff (Dancers)

The Hand of Fear

Written by Bob Baker and Dave Martin
Directed by Lennie Mayne

Also starring
Judith Paris, Stephen Thorne (Eldrad); Glyn Houston (Watson); Rex Robinson (Carter); Roy Boyd (Driscoll); Frances Pidgeon (Miss Jackson); John Cannon (Elgin); David Purcell (Abbott); Renu Setna (Intern); Roy Skelton (Rokon); Roy Pattison (Zazzka); Robin Hargreave (Guard)

Starring
Tom Baker (The Doctor)

The Deadly Assassin

Written by Robert Holmes
Directed by David Maloney

Also starring
Peter Pratt (The Master); Bernard Horsfall (Goth); George Pravda (Spandrell); Angus Mackay (Borusa); Erik Chitty (Engin); Hugh Walters (Runcible); Peter Mayock (Solis); Llewellyn Rees (The President); Derek Seaton (Hilred); Maurice Quick (Gold Usher); Michael Bilton, John Dawson (Time Lords); Helen Blatch (Voice)

Starring
Tom Baker (The Doctor)
Louise Jameson (Leela)

The Face of Evil

Written by Chris Boucher
Directed by Pennant Roberts

Also starring
David Garfield (Neeva); Leslie Schofield (Calib); Victor Lucas (Andor); Leon Eagles (Jabel); Mike Elles (Gebek); Brendan Price (Tomas); Colin Thomas (Sole); Lloyd Maguire (Lugo); Peter Baldcock (Acolyte); Tom Kelly, Brett Forrest (Guards); Rob Edwards, Pamela Salem, Roy Herrick, Anthony Frieze (Xoanon)

The Robots of Death

Written by Chris Boucher
Directed by Michael E. Briant

Also starring
Russell Hunter (Uvanov); Pamela Salem (Toos); David Collings (Poul); David Bailie (Dask); Miles Fothergill (SV7); Gregory de Polnay (D84); Brian Croucher (Borg); Tania Rogers (Zilda); Tariq Yunus (Cass); Rob Edwards (Chub); Peter Sax (Kerril); Mark Blackwell-Baker, John Bleasdale, Mark Cooper, Peter Langtry, Jeremy Ranchev, Richard Seager (Robots)

The Talons of Weng-Chiang

Written by Robert Holmes
Directed by Rodney Bennett

Also starring
John Bennet (Li H'sen Chang); Michael Spice (Weng-Chiang); Christopher Benjamin (Jago); Trevor Baxter (Litefoot); Deep Roy (Mr Sin); Chris Gannon (Casey); David McKail (Kyle); Conrad Asquith (Quick); Alan Butler (Buller); Patsy Smart (Ghoul); Judith Lloyd (Teresa); Vaune Craig-Raymond (Cleaner); Vincent Wong (Ho); Tony Then (Lee); John Wu (Coolie)

Contributor Biographies

WILL BROOKS is a designer, and digital artist responsible for several pieces of *Doctor Who* merchandise. Between 2015 and 2019 he was the resident 'photo' cover artist for Titan Comics, producing over 160 designs. He has also produced work for the likes of Big Finish Productions and the *Doctor Who Experience* in Cardiff Bay.

GRAEME BURK is a writer and author. He edited the memoirs of Sydney Newman, *Head of Drama*, for which he wrote a biographical essay. He is the co-author of several guides to *Doctor Who*: *Who is the Doctor* (2 volumes), *Who's 50: The 50 Doctor Who Stories to Watch Before You Die* and *The Doctors Are In*. Since 2013, he has been the host and co-producer of the *Doctor Who* podcast, *Reality Bomb*.

HANNAH COOPER, although a child of the 2005 revival, found it was UKTV Gold's *Doctor Who* omnibuses that first pushed her down a slippery slope of 1970s television. She lived through numerous weeks of the 1960s, 1970s and 1980s for backintimefortv.co.uk and has continued to explore a range of archive television while writing for blogs and guesting on various podcasts. Hannah passionately believes that television history should be accessible to as wide an audience as possible, aiming to share the parts she finds fascinating and enjoyable. She spends much of her time watching, reading, chatting and writing about television. Occasionally she visits present-day Earth.

MATT DALE was a Project Manager and part-time crazy cat man, who was best known for his musings on *Quantum Leap*. He co-hosted the long-running *Quantum Leap* podcast at quantumleappodcast.com and wrote several books on the show, available at forevertv.co.uk. He had been known to write about *Doctor Who* in the past, particularly at his website millenniumeffect.co.uk, which had been unearthing hidden corners of the universe for twenty-five years. Matt passed away in December 2023, shortly after completing his contribution to this book.

HAYDEN GRIBBLE was born just as *Doctor Who* was taken off the air in 1989. He then had to put up with sixteen years of rummaging at car boot sales, libraries and hassling parents to buy him videos and anything with Patrick Troughton and Cybermen in it to get his fix. He found the experience so harrowing he committed his memories to paper and released *Child Out of Time: Growing up with Doctor Who in the Wilderness Years* to a bit of acclaim. Nowadays he continues to write books, including the science-fiction *Captain Random* series and has been anything from a plumber to a radio DJ to make ends meet. He lives with his wife and son in Suffolk, is expecting another child very soon and is always looking for writing work. His pastimes include playing guitar, walking and talking all things *Doctor Who* on the *Diddly Dum* podcast.

SIMON GUERRIER is a writer and producer, and his most recent book is the biography *David Whitaker in an Exciting Adventure with Television* (2023). He's made documentaries for BBC Radio 3 and Radio 4, and produced two audio dramas for Big Finish starring Tom Baker and based on early draft scripts for what became *The Ark in Space* and *Genesis of the Daleks*.

TOBY HADOKE is an actor (*Coronation Street*, *Hollyoaks*, etc.), writer (Radio 4 plays, *Guardian* obituaries) and comedian (*Moths Ate My Doctor Who Scarf*) who has carved a niche for himself as a Z-List *Doctor Who* bore on TV, radio and DVD documentaries. He hosts BBC 4 Extra's *7th Dimension*, has his own series of podcasts – *Toby Hadoke's Time Travels* – and has taken 5 million years to write a book about *Quatermass*. Keep abreast of his frenzy of underachievements at www.tobyhadoke.com.

DAVID J HOWE has been involved with *Doctor Who* research and writing for over forty-five years. He has been consultant to a large number of publishers and manufacturers for their *Doctor Who* lines, and is author or co-author of many factual titles associated with the show, including *The Target Book* and *The Who Adventures*. He also has one of the largest collections of *Doctor Who* merchandise in the world. He is currently Editorial Director of Telos Publishing Ltd, a UK based independent press specialising in horror/science fiction novellas, crime novels, and guides to a variety of film and TV shows. In 2006 the company won the World Fantasy Award for their publishing work, and in 2010 received the British Fantasy Award for Best Small Press. The company celebrated its 20th anniversary in 2020.

ROBIN INCE is an award-wining up comedian and bestselling author. He has recently completed a tour of two hundred independent bookshops across Britain with his book *Bibliomaniac*, a love letter to books and book people. Robin writes and presents *Robin Ince's Reality Tunnel* for BBC Radio 4, for whom he also co-writes and co-presents *The Infinite Monkey Cage* with Professor Brian Cox. He is a founder of the annual festival of science and art, *Nine Lessons and Carols for Curious People*, and the Cosmic Shambles online network. He has a regular column in *The Big Issue* and is currently working on a book about neurodiversity. Find him at cosmicshambles.com/words/blogs/robinince

ALEX KINGDOM always wanted to be a footballer as a kid, but when he was diagnosed with Cerebral Palsy and learned he would have to use a wheelchair he figured that the players on the pitch probably wouldn't want to get their toes run over. This didn't stop his love for the game or even him wanting to be involved so he decided that he wanted to be a commentator and would always talk alongside the sport he was watching. Then eventually he was introduced to science-fiction, his dream changed, and his bizarre imagination kicked in. He recently graduated from university, where he was lucky enough to study in Cardiff for three years, doing a course about media production. He has wanted to work in television for some time now and his goal would be to eventually write for a fictional television series, and he hopes one day to achieve this. Who knows … he certainly doesn't.

EMMA KO has written extensively across scripted programming in film and TV, most recently on Netflix mystery series *1899*, the follow-up show from the team behind Netflix hit *Dark*. Her writing covers many genres, including animated cartoon series *Chopsocky Chooks* for Cartoon Network, *Dani's House* for CBBC, and *First*, which premiered at the British Horror Film Festival in 2018. Emma is a passionate advocate for better representation in the screen industry and is a founding member of EAST (easttv.org) a non-profit to help the career development and progression of British East and South East Asians creating scripted Television. Emma helped set up First Female Films to develop and produce female-helmed genre projects, and runs a Facebook group for Screenwriters of Colour in the UK.

TREY KORTE hails from Milwaukee, Wisconsin, USA, where he teaches high school English and drama, including a course in science-fiction. Growing up in a military family that moved frequently, he discovered *Doctor Who* as a child when he and his parents would watch it over Sunday dinner and has been a passionate fan ever since, influencing his interest in storytelling, critical analysis, and performance. He is a regular contributor to the *Outside In* anthologies and when not finding ways to incorporate *Doctor Who* into the classroom, he enjoys travel, theatre, fitness, LGBT activism, and spending quality time with his beloved husband Jamie. He'd like to dedicate his essay to his late mother – who taught him the importance of faith and belief.

AARON LOWE is a photographer and graphic designer living in Cardiff. Moving to the home of *Doctor Who* was an easy decision and has been a place that has fuelled their creativity and provided a lot of inspiration through their artwork and their LGBTQIA+ safe space, the group 'Friends of Ace' on Instagram, Facebook and X.

SOPHIA MORPHEW is a script editor and story producer. She began her career as an assistant at BBC Wales Drama, where her claim to fame was making the most disgusting cup of tea in the whole of the BBC. Since then she has worked in comedy and primetime and children's drama, across a variety of genres, most recently the Acorn detective series *The Chelsea Detective*.

PHIL NEWMAN is a freelance Set & Costume Designer who has designed and realised a wide range of productions both nationally and internationally for more than twenty-five years. He was Production, Set & Costume Designer on Reeltime Productions' multi-award-winning *Doctor Who* spin-off drama *Sil and the Devil Seeds of Arodor* (2019), designed the set for the documentary series *Doctor Who and the Collectors* for the *Doctor Who Collection* Blu-ray range and is Resident Designer (and occasional writer) at Colour House Children's Theatre in South London. He also presented *An Assignment with Grim Evil: An Interview with Chris Thompson* for the BBC Blu-ray/DVD release of *Doctor Who: The Evil of the Daleks*. Since the late 1980s, he has contributed numerous interviews and written features to such titles as *Doctor Who Magazine*, *TARDIS*, *Nothing at the End of the Lane* and, most recently, the latest issue of the much-acclaimed *Vworp Vworp!* magazine. He lives in Croydon.

KIM PFEIFER-ADAMS was born in Buffalo, New York, and is an artist and educator now living in Phoenix, Arizona. At the age of eleven, she won her first award for poetry and has been cursed to keep writing ever since. A self-proclaimed nerd, she has a Master's degree in Creative Non-Fiction and has contributed to *Hackwriters* online magazine as a science writer. She will someday finish her novel.

MICK SCHUBERT is a writer and editor specializing in science and science fiction. His past work includes chapters on *Doctor Who*, *Star Trek*, *Twin Peaks*, *Buffy the Vampire Slayer*, *The X-Files*, and more for ATB Publishing's *Outside In* series, as well as factual science writing for books, magazines, journals, websites, podcasts, and even Marvel Comics. He has written and lettered comics and graphic novels for the *New York Times* bestselling *FUBAR* series, Outré Press, Pilot Studios, 215 Ink, and others. When he's not writing or editing (which is almost never!), he's usually working on public engagement initiatives, advising on science and health communications, consulting on DEI and accessibility, or taking his dog on one million walks.

KENNY SMITH was born 11 days after Jon Pertwee regenerated into Tom Baker. He has worked as a journalist on several newspapers, including the *Rutherglen Reformer*, *Scottish Daily Record* and *Daily Mirror*. Kenny was editor of *Ayrshire Post* when it won Scottish Local Weekly Newspaper of the Year in 2017. He has been a *Doctor Who* fan for as long as he can remember, having edited numerous fanzines over the years, including *The Finished Product*, an unofficial Big Finish fanzine. He has been editor of Big Finish's official monthly magazine *Vortex* since 2014, and wrote the second volume of *The Big Finish Companion*. Kenny is also co-host of the *Doctor Who* podcasts *The Power of 3* and *Pieces of Eighth*. He currently works as a communications officer in NHS Scotland, and lives near Glasgow with his wife, teenager and cat, Nemo.

MATTHEW SWEET presents *Free Thinking* and *Sound of Cinema* on BBC Radio 3. His twenty-five years of programmes include *The Culture Show* (BBC2), *Checking into History* (C4), five series of *The Philosophers Arms* (Radio 4) and *1922: The Birth of Now*, a ten-part history of modernism (Radio 4). He is the author of *Inventing the Victorians* (Faber, 2001), *Shepperton Babylon* (Faber, 2005), *The West End Front* (Faber, 2011) and *Operation Chaos* (Picador 2018). He has been film critic of *Independent on Sunday*, photography critic of *Newsweek* and fashion columnist for *1843/The Economist*. His film *Liberation Radio* screened in the 2021 London Film Festival and at the Manzi gallery in Hanoi. In 2017 he and the baker Frances Quinn achieved a chocolate-related Guinness World record. He was Series Consultant on the Showtime/Sky Atlantic series *Penny Dreadful* and is now working on a biography of Barbara Cartland and co-writing, with Mark Gatiss, a detective show for Masterpiece/PBS.

MATTHEW TOFFOLO has been a *Doctor Who* fan and toy collector since the mid-1990s. In 2007 he combined both passions by making stop-motion animations based on the television series on his YouTube channel, *batmanmarch*. This led to reviews of the Character Options toyline, and a podcast called *The Review of Death*, which discusses *Doctor Who* across its history. Matthew's passion for film and television led to him graduating in Film Studies, and becoming a Content Producer for the Bristol-based gaming/video production company, The Yogscast. In 2018, work and hobbies crossed paths when Matthew was tasked with producing and co-presenting a series of preshows that coincided with *Doctor Who* on Twitch. He has written a fan-funded *Doctor Who* comic, *Fan Fiction Illustrated*, alongside former *Doctor Who* script editor Andrew Cartmel, and acted as a consultant on the *Doctor Who* figurine range from Big Chief Studios

IAN WINTERTON is a former film journalist who, having interviewed many big Hollywood names, has now become a fulltime scriptwriter. For the screen, he's written several short films, and his police/crime drama, *Blurred* is part of Saffron Cherry Productions Ltd development slate. In audio drama he adapted Ramsey Campbell's novel, *The Hungry Moon* and he's just written and recorded his first full-cast story for Big Finish Productions. Other audio work includes *Cracking the Feathers* and *All the Bens* for Bamalam Productions Ltd, a company he now serves on as a trustee. Also for Bamalam, Ian is co-producer and lead writer on *Scuttled*, an audio drama in association with the Museum of London Archaeology. As well as screen and audio work, Ian also scripts comics for Cutaway Comics, titles thus far including *Demons of Eden, Sutekh: The Heretic, Drax: London Calling* and *Gods And Monsters*.

With thanks to our Kickstarter backers

Nick Abadzis	Martin Glassborow	Christopher Payne
Richard Able	Scott Gordon	Simon Pedley
Nigel Adams	James Gould	Lisa Perella
Janet Adkins	Ian Greenfield	Barbara Peterson
Scott Armstrong	Bedwyr Gulling	Barry Simon Phillips
William Bain	Laurence Hallam	David Preston
Cameron Bain	Mark Healey	Gareth Pugh
Dan Baker	Stuart Henderson	Thomas Reid
Matt Betts	Wilfred Hewson	Joshua Richmond
Manjit Singh Bhail	Christopher Hill	Fin Robertson
William Boucher	Matthew Hills	Timothy Rodmell
Huw Buchtmann	Sam Hollingsworth	Ira Rosenblatt
Russell Anthony	Kevin Houston	Andrew Scott
Cammack	Malin Huffman	Andrew Shapton
Stephen Candy	Aneurin Jackson	Jason Skirvin
Richard Chalk	Blayne T Jensen	Brian D Smith
Roger Clark	Robert Jewell	Luke Smith
Christopher Colley	Mark Jobson	Kevin Christopher
James Cole	Dallas L Jones	Snipes
Russell Cook	Neil Kenny	Andrew Stark
Robert Corrigan	David Kill	Dave Stevens
Ian Curry	Gary Knowles	Richard Tarrant
Chris Daltrey	David Kocur	Phil Taylor
Luke Daniels	Phillip Lacey	Mitchell Alexander
Cyrus Deacon	Stephen Last	Tregale
Andrew Donkin	Mark Ledsome	Rob Turner
Earl Ecklund III	Joshua Liberty	Richard Unwin
Geraint Edwards	Sean Marsh	Vitas Varnas
Clay Eichelberger	Cameron Mason	Antony Wainer
Sam Fain	Joe McIntyre	Alistair Robert Wallace
Ian Fensome	John McLay	Stephen Walters
John Paul Fitzpatrick	Jamie Meharg	Noel Warham
Daniel Flannigan	Gareth Molyneux	Andrew Webster
Mark Gentile	Nathan Moore	Paul Webster
Harald Gehlen	Paul A Murphy	Alex Wilcock
Andrew Gilardi	Christopher Paul	Ian Williams
Richard Girl	Neale	Steve Young
	Terry Parker	